to Mina
with good wishes

Helen Taylor

New Orleans
24 March 1995

Southern Literary Studies
Louis D. Rubin, Jr., Editor

Gender, Race, *and* Region *in the* Writings *of*
Grace King, Ruth McEnery Stuart, *and* Kate Chopin

HELEN TAYLOR

Gender, Race, *and* Region *in the* Writings *of* Grace King, Ruth McEnery Stuart, *and* Kate Chopin

LOUISIANA STATE UNIVERSITY PRESS

Baton Rouge and London

Copyright © 1989 by Louisiana State University Press
All rights reserved
Manufactured in the United States of America

Designer: Laura Roubique Gleason
Typeface: Linotron Bembo
Typesetter: The Composing Room of Michigan, Inc.

First Printing

97   96   95   94   93   92   91   90   89   5   4   3   2   1

Library of Congress Cataloging-in-Publication Data

Taylor, Helen, 1947–
    Gender, race and region in the writings of Grace King, Ruth
  McEnery Stuart, and Kate Chopin / Helen Taylor.
        p.   cm.—(Southern literary studies)
    Bibliography: p.
    Includes index.
    ISBN 0-8071-1445-6
    1. American fiction—Louisiana—History and criticism.
  2. American fiction—Women authors—History and criticism.   3. Women
  and literature—Louisiana.   4. Louisiana in literature.   5. Sex role
  in literature.   6. Race in literature.   7. Local color in
  literature.   8. King, Grace Elizabeth, 1852–1932—Criticism and
  interpretation.   9. Stuart, Ruth McEnery, 1856–1917—Criticism and
  interpretation.   10. Chopin, Kate, 1851–1904—Criticism and
  interpretation.   I. Title.   II. Series.
  PS266.L8T39   1989
  813'.4'0932763—dc19   88-22040
                                                                     CIP

The paper in this book meets the guidelines for permanence and durability of the Committee
on Production Guidelines for Book Longevity of the Council on Library Resources. ∞

Contents

Preface

I am a grandchild of a lost War, and I have
blood-knowledge of what life can be in a defeated
country on the bare bones of privation.

—Katherine Anne Porter, *The Days Before*

Like Katherine Anne Porter, most southerners see the Civil War as a watershed for the South. The war itself, and the various stages through which the South passed after its military defeat, have powerfully shaped the collective imagination of southerners and have remained a reference point for southern writing of all kinds. This book makes an attempt to come to terms with some of the complex meanings of the Civil War and its aftermath, by focusing on the fiction that has been so crucial in interpreting, idealizing, and mythifying the ante- and postbellum South both to itself and to other sections of the United States.

More than any other section of the U.S.A., that imaginary community known as the South has been discussed and defined in mythic and fictional terms; and, as many critics have pointed out, it is the only region to have its own indigenous legendary female figure, the southern lady or belle. The "belle" is a cliché of popular literature and film. Although she has assumed very different forms—from tragic-romantic figures Scarlett O'Hara, Jezebel, and Blanche DuBois, to the comic failed belles in such novels as *Kinflicks* and *The Confederacy of Dunces*—she is understood as a special kind of creature, having a different history and quality from other women. Originating in the fictional reading and imagination of the white male planter, this idealized mythical figure is idle, leisured, long-suffering, sexually pure, innocent, and childlike, conspicuously consuming her husband's wealth, and symbolizing racial purity. She is, of course, white (a fact emphasized by her magnolia complexion and soft, creamy-white hands), and she bears almost no relationship to her black counterpart working in the fields or her white sister laboring in a factory.[1]

1. Margaret Mitchell, *Gone With The Wind* (New York, 1936); William Wyler (dir.), *Jezebel,* 1938; Tennessee Williams, *A Streetcar Named Desire* (Harmondsworth, England,

Indeed, given the many representational forms this symbolic figure has taken, it is perhaps surprising how little is known about southern women. While the "belle" image of the southern lady is celebrated, the diversity of southern white and black women's experience is as yet only sketchily documented. In recent years, feminist critics have followed the dominant concern of much nineteenth-century American scholarship in focusing attention on the Northeast. There is now an impressive body of publication devoted to the history of northern women's organizations, clubs, suffrage activity, as well as to major writers such as Margaret Fuller, Louisa M. Alcott, and Harriet Beecher Stowe. By contrast, there has been a dearth of scholarship on the history of southern women, their activities and organizations in specific states, and on the work of southern women writers. It is a fair reflection of the state of play that in *The Encyclopedia of Southern History* the subject of "Reconstruction" is allotted twice the space of "Women, Women's Colleges, and Women's Rights Movement."

In 1982, at a symposium on "Sex, Race, and the Role of Women in the South," the state of scholarship was reviewed and found sadly lacking. Southern historians identified huge gaps in knowledge, from the nature of the impact of the Civil War on women's lives to the importance of women's voluntary associations, while literary historian Anne Goodwyn Jones indicated fruitful directions in which research into diaries, slave narratives, and novels might proceed to illuminate the lives of literate women. It was emphasized that most of the evidence about southern women's lives before the twentieth century comes from letters, diaries, and memoirs, most of which were written by middle-class white women, and that very little is known of working-class whites or of black women of all classes. Anne Firor Scott, the historian who has most advanced the state of southern women's scholarship, pointed out that the typical southern woman does not exist: she "came in many varieties of class, race, and ability."[2] It is clear that a great deal of research remains to be done before the full range of southern women's lives, ideas, achievements, and conflicts can be seen in their heterogeneous complexity.

However, the work is underway. Historians have begun the major task

1959); Lisa Alther, *Kinflicks* (New York, 1976); John Kennedy Toole, *A Confederacy of Dunces* (Baton Rouge, 1980). For good summaries of the myth of the southern lady, see Anne Firor Scott, *The Southern Lady: From Pedestal to Politics, 1830–1930* (Chicago, 1970); Anne Goodwyn Jones, *Tomorrow Is Another Day: The Woman Writer in the South, 1859–1936* (Baton Rouge, 1981); Kathryn Lee Seidel, *The Southern Belle in the American Novel* (Tampa, Fla., 1985); and William R. Taylor, *Cavalier and Yankee: The Old South and American National Character* (New York, 1961).

2. Joanne V. Hawks and Sheila L. Skemp (eds.), *Sex, Race, and the Role of Women in the South* (Jackson, 1983), 110.

of recording and analyzing chronicles of women in various regions and states at different periods of the South's history. Scott's work, drawing on research in the 1930s by Julia Cherry Spruill and others, has provided a general context that later studies have fleshed out. And recent scholarship is producing interesting evidence that questions the relevance for southern women of the periodization of the Civil War and Reconstruction. Jean E. Friedman, for example, points to the "stability of kin networks . . . [which] enabled the southern community to survive the war," and she suggests that the family-centered community (among whites, at least) prevented the war from effecting that lasting change on women's self-image and role which earlier historians have described.[3]

Anne Goodwyn Jones's pioneering book, *Tomorrow Is Another Day: The Woman Writer in the South, 1859–1936,* is the only study to have attempted to construe "the female mind of the South" through examining the fiction of a group of southern writers from different states over a period of seventy-seven years. Its excellent introduction traces the historical sources of the contradictions and tensions in southern women's experience, and describes well the centrality of women writers in southern letters. Jones suggests a tradition of liberalism—often veiled rather than direct—in southern women's writings, one that she traces through "patterns of imagery, characterization, plotting, narrative stance, and theme" common to the seven writers discussed.[4] *Tomorrow Is Another Day* is required reading for any scholar of women's writing. It has mapped the field, demonstrated the variety of southern women's literary achievements, and suggested new directions for more detailed studies of individual writers and specific periods.[5]

This book, drawing on recent feminist research, is an attempt to extend Jones's project by examining selected women writers working in a single southern state over a period of roughly twenty years. My focus is on the three most successful women writers in Louisiana between the Civil War and 1900—Grace King, Ruth McEnery Stuart, and Kate Chopin. These women were publishing after the war, that crisis of regional difference

3. Julia Cherry Spruill, *Women's Life and Work in the Southern Colonies* (Chapel Hill, N.C., 1938); Scott, *The Southern Lady;* Hawks and Skemp (eds.), *Sex, Race, and the Role of Women in the South,* Bibliographical Essay, 11.

4. Jones, *Tomorrow Is Another Day,* 45.

5. For instance, the first symposium on Louisiana women writers was held at Loyola University, New Orleans, September 19–20, 1986. Drawing on symposium papers, a special issue of *New Orleans Review* as well as a book collection are currently being prepared. See Dorothy Brown and Elizabeth Sarkodie-Mensah (eds.), *A Selected Bibliography of Louisiana Women Writers* (New Orleans, La., 1986).

which had ostensibly been resolved and was being replaced by urgent demands for national reconciliation and harmony. As a separate region of the United States, the South ceased to exist after the Civil War. North/South divisions, exacerbated by enormous economic and social differences as well as by the southern slave system, were brought to a head by southern states' secession from the Union and were ostensibly healed with the Union forces' triumph in 1865. The events of the subsequent decades until 1900 demonstrated how fragile was that healed breach, and how precarious the new sense of national unity. But increasingly there was a desire to validate the importance of "One Nation," a socially, economically, and racially harmonious national culture.

Along with other forms of representation, fiction played a significant role in this process of ideological construction and consolidation. It did so paradoxically through its celebration of *difference*: the "Local Color" fictional movement recorded the nation's diverse regional characteristics, peoples, and dialects, but mostly in such terms that these could be patronized and thus marginalized by a northeastern literary establishment and the readers for whom it was aiming. The great majority of this fiction was written by white middle-class women, and the largest number of works and most of the critically acclaimed writers came from the South. And as the very real economic, racial, and social divisions between North and South were forcibly eliminated or modified (albeit unevenly, and with variable success) in the postbellum decades, so northeastern editors began to encourage mythic and romantic interpretations of southern states. The writers I discuss here all benefited from this encouragement and were urged to participate in this new idealization of the South.

Grace King, Ruth McEnery Stuart, and Kate Chopin were all acclaimed in northern letters as significant southern writers of Local Color fiction. They were examples of the first group of women to be accepted by northern editors and publishers as professional writers; all of them earned a considerable income from their writing and regarded themselves as serious writers. The aim of this book is not primarily to evaluate their fiction, nor to argue a case for reprinting their neglected works (the more usual preoccupations of feminist criticism focusing on forgotten writers). My analysis of the three writers is not intended as an apology for or celebration of southern Local Color, nor their now unacceptable political caricatures of Reconstruction and the southern black. Finally, I am not arguing for an incorporation of these writers in a canon, be it of American southern or feminist literature.

Clearly there are difficulties inherent in any liberal confrontation of fictional texts written in the South of the 1880s and 1890s. Although all three writers can be seen to have expressed radical ideas in relation to women and feminism, nonetheless they were all politically conservative and—to a modern sensibility—deeply racist. This book has encountered the kinds of difficulty that Alan Sinfield argues face radical teachers of reactionary literary texts. Acknowledging that most "canonical" texts are unlikely to produce socialist readings, Sinfield argues that the task of radical criticism should be to examine an author's "project"—"his or her attempt to negotiate and promote a preferred version of reality from a particular position in society. The contradictions and closures, the disturbances and indirections . . . will emerge as strategies which aim to make vivid, coherent and persuasive a particular view of reality. The text is thus opened up to *understanding*—as a project conceived at a specific conjuncture; and so to *questioning*—of its values."[6]

This process of defining the project and thus understanding the text is one that I will use with all three writers, especially in discussing their views on the purpose of their writing as expressed in correspondence and private papers. But an author's *conscious* project (which cannot be seen in isolation) rarely develops in the ways s/he conceived it, and is always transformed through its readings both at publication time and in subsequent critical exegesis. Thus, the "understanding" and "questioning" must also take into account the unconscious and contradictory elements of these writers' projects, which can only emerge from close readings of the texts themselves, not simply from historical knowledge. One must also ask if there is a regional and/or national project in which the writer was (knowingly or innocently) participating. And I read the texts not as passively embedded in a particular society and historical situation, but as dialectically constructed by *and* constructing versions of that society and history.

This book, drawing as it does on southern scholarship and on Anglo-American and French feminist theoretical and empirical studies attempts to produce an examination of women's writing around a particular historical period/crisis to explore the interrelationships of gender, race, and region. My choice of women writing about Louisiana after the Civil War is intended to suggest new links between regionalism and feminism, by analyzing the specific ways women related to the Local Color movement and explored the meanings of Louisiana's historical, cultural, and mythic heritage and problems. The book aims to document the contribution of women writers to Louisiana at a singularly fascinating and successful

6. Alan Sinfield, "Four Ways with a Reactionary Text," *LTP: Journal of Literature Teaching Politics,* II (1983), 92.

period of its social and literary history, in order both to enrich our understanding of the ways in which "southern letters" encompasses a multiplicity of literary discourses and publication histories, and also to extend our knowledge of the specific experiences and achievements of nineteenth-century women writers.

Acknowledgments

I am indebted to the American Council of Learned Societies for granting me an American Studies Fellowship, 1980–81, to undertake research in the United States; to the English Department, Louisiana State University, for its hospitality; and to Bristol Polytechnic for allowing me study leave and supporting my research in many ways.

The following individuals (listed alphabetically) have been especially helpful: Jan Andrews, Professor Isobel Armstrong, Homi Bhabha, Elizabeth Bird, Panthea Broughton, Robert Bush, Frank de Caro, Mark Conroy, Margaret Culley, Marie Ingram, Donald Jones, Rosan Jordan, Peter M. Lewis, members of Literature Teaching Politics, Mrs. D. Macey, Mrs. Mildred McCoy, the Marxist-Feminist Literature Collective, Peter Nichol, Per Seyersted, Elaine Showalter, Ida and Eric Taylor. Susan Millar Williams undertook valuable extra research into Louisiana women writers. John M. Coxe and Mary Coxe were generous in sharing their private Grace King collection with me, and in giving permission for me to use the Grace King Papers at LSU.

I am deeply grateful to Professor Lewis P. Simpson for his friendly encouragement over many years, and to Professor Louis D. Rubin, Jr., for his detailed criticisms of the manuscript. I owe a special debt to long-suffering colleagues Madge Dresser and Margaret Kirkham, and to long-standing friends Louise Reverby, and Marie and Neal Blanchard. Margaret Fisher Dalrymple proved a most perceptive and meticulous editor.

Two special people made this possible. Cora Kaplan inspired me and improved my writing at every stage. Derrick Price (to my pleasant surprise and his great credit) has lived it all with me.

Gender, Race, *and* Region *in the* Writings *of*
Grace King, Ruth McEnery Stuart, *and* Kate Chopin

Introduction

The women who are the subject of this study were all old enough to understand the disruptions and suffering caused by the Civil War. Grace King (1852–1932) and Ruth McEnery Stuart (1849–1917) lived in New Orleans through the war and Reconstruction (which lasted in Louisiana from approximately 1862 to 1877), while Kate Chopin (1850–1904), who was part of a pro-Confederate family living in St. Louis, a major Union stronghold, moved to New Orleans for the last seven years of Reconstruction. As with other southern writers, the three women's experiences of this turbulent and politically charged period of Louisiana's history stirred their imaginations and to some extent structured the political and racial ideological positions that their fiction was to explore. It is significant that they all began to write between 1883 and 1884, some half-dozen years after Republican carpetbag governments had been permanently driven from the state by Louisiana's traditional white ruling class, and also at the time of the state's greatest popularity in the nation's cultural life. I will discuss later the way the writers were influenced by Louisiana's mythic construction as romantic paradise. Of significance here is the fact that these women were strongly influenced by the contemporary definitions of the causes and effects of the war, Reconstruction, Counter-Reconstruction, and Redemption.[1]

1. The history of southern women is not the only lacuna in southern historiography. Although there have been historiographical controversies centering on the quarter-century following the Civil War, as late as 1980 the Reconstruction scholar John Hope Franklin deplored the absence of a considered overview of the period and the lack of new scholarship that would fill the many gaps. He argues that, of all periods in American history, Reconstruction arouses most passionate feelings, and that the "objective" scholarship he seems to believe possible has been hampered by a legacy of sectional bitterness, racial animosity, and bigotry, together with conflicting political analyses of a number of issues, especially abolition. See

All three writers lived in Louisiana during a period of crisis and dramatic transformations of political, economic, and social life. Louisiana was much affected by the Civil War.[2] One-fifth of all her Confederate troops were killed in battle, and many more wounded or crippled for life. Most families lost at least one member. Around six hundred military engagements took place in the state, leaving considerable destruction of property and land. With freed slaves counted as lost property, the banking system shattered, and Confederate paper money and bonds worthless, Louisiana lost one-third of its wealth. In 1860, in terms of (white) per capita wealth, the state ranked first in the South, second in the nation. By the first census after Reconstruction, Louisiana was thirty-seventh among all American states and territories. Plantations and farms were badly damaged and pillaged; crumbling levees, rusting equipment, and neglected, scattered farm animals meant that the mainstays of Louisiana's antebellum prosperity, its sugar and cotton plantations, were badly hit. Before the war, Louisiana had produced 95 percent of the South's sugar crop; by 1877, it was producing a mere one-third of that output. Furthermore, after Radical Republican and then Bourbon misrule throughout the 1870s, the state's reputation for fraud, corruption, lawlessness, and violence was unparalleled. By the 1880s, northern businessmen who had formerly invested heavily in Louisiana were wary of its political corruption, fraudulent ballot box practices, and high crime rate—especially in New Orleans. In the 1880s and 1890s, the state had the dubious distinction of boasting the highest rate of illiteracy in the South, and the worst national record for public institutions—schools, asylums, and prisons.

The New Orleans in which the three women lived—and of which King and Stuart were natives—had long been an important world port and commercial, cultural, and social center. From 1800 to 1861, a large proportion of the world's goods in transit had gone through New Orleans, and (while the rest of Louisiana was rural and unsophisticated) the city in which Grace King and Ruth McEnery grew up had a large population with a cosmopolitan atmosphere because of its many ethnic groups, including

John Hope Franklin, "Mirror for Americans: A Century of Reconstruction History," *American Historical Review*, LXXXV (February, 1980), 1–14. The absence of authoritative accounts of the period makes a literary scholar's work doubly difficult.

2. The following information is summarized from C. Vann Woodward, *Origins of the New South, 1877–1913* (Baton Rouge, 1951); John D. Winters, *The Civil War in Louisiana* (Baton Rouge, 1963); William Ivy Hair, *Bourbonism and Agrarian Protest: Louisiana Politics, 1877–1900* (Baton Rouge, 1969); Joe Gray Taylor, *Louisiana Reconstructed, 1863–1877* (Baton Rouge, 1974); Mark T. Carleton, Perry H. Howard, and Joseph B. Parker (eds.), *Readings in Louisiana Politics* (Baton Rouge, 1975); Bennett H. Wall (ed.), *Louisiana: A History* (Arlington Heights, Ill., 1984).

the largest community of free blacks in the South. It was occupied by Union troops as early as 1862, and during the course of the war lost most of its wealth and commercial functions. Although its postbellum fortunes revived, especially when it resumed its functions as an exporting depot, by 1870 the city's financial crisis (begun by the war) had increased. It was deeply in debt, and for decades continued in economic chaos, due largely to the activities of corrupt businessmen, politicians, and companies (notably the Louisiana Lottery Company). A mecca for the hungry, vagrant, and sick (including thousands of freed blacks fleeing from plantations), the city became a center of violent crime, social problems, and disease. Yellow fever epidemics, unwholesome sanitation, and frequent floodings, which all went untreated until the late 1890s, meant that in economic, social, and racial terms New Orleans was a tense, difficult, and dangerous city in which to live—hardly the "Paradise Regained" Edward King hoped it would be by the 1890s, nor the "place so full of romantic sentiment" that William Dean Howells imagined it to be in the late 1880s.[3]

But in some ways, in the years following the Civil War, it was business-as-usual. The image that white Democrats perpetuated of the carpetbag southern governments was grossly exaggerated. Not only was most confiscated land restored to its former owners within a few years after the war—on condition the loyalty oath was signed or a presidential pardon given—but the temporary advantages conferred on freed blacks (suffrage, public education, minimal land ownership, or sharecropping) were soon brutally removed. As John Hope Franklin points out, "effective political power therefore remained where it had been before the war—with an oligarchy, a small ruling clique, which wielded power far out of proportion to its numerical strength. . . . Contrary to the widely held view, there was no significant breakup of the plantation system during and after reconstruction."[4] When the Constitution of 1868 was written by the state conventions of 1867–68, Louisiana agreed that blacks were to constitute 50 percent of the delegates, hardly a clear majority as some whites implied. Indeed, political participation by blacks in the South during Reconstruction was "never more than a thin veneer of integration." Though they had unusually high rates of literacy and status within the community, black politicians in Louisiana had little capital, few contacts, minimal patronage, and therefore derisory power. The lot of the southern black man (and to a lesser extent and in different ways, black woman) can be summarized by the new regulations and events of Reconstruction: black codes regulating

3. Edward King, *The Great South,* ed. W. Magruder Drake and Robert R. Jones (Baton Rouge, 1972), 17; Grace King, *Memories of a Southern Woman of Letters* (New York, 1932), 85.
4. John Hope Franklin, *Reconstruction After the Civil War* (Chicago, 1961), 219.

black vagrancy, labor, and legal rights (modeled on slave codes); the unenforced Civil Rights Act of 1865; the lack of federal support given the few scattered Freedmen's Bureaus; the convict-leasing and contract labor systems that returned freed blacks to the conditions of slavery; the failure of black trade unions and free integrated public education; intimidation and violence at the ballot box; extreme rural poverty because of a lack of capital and land, resulting in badly paid labor on the land or shabby sharecropping agreements; unemployment in towns and cities; and the constant harassment, victimization, and murder of individual blacks in all parts of the southern states.

In terms of race, Louisiana had long been a far more relaxed and mixed state than any other. In New Orleans, for decades there had been an unusually large community of free blacks with a sophisticated and economically and culturally varied lifestyle. Both in the city and throughout the state, the integration of public places and interracial sexual contacts were fairly common before and after the war. The population of Louisiana in general, and of New Orleans in particular, had the highest percentage of mixed-race ancestry of any American city or state.[5] Since New Orleans had a heterogeneous citizenry comprising Italians, Spaniards, and French as well as blacks and people of mixed race, it was impossible to differentiate people simply by color or language—free mulattoes, for instance, were usually French-speaking. The practice of "passing for white" was common, and as racial tensions increased during Reconstruction this practice accelerated considerably. Also, miscegenation (usually between white men and black or mulatto women) had been a tolerated feature of city life before the war—through *plaçage* (the common-law alliances formulated mainly at quadroon balls, a practice popular in the 1820s and 1830s, though in bad repute by the 1850s), and the many casual alliances between whites and free blacks. By 1860, New Orleans had adopted a fairly liberal attitude toward black-white relations, which was soon to be eroded.

Soon after the war began, especially with the Emancipation Proclamation and the Federal occupation of New Orleans, whites began to turn on blacks, blaming them for the humiliation and devastation that the fighting and occupation were causing. The increasing riots, tensions, and diseases caused by black migration into New Orleans from the plantations, and the subsequent imposition of the black codes between 1865 and 1866, caused much interracial hatred and suspicion. That very tolerance between the races in antebellum New Orleans was seized on by the old white ruling class as one of the main cards that had played into the carpetbaggers' hands, and as a major threat to the reestablishment of white supremacy and (in

5. John W. Blassingame, *Black New Orleans, 1860–1880* (Chicago, 1973), 201.

eugenicist terms) the maintenance of a "pure" race. This new suspicion and tension turned even more uncompromisingly to violence as soon as the Reconstruction period began.

After the notorious New Orleans riot of July, 1866, when thirty-four blacks were shot dead by white citizens furious at the reconvening of a black suffrage convention, armed bands of whites roamed Louisiana. In the 1860s, over three thousand people, mostly black, were killed or wounded in massacres, and the process of "whitecapping" (terrorizing blacks at random) continued long after the end of Reconstruction.[6] When the disputed state governorship election of 1872 was settled by presidential fiat in favor of the Republican candidate William Pitt Kellogg, Democratic fury ran high. Kellogg's authority was challenged by the newly organized White Leagues—paramilitary groups dedicated to the restoration of white supremacy. Their numbers rose rapidly to approximately 25,000, with many large property-holders and respected citizens in their ranks—including Grace King's brother and Kate Chopin's husband. The White Leagues were crucial both in helping destroy Louisiana's Reconstruction government and also in preventing plans, laboriously worked out in the early postwar governments, to desegregate schools, churches, and other public places. Whites had opposed school integration as soon as it began in 1869, but only in 1874 did the leagues' concerted attacks on schools in the form of parental boycotts and the forcible removal of black children from classrooms persuade the school boards to close schools and drop plans for full integration. Although the Catholic Church officially opposed segregation, many priests supported the White Leagues. In 1875 priests in New Orleans' Saint Louis Cathedral tried to segregate their parishioners. The league was also very vocal in defending the purity of white women. John Blassingame argues that the rage that interracial marriage aroused in white supremacists "lay at the foundation of almost all white opposition to the Negro's acquisition of civil and political rights."[7]

In 1874, at the Battle of Liberty Place, the White League staged a violent, bloody confrontation in Canal Street against Kellogg's militia and police, which was quelled only when Federal troops were called in. Reconstruction was already collapsing, and two years later the federal govern-

6. Ruth McEnery Stuart's story *Napoleon Jackson* features this group's activities.

7. See H. Oscar Lestage, Jr., "The White League in Louisiana and Its Participation in Reconstruction Riots," *Louisiana Historical Quarterly*, XVIII (July, 1935); Walter Prichard (ed.), "The Origin and Activities of the 'White League' in New Orleans (Reminiscences of a Participant in the Movement)," *Louisiana Historical Quarterly*, XXIII (April, 1940). Both articles were read in reprinted monographs, so pagination was different from the originals. Also, see Richard Hofstadter and Michael Wallace (eds.), *American Violence: A Documentary History* (New York, 1971), 101–105; Blassingame, *Black New Orleans*, 204.

ment refused to support Louisiana's Radical Republicans against such militant Democratic insurrection. "Redemption" had begun. From being one of the most racially harmonious cities in the Union, the New Orleans of the 1870s and 1880s became one of the most racially violent and explosive. In addition to the clashes provoked by the leagues and new proscriptions on interracial contacts in public meeting places, there were many labor strikes with blacks used often as "scabs" and angry fights between white and black workers (especially in the docks). White newspapers encouraged bitterness and whipped up angry feelings toward blacks and against integration. Free blacks, regarded for the first time with considerable suspicion, turned angrily on the many homeless, penniless freedmen coming into the city from rural plantations and tried to maintain a difference of status.

It is important to emphasize that Grace King, Ruth McEnery, and Kate Chopin were all living in New Orleans at the time of these disturbances. King's correspondence in particular discussed many of these tensions, and when she began to correspond with northern editors and friends in the late 1880s and early 1890s she often attacked carpetbag governments and New Orleans' black community. King's brother was a sergeant in the city's White League, and he and Oscar Chopin, who was also prominent in league activities, fought in the Battle of Liberty Place. The Chopins later moved to Red River Parish in northwest Louisiana, site of the other most violent white supremacy demonstration of Reconstruction, the Coushatta Massacre, where Oscar Chopin's New Orleans activities found considerable approval.

Although, as Jean E. Friedman argues, traditional kin ties held through the Civil War, enabling the southern community to survive, nevertheless the lives of southern white women were in many ways dramatically altered by the war and the years that followed. A significant number (like pioneer women) gained confidence and strength from the hardships and challenges they were forced to encounter. By 1890 there were around sixty thousand Confederate widows in the South; in every state women outnumbered men in all age groups. During the war, men's absence from plantations, farms, and cities had meant that white women either took over jobs they had previously left to black women and men or else assumed total control of jobs they had hitherto shared with fathers, brothers, and husbands. Among other occupations, women became planters, merchants, millers, business managers, overseers, and teachers. In Louisiana as elsewhere, they organized societies for soldiers' aid and ran hospitals for wounded soldiers; held "calico balls" and "starvation parties"; and made costumes for Ku Klux Klan and White League night-riders. Male writers extolled the women's readiness to turn their hands to new responsibilities and to improvise with meager resources. The major ideological function that women fulfilled during the war was that of Confederate cheerleaders. Their uncritical support (in public, at least) of Confederate troops and their intransigent hostility toward Federal soldiers was made famous by the "harridans" of Louisiana, who are discussed in every war journal and many newspaper accounts.[8]

It is not surprising that women's fiction of the period emphasizes the importance of and need for education for women and (to a lesser extent) for blacks. One of the main women's lobbies during postwar decades was for better schools for white girls and for vocational training and education for blacks. White middle-class women knew well that the deprivation of thorough schooling led men and women into ignorance, foolish judgments, and ultimately injudicious action (especially worrying to them in terms of freed blacks). Southern families had traditionally sent their sons to northern and European schools and colleges and had also established centers of learning within the South, but until the twentieth century southern women were given little formal education outside their fathers' libraries and various private academies and seminaries in which greater emphasis was placed on social skills than scholarship. Although the long-established Ursuline Convent in New Orleans had a high reputation, it was not until the 1880s that some good colleges for women were established, notably Baltimore's Goucher College and Sophie Newcomb College, which opened in New Orleans in 1888. The black institution Straight University accepted women students after Reconstruction; Alice Dunbar-Nelson was educated there. Although by 1885 women constituted the majority of teachers in Louisiana, formal training took much longer to be properly set up.

Informal education for women, however, flourished after Reconstruction. The women's club movement had begun in 1868 in New York (with "Sorosis") but only started in New Orleans in 1884. This was the year of the World's Cotton Centennial Exposition, held in the city, and there was a popular demand for a significant contribution by women. A Woman's Department was set up under the commissionership of Julia Ward Howe of Massachusetts, with representatives from all other states. The city was

8. See Kathryn Reinhart Schuler, "Women in Public Affairs in Louisiana During Reconstruction," *Louisiana Historical Quarterly*, XIX (July, 1936); Scott, *The Southern Lady;* Ellen Carol DuBois, *Feminism and Suffrage: The Emergence of an Independent Women's Movement in America, 1848–1869* (Ithaca, N.Y., 1978); Hawks and Skemp (eds.), *Sex, Race, and the Role of Women in the South;* Jones, *Tomorrow Is Another Day.*

certainly ripe for an educational society, since it had established the National Press Association, a Christian Woman's Exchange, a Southern Art Union, and a Woman's Industrial Association. The New Orleans Woman's Club, formed that year under Howe's direction, was a natural successor to soldiers' relief groups, ladies' aid societies, and church and temperance groups. Other groups formed rapidly after Howe's club, and although women's concerns were first with self-education, mainly of a literary kind (focusing on some feminist literature and "dangerous" European authors such as Ibsen), they later branched out into political discussion and work for issues such as children's education. In the mid-1890s federations of women's clubs formed in all southern states, working for reforms of child labor, sanitation, libraries and—most controversially—woman suffrage. It is partly due to the confidence gained at Howe's club that Grace King began to write and to publish.

However, although their lives were dramatically different from those of women before the war, by the turn of the century white southern women were little further forward in legal and constitutional terms than before 1860. In terms of employment, economics, legal status (much hampered by the conservative Napoleonic Code), education, and domestic role, only small improvements had been made as a result of individual and group pressure. The ideology of white southern femininity was still at odds with the new realities of women's lives and the demands of southern feminists. As Anne Goodwyn Jones points out, the southern lady was still expected to represent "her culture's idea of religious, moral, sexual, racial, and social perfection." Whatever new roles and work they experimented with, southern white women were still called upon to keep alive the memory of the Confederate cause and its dead; the ideology of the Lost Cause was to be defended and immortalized in women's lives and writings. The increasing encouragement given by members of the city's white ruling class to women poets, fiction writers, and journalists bears testimony to the fact that women were recognized as having a major role to play in keeping alive in popular imagination the Old South, antebellum class and race relations, and a nostalgic idealized version of southern femininity.[9]

When one examines the lives of black women in postbellum Louisiana, a very different picture emerges, one that casts many shadows over their

9. Louisiana is the only state to adhere to the old French legal system. In the nineteenth century, this code was particularly oppressive in the marriage contract, since all of a wife's property (before and after marriage) belonged to her husband, who was also guardian of her children. Women had no legal or personal rights. Margaret Culley, "The Context of *The Awakening*," in Kate Chopin, *The Awakening*, ed. Margaret Culley (New York, 1976), 118; Jones, *Tomorrow Is Another Day*, 9.

white contemporaries. John Blassingame quotes Reconstruction New Orleans newspapers to show that many black women joined with white women in demanding equal rights with men in education, jobs, and property and political rights. Using the same rhetorical devices as their white contemporaries, black women argued that the only way to give dignity to the black race was "to elevate the Negro woman." The 1871 visit to the city of Frances Harper, northern poet and orator, inaugurated an active black women's rights campaign, which was given some support by the black newspaper the *Louisianian*. After the war, there were far more black women than black men in New Orleans, and partly out of necessity, partly because of tradition, a large number of women worked to support themselves and their children. In the 1880s census, one-third of black women were in paid employment. This practice of working gave them higher status within their own community than white women had in theirs, though it also led to multiple exploitation. Black women were expected to work at often menial jobs, for worse pay than any other group; they had to take the main responsibility for child-care and domestic labor; and in the slave South (and also in postwar years) they had to endure sexual abuse and humiliation from white planters and their sons. As Gerda Lerner argues, in economic, political, and social terms, black women were (and still are) "the most powerless group in American society." The ideology of southern womanhood, however restrictive, did ensure that white bourgeois women (in the last instance, always participating and/or colluding in the slavocracy) were protected from the worst kinds of exploitation in the work force and domestic life. Black women, however, suffered exploitation from which their reproductive role and femininity gave them no respite.[10]

Furthermore, as Angela Davis argues, white women suffragists capitulated to the racist and imperialist mood of the 1890s and early twentieth century, at an historical conjuncture when new monopolist national expansion required more intense forms of racism than ever before. At the very time when black women most needed white women's support to condemn lynching and other interracial violence (including rape of black women), and to support black women workers, trade unions, and clubs, these white women (Davis argues) were obsessed with securing the vote for themselves only.[11]

Angela Davis' critique of white suffragists (shared by others) has some justice, especially since Elizabeth Cady Stanton's NAWSA (National Woman Suffrage Association) repudiated the Fifteenth Amendment and

10. Blassingame, *Black New Orleans,* 88–89; Gerda Lerner (ed.), *Black Women in White America: A Documentary History* (New York, 1972), xxiii.
11. Angela Davis, *Women, Race and Class* (London, 1982).

took an increasingly racist and elitist line. But it must be remembered that the abolition movement and the Republican party deliberately marginalized women, black *and* white, after the Civil War. With the passage of the Fifteenth Amendment and especially after the Republican election victory of 1872, Republicans abandoned the issue of woman suffrage altogether. As Ellen DuBois points out, as early as 1868 Edwin Stanton argued that by appropriating for themselves the Garrisonian philosophy of universal moral equality, the Radicals and abolitionists had blocked women's access to their only democratic ideology: "It literally deprived feminists of a political language in which to make their case." The exclusion of women from the suffrage campaign led some women to abandon their own fight, maintaining, like Julia Ward Howe, that they would only argue their own case when blacks had secured the vote, and some to seek alliances with the more unsavory elements of the Democratic party, which were eager to use woman suffrage to disfranchise blacks. The most tragic result of these splits and of the racist company that NAWSA kept was that by the 1890s a vast divide had opened between black and white women. Clubs were segregated, so there was little social contact even between professional women of both races; and in however fond and sentimental terms white middle-class women spoke and wrote of their former slaves and domestic servants, few of them had black women friends or were involved in political struggles around black women's rights and conditions. Furthermore, worried by the declining white birthrate, the 1890s suffragists actively campaigned for birth control measures for poor, immigrant, and black women.[12]

Such racial divisiveness, and thus distrust, were further fueled by the white supremacist rhetoric of Reconstruction and Counter-Reconstruction, which posed every black man as potential rapist. Michel Foucault argues that the nineteenth century saw a "multiplicity of discourses" around sex and that this discursive explosion has to be seen as "the self-affirmation of one class rather than the enslavement of another: a defense, a protection, a strengthening, and an exaltation that were eventually extended to others . . . as a means of social control and political subjugation." But Foucault does not directly address the problem of racism. In terms of the southern white ruling class, self-affirmation worked simultaneously with control and subjugation of blacks. Thus, hard upon emancipation and increasingly thereafter, the white fantasy of the black man as voracious sexual being was used as a weapon of social and racial domination. From the early days of the Civil War, discourses about the freedman made him a specter for every white girl and woman in the South, despite the fact that not a single black rape of a white woman was reported during

12. DuBois, *Feminism and Suffrage,* 106, 169.

the war. A New Orleans schoolgirl, Clara Solomon, spoke for many women between 1860 and 1900 when she confided to her diary, "I fear more from the negroes than Yankees and an insurrection is my continual horror." It could be argued that it was this fantasy, out of all proportion to the actual statistics of black crime against whites, that led so many white women to attempt to control or exorcise their fears by resorting to the written word. Certainly, the tamed black figure—loyal, affectionate, desexualized—is celebrated in every kind of female discourse of the period; as I will demonstrate in the works of King, Stuart, and Chopin, it becomes a recurrent and almost obsessive fictional motif.[13]

Significant as this theme of racial and sexual fear was, the "discursive explosion" by women around and after the Civil War can be explained in various other ways. Apart from the increasing interest in and demand for southern materials by northern publishers, there was an urgent need on the part of many women to write private documents to record their extraordinary experiences, and the influence of feminist ideas—initially arising within the abolition movement—stressed the great importance of public discourse for blacks and for women. Often the women began to write diaries for personal perusal but soon recognized their potential historical importance. As C. Vann Woodward points out in his edition of Mary Boykin Chesnut's diary, this apparently immediate, spontaneous document was written from notes twenty years after the war, between 1881 and 1884; Edmund Wilson was closer to the mark than he knew when he said her style was that of a "writer who is not merely jotting down her days but establishing, as a novelist does, an atmosphere, an emotional tone." Chesnut bequeathed her diary to a friend, while the Louisiana diarist Julia LeGrand wrote her wartime journal especially for her niece Edith Pye Weedon; two other Louisiana women used their personal memories as the basis for collected reminiscences.[14]

From the large number of published and untranscribed diaries, it is

13. Michel Foucault, *The History of Sexuality, Vol. 1: An Introduction* (Harmondsworth, England, 1981), 33, 123; Clara Solomon Diary, 1861–1862, p. 217, quoted in Blassingame, *Black New Orleans,* 27.

14. C. Vann Woodward, "Introduction," *Mary Chesnut's Civil War* (New Haven, 1981), xvi. Chesnut wrote two novels during the 1860s that can be seen as preparations for the Diary. Also see Anne Goodwyn Jones, "Southern Literary Women as Chroniclers of Southern Life," in Hawks and Skemp (eds.), *Sex. Race, and the Role of Women in the South,* 75–94; Edmund Wilson, *Patriotic Gore: Studies in the Literature of the American Civil War* (New York, 1962), 279; *The Journal of Julia LeGrand: New Orleans 1862–1863* (Richmond, Va., 1911); Eliza McHatton-Ripley, *From Flag to Flag: A Woman's Adventures and Experiences in the South During the War, in Mexico, and in Cuba* (New York, 1896); Caroline E. Merrick, *Old Times in Dixie Land: A Southern Matron's Memories* (New York, 1901).

apparent that several white middle-class women, usually of planter families, confided their wartime experiences to print. Diary writing provided both an outlet for women's feelings and also a crucial sense of being part of, rather than excluded from, imaginatively lived history: Sarah Morgan Dawson referred to hers as a "necessity," a "resource in these days of trouble," "relief to me where my tongue was forced to remain quiet!" Julia LeGrand wrote in 1863, "I have some right to make cry go up with the general voice, more especially that I feel indeed that I 'have no language, but a cry.' "[15]

Private diaries provide considerable insight both into the daily life of women of the planter class and also into the kinds of aspirations, dissatisfactions, and fantasies that such women entertained at this historical conjuncture. These insights are especially interesting when one comes to examine the more public, thus usually more allusive and mediated discursive practice of fiction. The main points that emerge repeatedly are: a new sense of self-importance (often expressed as self-dramatization) arising from new responsibilities and freedom because of the absence of male members of the family; mingled enthusiasm for and horror of Confederate jingoism; and excitement at living through a major historical crisis that they sensed was changing many familiar class, race, and gender relations. The women describe in detail the wartime tasks in which they had to engage, from animal husbandry to fishing, sewing soldiers' clothes, and endless letter writing to soldier relatives. A new kind of southern woman emerges from the diaries, one the fiction was increasingly to represent: a plucky, courageous, and practical creature in homespun dress who no longer yearned to live up to the antebellum ideal of a fastidiously feminine southern belle. The poem "The Southern Girl" was copied into many young women's notebooks and diaries, including Grace King's:

> . . . We scorn to wear a stitch of silk
> Or a stripe of Northern lace
> But make our homespun dresses up
> And wear them with such grace . . .

This defiant southern woman (the same kind who harassed Butler in New Orleans) became legendary throughout the nation, and the women express in their diaries and private papers a sense of themselves as representative southern figures, who—despite being unable to fight—were nonetheless fiercely loyal to the Confederate cause. As Sarah Dawson wrote, "I have lost my home and all its dear contents for our Southern Rights. . . .

15. Sarah Dawson, *A Confederate Girl's Diary*, ed. James I. Robertson, Jr. (Bloomington, Ind., 1960), 76–78; *Journal of Julia LeGrand*, 160.

Well, I boast myself Rebel, sing 'Dixie,' shout Southern Rights, pray for God's blessing on our cause, without ceasing . . . I am only a woman, and that is the way I feel."[16]

This pride in their own loyalty was only matched by a disappointment in their men's contribution. If it was woman's role to sit and wait, urging husband and sons to go to fight, she was bound to have high expectations of those men. Kate Stone comments angrily on the men reluctant to fight, prepared to "rest quietly at home" while others fought in their place. She later admits wryly to her shattered illusion about soldiers' battlefield activity: "The gloves with the open fingers were a flat failure. It seems soldiers are not always in a hurry or always shooting guns. They always have time to take off the gloves when necessary to use their fingers." Caroline Merrick noted that it was "the woman who brought her greater adaptability and elasticity to control circumstances, and to lay the foundations of a new order," and in the aftermath of the war she noted, "the women in every community seemed to far outnumber the men; and the empty sleeve and the crutch made men who had unflinchingly faced death in battle impotent to face their future."[17]

The sexual incapacity and emasculation suggested here by the word *impotence* and the empty sleeve indicate a kind of sexual wounding that Sandra Gilbert argues post–World War I women writers also found in their men.[18] Discussing Alice Meynell and H.D., Gilbert argues that the women saw themselves as survivors, contemptuous of the men who seem to have been punished for their very maleness. The men were both invalid and in-valid; by contrast, the women discovered a new power and vigor. Both wars were perceived—however inaccurately—by women writers as having feminized men and strengthened women (a perception perhaps strengthened in 1918 when some British women won the vote).

Although the Civil War brought few immediate gains to bourgeois white women, it certainly forced them to make judgments about political and social matters they had hitherto taken for granted. In many diaries, letters, and some fiction, there is an uneasiness expressed about the value of the war, the reliability of men, and the stability and validity of all their

16. Kate Stone, *Brokenburn: The Journal of Kate Stone, 1861–1868,* ed. John Q. Anderson (Baton Rouge, 1955), 24; Matthew Page Andrews (ed.), *The Women of the South in War Times* (Baltimore, 1927); Grace King, December 11, 1865, in Grace King Papers, Louisiana and Lower Mississippi Valley Collection, Hill Memorial Library, Louisiana State University, Baton Rouge; Dawson, *A Confederate Girl's Diary,* 318–19.

17. Stone, *Brokenburn,* 87, 106; Merrick, *Old Times in Dixie Land,* 75–76.

18. Sandra M. Gilbert, " 'Soldier's Heart': Literary Men and Literary Women, and the Great War" (paper presented at the annual meeting of the Modern Languages Association, December 28, 1980).

previous relationships—with family and with slaves. As Christians, some women were shocked at the strength of their contemporaries' hatred of the Union troops. Traditional female values of nurturing and caring were challenged by the new necessity to hate the enemy and distrust all blacks, however close and loyal they might have seemed. Blacks were praised for loyalty to their masters and especially mistresses, but feared and despised for signs of restiveness or ingratitude. The expectations with which women had been reared, that they would be cared for and supported economically, were now revealed as precarious, especially when male relatives were killed or wounded. And the class alliance between bourgeois women, which they had previously taken for granted, was now seen to be nonexistent; not only had a northern woman, Harriet Beecher Stowe, attacked the South and by implication southern women, but many Yankee women were known to have played an active and significant part in abolition, a movement a great number of southern women blamed for their current plight. Thus, in terms of class, gender, and race relations and issues, southern women were confused and pulled in different directions; their contradictory experiences are thus explored and lamented in the "private" discourse of journal and diary writing. Autobiography was used to construct a tragic myth of the postbellum southern woman, a myth that women used increasingly to justify a struggle for women's rights to the exclusion of those of blacks.

Ironically, in order to describe their situation, one of the most frequent analogies made by white women is with slavery. Indeed, the condition of slavery is used metonymically (usually without irony) to discuss their state of helpless dependence, lack of economic and personal autonomy, and generalized Confederate humiliation by Union troops. This metonymy is not new to the South or to the discourse of women. British women writers from Mary Wollstonecraft to Jane Austen, Charlotte Brontë, and Elizabeth Barrett Browning had already made considerable ironic use of it, while the early American feminists had equated marriage or (in the case of the Lowell mill-workers) women's economic oppression with the condition of slavery. The Grimké sisters were the first systematically to explore such comparisons; their analysis was relatively subtle and sophisticated, recognizing "the dialectical character of the relationship between the two causes." Angela Davis argues that there were many political and historical distortions in the discourses of white women, who assumed they were treated no better than slaves; as she demonstrates, the hostility toward black suffrage without woman suffrage derived from a blinkered view of the relative oppression of white women and of black women and men. That there were some specific similarities between the states of white bourgeois marriage and black slavery is undeniable; to suggest that the two can be equated is clearly outrageous.[19]

White women diarists and many fiction writers persisted in interpreting the war and the events that followed as a tragedy primarily for the ruling class. Their view of themselves as suffering and humiliated more than any other class or group was derived partly from interpretations of the Yankee as a black-loving, humane liberator of slaves, partly from sheer ignorance of the condition of freedmen and women after the war. The suffering of women of the planter and professional classes, however acute, was in no way comparable with the full-scale poverty, ill treatment, and destitution of a large number of freed blacks, as well as ruined yeoman farmers with no reserve resources or family contacts on which to fall back.[20] But this desire on the part of bourgeois white women to compare their conditions with those of black slaves should not simply be dismissed as false consciousness. In terms of their emotional loyalties and ties to blacks, especially black women, the juxtaposition of their own kinds of bondage with slavery inevitably led to an unconscious or conscious identification with black women that could perhaps only emerge in the contradictions, curious absences or eruptions, and unsatisfactory closures of women's postbellum fiction. And the fact that the women spoke of the two bondages in the same breath in various kinds of writing kept before their eyes those problems of their own subjectivity as it had been constructed through the discourses of slavery, abolition, black and woman suffrage, and women's rights. Beginning with the war diarists and letter-writers and continuing through the post-Reconstruction fiction, women returned directly or obliquely to these urgent questions that could be resolved neither through turning their backs on the lessons of contemporary history, nor by settling into a comfortable, blind loyalty to their own "redeemed" class.

Southern writers in the nineteenth century found few opportunities for publication in their own region. The South had always looked to the North for publishers and publications, even though there were pockets of southern writers long before the Civil War. But the "gifted gentlemen amateurs" who were writing in the antebellum South met with indifference from their peers and an absence of publication opportunities in

19. Cora Kaplan, "Introduction," in Elizabeth Barrett Browning, *Aurora Leigh* (London, 1978); Margaret Kirkham, *Jane Austen, Feminism and Fiction* (Brighton, 1983), chapter 17, "Mansfield Park"; Davis, *Women, Race and Class,* 44.

20. Ellen Glasgow is the only author to have concerned herself centrally with this latter group in the last decades of the nineteenth century.

their region. The only literary center was Charleston, and in 1859 one of the "Charleston School," Henry Timrod, spoke of the southern author as "the Pariah of modern literature." For a short time during the war, deprived of northern and European books and magazines, the South developed its own printers and publishers, and encouraged native material. Although most of this activity ceased shortly afterwards, nonetheless southern letters, newly fashionable in the North, took upon itself the task of rewriting its own history and defending its defeated values. As Daniel Aaron argues, "the literature of the embattled Confederacy was a patriotic literature, predominantly polemical and shrill, occasionally elegaic," much of it "shot through with sentiment, moonshine, and special pleading."[21]

Although the main antebellum southern apologists and creators of the Cavalier legend—William Gilmore Simms, Timrod, and John Pendleton Kennedy—were dead by 1870, other writers such as Thomas Nelson Page assumed the role of southern men of letters, denouncing the New South in favor of an idealized, "organic" antebellum South whose passing they bemoaned. Dozens of women writers, encouraged by the huge success of two southerners, Augusta Evans and Mrs. E.D.E.N. Southworth, took their sectional and professional responsibility seriously and responded eagerly to northern demands for fiction and poetry. The fictional fashion of "Local Color" was the result.

There is much critical writing about regional and Local Color fiction, but no full-length treatment of its historical and ideological function. One critic who has continually explored questions of literary regionalism, Raymond Williams, confines his work to British literature and problems of class. Williams has pointed out that in British letters since the nineteenth century any fiction set in London and the Home Counties would never be regarded as "regional," unlike a novel set in the Lake District or mid-Wales: "The life and people of certain favoured regions are seen as essentially general, even perhaps normal, while the life and people of certain other regions . . . are, well, regional." He argues that this is not merely a value judgment, but rather "an expression of centralized cultural dominance." Although the United States presents different problems, Williams' thesis holds true of American belles-lettres, and I shall attempt to argue

21. See Jay B. Hubbell, *The South in American Literature: 1607–1900* (Durham, N.C., 1954); Taylor, *Cavalier and Yankee;* Jean Fagan Yellin, *The Intricate Knot: Black Figures in American Literature, 1776–1863* (New York, 1972); Lewis P. Simpson, *The Man of Letters in New England and the South: Essays on the History of the Literary Vocation in America* (Baton Rouge, 1973); Daniel Aaron, *The Unwritten War: American Writers and the Civil War* (London, 1973), 231, 228; Henry Timrod, quoted in Thomas D. Young *et al.* (eds.), *The Literature of the South* (Glenview, Ill., 1968), 93.

this point in terms of a hegemonic national culture, language, and nationalist ideological formations.[22]

The term *Local Color* derives from the name applied to Théophile Gautier's school of writers in 1830s France. "La couleur locale" denoted the exotic romanticism of Gautier, Prosper Mérimée, and the Flaubert of *Salammbô*. The term was later used by French realists—notably Flaubert and Maupassant—to refer to the essence of realism, the details and motifs characteristic of and appropriate to a particular setting. According to scholars of American Local Color, the term was used in postbellum America to describe three phases of fictional writing—especially the picturesque (epitomized by Bret Harte), and less frequently the scientifically observant (by Mark Twain) and the serious contemporary (Hamlin Garland). Robert Bush summarizes the importance of Local Color in terms of the reading public's cultivation of a taste for native materials rather than English imports; its preparation of the ground for native American naturalism; the prestige it gave the American short story; and its influence on major early twentieth-century novelists such as Willa Cather and Ellen Glasgow.

While these arguments go some way to pointing out the significance of Local Color in terms of American letters, they do not explain why such a literary movement enjoyed the vogue it did in the 1880s and 1890s. Robert Bush argues that this fiction was disparaged as mere "touristic localism" by 1900, but this hardly accounts for its serious treatment by northern editors for the preceding quarter-century. Indeed, if one examines the use of the term *Local Color* and the relationship of writers to the genre, it becomes clear that there was a great deal at stake in the critical popularity and editorial encouragement of such work. The words themselves, used by the northern literary establishment to define regional literature, speak their own ideological assumptions. *Local* denotes any "abnormal" literary subject decentered from the northeastern literary centers (especially Boston and New York) and far removed from northern industrial and commercial cities. The second word, *color*, indicates the exotic flavor required of such fiction. Not only must it provide a sense of lived experience in rural and small-town America; it must also construct those areas in ways that would confirm their very strangeness and curiosity to a "normal" northern reader. This reader, understood to be cosmopolitan and urbane (whatever his/her origins, definitely *not* identified with a region), was to be entertained by the dialects, peoples, and customs of a heterogeneous

22. See Louis D. Rubin, Jr., *George W. Cable: The Life and Times of a Southern Heretic* (New York, 1969); Raymond Williams, "Region and Class in the Novel," in Douglas Jefferson and Graham Martin (eds.), *The Uses of Fiction: Essays on the Modern Novel in Honour of Arnold Kettle* (Philadelphia, 1982), 60.

United States now designated as a mythic Other Place, subject of literary-anthropological fascination only.[23]

Local Color fiction is generally said to be primarily about reconciliation and nostalgic celebration, and the South is seen as the ideal setting for such work. Paul Buck asserts that "no section of America had such an abundance of picturesque detail. Local color was to be found in every corner of Dixie . . . a background of rich and varied charm." But as a literary movement Local Color was by no means so innocent. In 1892 Thomas Nelson Page claimed that the Old South owed "her final defeat" to the lack of an antebellum literature, since "in the supreme moment of her existence she [the South] found herself arraigned at the bar of the world without an advocate and without a defense." In the New South, Page (significantly a lawyer before a novelist) and other southerners were quick to understand the political potential—indeed, urgency—of sectional fiction, especially as a means of setting straight a record which, it was felt, had been left to the North to write. Repeatedly in postbellum southern fiction, authors returned for subject matter to the antebellum South, their sentiments according with those of Virginia Frazer Boyle's black character who exclaims, " 'dey was good ole days, dose times befoah de wah!' "[24]

Although there were a few writers (notably Mark Twain) who used antebellum materials critically, especially in relation to questions of race, some were forced into obscurity by the early 1880s (like Albion Tourgée) or gradually encouraged to change tack in later work (George W. Cable). The writers whose nostalgic, defensive, but conciliatory versions of southern political and social history were embraced by the northern literary establishment of the 1880s and 1890s were conservative figures (now regarded as minor), like the poet Sidney Lanier and fiction writers such as John Esten Cooke, Page, Joel Chandler Harris, Mary Noailles Murfree, and the three subjects of this study.

Just as the Old South had had no literary center where writers could congregate and publishing houses flourish, so in the New South writers still relied on northern publishers and reading public. By the late 1870s the northern magazines were very keen to foster a fresh sense of nationalism, and the major publications adopted a policy of reconciliation that meant deliberately seeking copy from regions hitherto little known or courted

23. Robert B. Bush, "Louisiana Prose Fiction, 1870–1900" (Ph.D. dissertation, State University of Iowa, 1957), 12–15, 16.

24. Young *et al.*, *The Literature of the South,* 433–35; Larzer Ziff, *The American 1890s: Life and Times of a Lost Generation* (New York, 1967); Paul H. Buck, *The Road to Reunion, 1865–1900* (Boston, 1937), 196; Thomas Nelson Page, *The Old South: Essays Social and Political* (New York, 1892), 50; Virginia Frazer Boyle, "How Jerry Bought Malvinny," *Century,* XL (1880), 892.

for their literary output. Around the Civil War there had been indifference or hostility to southern materials, but in the late 1860s and 1870s, as sectional bitterness faded, reporters and travelers began to drift South and sent back bulletins on the progress of Reconstruction. The first substantial accounts were published through the 1870s in newspapers, magazines, books, and official reports by writers such as Robert Somers, James S. Pike, Charles Nordhoff, and Edward King. The 1880s saw an even greater number of writers, who were becoming increasingly uncritical and encomiastic. In terms of southern writings, *Scribner's* (which became *Century* magazine in 1881) was the most important journal. In 1891, its editorial creed was "a sane and earnest Americanism" that sought "to increase the sentiment of union throughout our diverse sisterhood of States"; this had in fact been its policy for almost two decades. *Scribner's* had commissioned articles from the journalist Edward King who, during 1873 and 1874, published a series based on his travels, called "The Great South." Louis Rubin says of these popular articles that as "the first extended treatment of the South during Reconstruction to appear in the national magazine press, [they] helped to prepare readers and editors for the literary use of Southern material." King is now best remembered for his patronage of George W. Cable, and I will return to him in the chapter on Grace King.[25]

Though supporting the Republican cause, *Scribner's/Century* built on its successful series by fostering and seeking out southern literary talent. Richard Watson Gilder, who was by the mid-1880s virtually the most influential magazine editor in the country, discovered many southern writers, such as Cable, Sidney Lanier, Joel Chandler Harris, Thomas Nelson Page, and Mary Johnston. By the late 1880s, *Century,* dominated by Harris, Page, and Cable, was saturated with southern fiction and illustrations, and other magazines followed suit. *Lippincott's,* the fiercely Republican *Harper's Monthly Magazine,* and *Atlantic Monthly* had all capitulated by 1890, and since many magazines had close links with publishing houses they were also able to offer book publication to southern authors. Editors such as Gilder and Charles Dudley Warner visited the South to look for new authors (Grace King and Ruth Stuart were both "discovered" in this way), and northern writers, caught up in the trend, went South or wrote southern fiction.[26] Uncritical enthusiasm and appeasement were the order

25. W. Magruder Drake and Robert R. Jones, "Editors' Introduction," in Edward King, *The Great South,* xxi–lxii; "Editorial," quoted in Buck, *The Road to Reunion,* 221; Rubin, *George W. Cable,* 14.

26. Some of the best known are Constance Fenimore Woolson, *Rodman the Keeper: Southern Sketches, 1880* (New York, 1880), which attracted Henry James's attention; Maud Howe, *Atalanta in the South: A Romance* (Boston, 1886); Sarah Orne Jewett, "The Mistress of Sydenham Plantation" (1888), in *Strangers and Wayfarers* (Boston, 1896), 18–35.

of the day. The courageous Albion Tourgée, who had written novels and treatises on the plight of freedmen in his adopted state of North Carolina, and George W. Cable who did the same for his native Louisiana, found to their cost that the North was swallowing whole a white racist Democrat line on the war and Reconstruction. As Tourgée wrote bitterly in 1888 (the year in which two-thirds of all stories furnished by syndicates to newspapers were "southern stories"), "our literature has become not only Southern in type but distinctly Confederate in sympathy." Paul Buck argues that the cumulative effect of these prosouthern publication policies was to "soften the tension of sectional relations and produce a popular attitude of complacency to Southern problems."[27]

Much of this softening and conciliation was enhanced through the extensive publication of short fiction featuring black dialect. The first black dialect sketch, "Gran' mammy" by Sherwood Bonner, was published in 1875, and she was succeeded by many other writers such as Mollie Moore Davis (in *Wide Awake,* 1876), Irwin Russell ("Christmas Night in the Quarters," 1876) and Thomas Nelson Page ("Marse Chan," 1884). Ruth McEnery Stuart is an important example of a writer in this genre, and the chapter on Stuart will discuss in detail the significance of dialect fiction to northern letters. It is important to note here, however, that the invention through dialect of a tamed, quaint black folk-hero contributed in large measure to popular complacency about the condition of southern blacks in postbellum America. In his 1888 essay, Albion Tourgée commented that a foreigner judging American civilization by its fiction "would undoubtedly conclude that the South was the seat of intellectual empire in America, and the African the chief romantic element of our population." Thomas Nelson Page was a successful dialect writer, and his portraits of "ancient ex-slaves still hankering for the days of blissful servitude and 'keening in Negro dialect over the Confederacy's fallen glories'" was very influential. Both Paul Buck and Edmund Wilson comment on the dreadful irony of New Englander Thomas Wentworth Higginson (intellectual abolitionist and subsidizer of John Brown) weeping over Page's "Marse Chan," a tale of a faithful black man grieving at his Confederate master's death. As Wilson says, Page's stories, like those of other dialect writers, were "applying soft poultices of words not merely to the suppurating wounds of the South but also to the feelings of guilt of the North."[28]

27. Albion Tourgée, "The South as a Field for Fiction," *Forum,* VI (1888), 405; and see his novel, *Bricks Without Straw* (Baton Rouge, 1969); Buck, *The Road to Reunion,* 235.
28. Tourgée, "The South as a Field for Fiction"; Aaron, *The Unwritten War,* 286 (the quotation is from James Branch Cabell, *Let Me Lie* [New York, 1947], 241); Wilson, *Patriotic Gore,* 615.

The limited possibilities available to a southern writer who rejected soft poultices in favor of opening up deep wounds are exemplified in the fate of George W. Cable (1844–1925). His courageous radical critique in fiction, polemical tracts, and public speeches on the treatment of blacks in Louisiana forced him to leave his native state and live permanently in exile. *The Grandissimes* (1880), his strongest fictional attack on Louisiana's class and race hierarchies, was so heavily pilloried that after settling in the North, he divided his work into two parts, writing anodyne sentimental fiction to make a living, while using lectures and tracts as the medium through which to expose southern racism. I will discuss Cable in more detail in the chapter on Grace King, but it is important to cite his case here. It demonstrates the powerful proscription by northern editors from the 1880s onwards of overtly political southern fiction that did not present an idealized, harmonious view of the South and the race question. It is not surprising that as Cable's career in New Orleans declined, Grace King's began to rise, and that unlike his, her reputation remained secure until the early 1900s, especially in New Orleans. The fact that both Cable and King, with their polarized views of the South and the "peculiar institution," could be welcomed and acclaimed by the reputedly radical Hartford community, within a few years of each other, is further evidence of the rapid move in the postbellum North toward a catholic, uncritical stance in relation to the war and the problems of the southern freedman. In 1894, Theodore Roosevelt denounced "that unwholesome parochial spirit, that over-exaltation of the little community at the expense of the great nation," and by 1900 Local Color's literary and political project was complete. It had celebrated the nation's diversity while reassuring a national reading public that this need not mean division, and that sectional differences had been reconciled or contained in favor of a unified United States.[29]

There has been little attempt to theorize or historicize women's Local Color writing. Most critics have neglected or dismissed postbellum regionalist fiction as minor, concerned with small details of little general significance; feminist attention to such writers has therefore responded by attempting to rectify such undervaluation through attention to a few "classics" of the genre. While the political dimensions and contradictions of male "regionalist" writers from Twain to Faulkner have been well explored, in relation to women writers such considerations have been neglected for formalist and thematic considerations. Furthermore, women regionalist writers are discussed as if the specific concerns of their regions can be homogenized and differences erased through feminist interpretations and the construction of an alternative female canon from Jewett through Cather to Flannery O'Connor. Ann Douglas Wood typifies a

29. Theodore Roosevelt, "What 'Americanism' Means," *Forum*, XVII (1894), 198.

feminist response that has apparently closed discussion: describing women Local Colorists as "corpse watchers," she argues they wrote out of nostalgia and despair because of their own declining class status and their awareness of women's increasing isolation and irrelevance in a new male-dominated technological postbellum society. These writers—hostile to the women's movement—are characterized as representing bleak impoverished worlds lacking in energy and optimism. The article over-schematizes an extremely complex movement and obscures the important features for feminist scholarship; for while Wood acknowledges the persistence of Local Color through modern women writers such as Flannery O'Connor, Carson McCullers, and Eudora Welty, she cannot explain why (especially in southern letters) women have continued to focus on the regional and local. The value of Local Color and regionalism for women writers in the South and the uses that women of different periods have made of their "parochial" experiences are therefore undermined and ultimately trivialized.[30]

In an 1891 article in *Century,* Wilbur Fisk Tillett celebrated the previous thirty years of southern female literary production. Citing a book published in 1869, *The Living Writers of the South,* he noted that roughly half those listed were women, most of whose books and articles had been written and published after the war began. His comment is significant: "[The writings] had been called forth by the war and the trying experiences following it. Whether the changed conditions under which we live have anything to do with it, it is nevertheless certainly true that there have been more literary women developed in the South in the thirty years since the war than in all our previous history." There was a considerable amount of literary activity among Louisiana women after the war, and the number of women publishing fiction rose steadily in the 1880s and 1890s. In the most complete bibliography of Louisiana fiction, Lizzie McVoy and Ruth Campbell list 199 works by Louisiana women (native to or at least resident in the state) published between 1865 and 1919. They name sixty-seven women and thirty-two male writers, though the wide use of masculine pseudonyms by women suggests that many of those thirty-two were in fact female. Also, by 1890 many women were contributing regularly to

30. See the significantly titled Cynthia Griffin Wolff (ed.), *Classic American Women Writers* (New York, 1980), which contains works by Jewett, Chopin, Wharton, and Cather, and Heather McClave (ed.), *Women Writers of the Short Story* (Englewood Cliffs, N.J., 1980), with essays on Jewett, Wharton, Cather *et al.;* Ann Douglas Wood, "The Literature of Impoverishment: The Women Local Colorists in America, 1865–1914," *Women's Studies,* I (1972), 31–32.

New Orleans newspapers—poets like Mary Ashley Townsend and fiction writers Mollie Moore, Bessie Bisland, and "Pearl Rivers." In 1876 Eliza J. Nicholson became chief owner and manager of the *Picayune*; at the time, the *Times-Democrat* was also owned by a woman. Soon after the war, New Orleans established a National Women's Press Association. The vast majority of fictional works listed in the McVoy-Campbell bibliography were published outside the South, most by publishing houses in New York, Boston, Philadelphia, Cleveland, and Chicago. Twenty-one came out of Louisiana, most from newspaper publishers in New Orleans, and seven from other southern cities such as St. Louis. Despite interest in and enthusiasm for southern writing demonstrated by various anthologies, most writers who wished to publish southern materials were wooed by northern publishers, and the majority seized their opportunity.[31]

The women who were writing in postbellum Louisiana shared many characteristics. They were white almost to a woman; the black writer Alice Dunbar-Nelson (1875–1935) is the only known exception, and she began to write only when she moved to New York. All the white writers were daughters of wealthy professional men or planters; all had been given a considerable education at home in their fathers' libraries, supplemented by some boarding-school attendance and foreign travel. Many had positive encouragement in their writing from members of their family, including husbands who often provided publishing contacts. Most had one or more male mentor who was interested in them at both a personal and professional level, and who helped build their careers. The usual model for nineteenth-century women writers, established by feminist critics, is that of a woman beginning to write or publish in spite of, or indeed after sloughing off, male friends and relations. Anne Goodwyn Jones has suggested very usefully that southern white writers do not conform to romantic feminist notions of "anxiety of authorship" and female subculture; as she points out, southern white women writers have had "an active and highly visible history since colonial times" and the southern community has "historically accepted and praised its women writers." Postbellum Louisiana women writers are no exception. Not only were they positively encouraged by male relatives, but they were also significant and acknowledged contributors to the literary revival after the Civil War. The common pattern of their literary development was to begin by writing verses and

---

31. Wilbur Fisk Tillett, "Southern Womanhood as Affected by the Civil War," *Century Magazine,* XLIII (November, 1891), 16; Lizzie Carter McVoy and Ruth Bates Campbell, *A Bibliography of Fiction by Louisianians and on Louisiana Subjects* (Baton Rouge, 1935). An example of an anthology of southern writing is Ida Raymond (ed.), *Southland Writers: Biographical and Critical Sketches of the Living Female Writers of the South* (Philadelphia, 1870).

short stories for publication in local newspapers and magazines; then to attempt to get published in national magazines; and finally to write one novel—after which most of them ceased writing and publication altogether. Many adopted a pseudonym—some masculine, others with romantic or regional associations ("Creole," "Filia," "Louisiana")—but reverted to their own names when they experienced some literary success.[32]

Writers frequently expressed anxiety about the possibility of being defeminized through the very act of writing for publication and thus engaging in public discourse, and several apologized profusely for putting pen to paper at all. Elizabeth Bisland Wetmore wrote in a preface, "timidly we launch . . . upon the broad stream of universal criticism, this simple little story. . . . Our mind may not be stored with lore or logic, and far from brilliant, yet we disdain useless pollysyllables [sic], aiming but to indite a plain sensible recital." Critics too praised women for not neglecting their families while writing (something Grace King found most trying); the dangers associated with becoming a professional southern woman of letters lay in family disapproval and ultimately censorship. As Mary Tardy wrote of Eliza Pugh, mother of one child and author of two novels, "she has not sunk the woman in the author, and has unhesitatingly declared her purpose to relinquish the pleasure of the pen should a word of reproach from those she loves warn her of such a probability."[33]

They appear to have rehearsed almost to the point of obsession familiar themes and preoccupations: most of the works are set around the Civil War and/or Reconstruction, and feature white families on large plantations, surrounded by loyal slaves or freedmen and women. Blacks rarely feature as other than supportive and consolatory figures in the drama of reversed white fortunes; if they do, it is in the familiar contexts of the female mulatto story (the heroine tragically doomed by her black blood or else triumphantly revealed to be white and therefore marriageable), or the black as subject of white curiosity—superstitious practitioner of voodoo or speaker of quaint and comic dialect. The predominant form is romance heavily spiced with gothic motifs, with elements of brutal realism and naturalism. The narrative usually features a central female protagonist whose major life crisis is the Civil War with all its inevitable disruptions to

32. For the following information, I am indebted to the research undertaken by Susan Millar Williams of the English Department, Louisiana State University, 1982–83. Also see her excellent dissertation, "Love and Rebellion: Louisiana Women Novelists, 1865–1919" (Ph.D. dissertation, Louisiana State University, 1984); Jones, *Tomorrow Is Another Day*, 41.

33. Elizabeth Bisland Wetmore [Louisiana], *Blue and Gray, or, Two Oaths and Three Warnings* (New Orleans, 1885), 4; Mary T. Tardy, in Raymond (ed.), *Southland Writers*, 296.

her marriage chances and her relations with blacks. The stereotypes of the conventional plantation novel are rife: southern women identifying strongly with the Confederacy, supporting their men and often wishing to be men themselves so they can fight; southern men who are brave, kind, and high-principled though in a significant number of cases broken by their war experiences and dependent on their women; northern men who are invariably crass, rude, and destructive. The book that Grace King claimed was shunned by decent southern women—*Uncle Tom's Cabin*—is the most frequently cited literary allusion, but the writers avoided the popular reconciliation motif in postbellum fiction, symbolized by the marriage of northern man and southern woman. They tended instead to vindicate the Confederate position and emphasize the devastating and demoralizing effect of the war and Reconstruction on Louisiana and its citizens. The most common conciliatory theme in relation to blacks is the timid liberal argument for a need for education and training—activities in which a few heroines participate.

It is clear that Louisiana, especially New Orleans, was identified as an appropriate site for romance and dramatic incident, and that writers from both Louisiana and other states, including the North, used to full fictional effect the regional peculiarities and different ethnic groups of the state. Indeed, the apparently exotic appeal of Louisiana was chosen by at least two non-Louisiana writers as the setting for politically sensitive problems such as the changing nature of postbellum gender definitions and roles, and the function of women in relation to blacks' education and work. One such work is by Maud Howe, who visited New Orleans with her mother in 1884 and then published *Atalanta in the South: A Romance,* a work heavily influenced by George W. Cable's critique of race relations but also including feminist themes he never attempted. Howe views southern chivalry with a skeptical feminist eye, seeing it as a virtue of shrewd, self-sacrificing *women* rather than of weak, dependent men. Indeed, perhaps because of her feminist training and family links, Maud Howe demonstrates unequivocally in this novel a point of view that many Louisiana women only imply or skirt around in their fiction—namely, contempt or pity for those men broken in body and spirit as a result of the upheavals of the war and Reconstruction, together with strong admiration for the strength and resourcefulness of women, and the loyal devotion of blacks. The novel indicts the neglect and maltreatment of both women and blacks, urging greater independence and self-reliance on the former, and arguing a standard liberal line about better education and opportunities for blacks. The latter theme is echoed in several women's novels of the period, though the preoccupation of southern women with the need for black education (with distant echoes of the Grimké sisters and *Uncle Tom's Cabin*) is usually clumsily incorporated into the narratives.[34]

But the racial themes are by no means always bland, or liberally incorporated within a romance framework. There are overtly unexamined racist elements in many works, and a few use racist subplots to spice their romantic central narrative. In one work, Mrs. Jeanette Coltharp's 1896 novel, *Burrill Coleman, Colored: A Tale of the Cotton Fields,* a white love story takes place against a black conspiracy to take over a parish and exterminate whites in the name of "negro supremacy." The love story gains a *frisson* of dangerous excitement from this affair, and once the conspirators are lynched by a white mob the white lovers are finally free to marry. The male black figures are all irresponsible, drunken, improvident, faithless, stupid, with an " 'invariable ill oder.' " The only good blacks are female—the young, trusting Ella who loves and helps the married Burrill Coleman, and kind Aunt Harmony who keeps a clean cabin. The novel's racism is confirmed in a way common to southern postbellum writers: it arises within a community which (the reader is to believe) wishes fervently to love and trust its blacks as it always has done, but has come to recognize gradually that such bonds can no longer be guaranteed between white and black. The relations of the romance are applied to black-white conflict, and the bonds of love, loyalty, and respect due between classes that recognize a strict hierarchy of relations are shown to have broken down. With political argument or analysis firmly excluded, the novels can depict blacks as insidious and ungrateful, their legitimate dissatisfactions or outright revolt as outrageous disloyalty. A writer such as Mrs. Coltharp can thus vindicate lynching as a justifiably defensive measure against the rise of black "untrustworthiness" and ingratitude to their natural superiors.[35]

It is in the context of those political, social, and literary developments in the postbellum South outlined above that I intend to discuss three writers in detail. Grace King, Ruth Stuart, and Kate Chopin became the most successful women writers about Louisiana, and enjoyed limited national success. In many ways they provided the North with the kinds of fictional interpretation of the South and Louisiana that it was demanding, and to that extent the writers conformed to editorial demands. But in significant ways the work of all three departs from and challenges conventional forms and themes. To varying degrees, they reinterpreted elements of southern

34. For example, Mrs. J. H. Walworth, *Without Blemish: Today's Problem* (New York, 1886), and Alice Ilgenfritz Jones, *Beatrice of Bayou Têche* (Chicago, 1895).

35. Mrs. Jeanette Coltharp, *Burrill Coleman, Colored: A Tale of the Cotton Fields* (Franklin, La., 1896), 145.

life and history in original ways that indicate fresh possibilities and breaks with orthodoxies, especially around issues of gender. My discussion of the three writers will attempt to demonstrate this both through reinterpretation of the biographies and through new readings of their fiction.

I

Grace King

The writings of Grace King are of considerable relevance to modern literary scholars, since she is one of the very few American women writers who have confronted the problems of race and gender in relation to regional political and social concerns. While her nonfiction takes a predominantly orthodox line, the fiction demonstrates a skeptical and critical view of gender definitions and relations between the sexes and races. Indeed, the fiction moves increasingly toward some brave, contentious feminist positions. And although she never *consciously* takes anything other than a standard southern white supremacist line on questions of race, much of her work probes that line through its very choice of subject matter, narrative tone, and unsatisfactory closures. The texts are rich with the contradictions and confusions within postbellum southern racial ideology—especially as inflected through questions of gender.

King gained a certain amount of critical acclaim, popular success, and international recognition in her lifetime as a fiction writer, biographer, and historian of Louisiana. However, most standard works on southern history and literature ignore her. If her name appears, it is usually as an example of the literary response to the Civil War, or as epitomizing Louisiana's hostility toward its notorious native son, George W. Cable. Her exclusion from standard histories was noted by one of the most eminent southern scholars, Arlin Turner, who argued the need for a full biography of King that would elucidate literary relations in Louisiana and "the literary lines from one remote region to the main literary centers." The literary scholar Robert Bush has done more than anyone else to further King scholarship: he has published the biography that Turner recognized was necessary, as well as a selection of King's writings and several articles in which he has illuminated her position as southern writer in postbellum

Louisiana and her relations with writers such as Mark Twain. There is only one full-length work on Grace King and her writing, a psychological study by David Kirby. Though both Bush and Kirby recognize a feminist strength in King's work, they do not explore this aspect of her writing, and both steer clear of examining her racial attitudes. Bush is aware of her staunch advocacy of the Lost Cause but tends to excuse or obfuscate her racism. Kirby ignores the issue of race and makes the extraordinary claim that her autobiography reveals King's "determination to become—and her success at becoming—a 'man of action' " (my emphasis). A modern critic interested in the history of American women's writing and the significance of postbellum southern letters must examine why King was so successful in bringing her particular political version of Louisiana to a northern reading public.[1]

Grace King's biography is quickly sketched. She was born in 1852 in New Orleans, where (apart from some years during the Civil War on the family plantation) she lived all her life and died just before her eightieth birthday. She began to write in 1884, and after her first published story, "Monsieur Motte," was in considerable demand from magazine and book publishers, enjoying a successful literary career until early in the present century. She published as much nonfiction as fiction: six historical and two biographical books on aspects of and figures in Louisiana history, as well as five novels/novellas, two short story collections, one play, and her auto-biography. She also published numerous short stories and articles on specific historical topics that were never anthologized. She was celebrated in her native city and known in intellectual circles in the Northeast and Paris; in the words of the Louisiana Historical Society, she died a respected "Scholar, Historian, Essayist, Writer of Fiction."[2] She never married, and lived throughout her life with her sisters and brothers.

In many ways, Grace King is typical of nineteenth-century women writers. Single and childless, she always lived in the family home; and she began to write after her father's death and her favorite sister's marriage (which she called "a form of bereavement"). She published her first article anonymously under the initials P.G., and resisted acknowledging authorship of her first published story, "Monsieur Motte," until a year after

1. Arlin Turner, "Dim Pages in Literary History: The South Since the Civil War," in Louis D. Rubin, Jr., and C. Hugh Holman (eds.), *Southern Literary Study: Problems and Possibilities* (Chapel Hill, N.C., 1975), 41; Robert Bush (ed.), *Grace King of New Orleans: A Selection of Her Writings* (Baton Rouge, 1973), and *Grace King: A Southern Destiny* (Baton Rouge, 1983), and see Bibliography for a full list of Bush's articles; David K. Kirby, *Grace King* (Boston, 1980), 24.

2. King, *Memories,* 398.

its considerable success.[3] Though financially supported by legacies from her father and uncle and by her brothers' earnings, she resented the dependence this involved and often chafed against her inevitable duties as household manager, seamstress, and sicknurse to her mother and sister. Like many women, she looked to her mother, sisters, and female friends for moral support, emotional intimacy, and necessary research and typing. And along with most successful women writers of the century, she was indebted to male authority and power for the encouragement and opportunity to publish her work. These different relationships to the men and women in her life are reflected in her style of address to each: self-deprecatory and flirtatious in her letters to male editors and critics, while to women more honest and direct in her revelations of ambition and self-esteem.

But while she shared many of the characteristics of other women writers, in crucial ways Grace King was atypical. Although many southern women published fiction, King was rare in nineteenth-century America in achieving the status of *southern* woman of letters, and I know of no other woman who achieved Grace King's sheer range of publication. More like some French women writers, King attempted and became successful in several different genres: the short story, novel, historical narrative, romantic historical fiction, literary criticism, biography, and autobiography. She even became a minor literary agent for French writers who wished to publish in America. Unlike her precursors, moreover, she remained in her birthplace all her life (apart from occasional travels) and took upon herself the role of southern/Louisiana spokesperson. In this way, and in her intense involvement with her own region, she anticipated southern women writers of later generations: Ellen Glasgow, who lived in Virginia all her life; Flannery O'Connor in Georgia; and Eudora Welty in Mississippi—all with strong roots in those communities that provided material for their fiction.

King is also unusual in the enormous range of acquaintances she had among writers, editors, and public figures in the United States and Europe. Of American figures, she knew such writers as the Louisiana historian Charles Gayarré; Edward King, correspondent of *Scribner's*; William Sloane, biographer of Napoleon; editors Hamilton Mabie and Henry Mills Alden; author-editors William Dean Howells and Charles Dudley Warner; the poet Richard Burton; New Orleans author Lafcadio Hearn; Virginia novelist Thomas Nelson Page; and Mark Twain. In France, among others she knew Th. Bentzon (Madame Blanc), critic and trans-

3. *Ibid.*, 49; and see Tillie Olsen, "Silences in Literature," in *Silences* (New York, 1978); Grace King, "Heroines of Novels," New Orleans *Times-Democrat*, May 31, 1885.

lator for *La Revue des Deux Mondes*; her son Edouard Blanc, lecturer and traveler; the poet Edouard Grenier; Pasteur Wagner, author of *The Simple Life*; and the poet Comtesse de Noailles. In New Orleans, she became a considerable literary celebrity and in the latter years of her life held a weekly salon, playing host to young writers such as Sherwood Anderson and Edmund Wilson. As one student of her life, John Kendall, has suggested, "probably no woman that America has produced, ever knew intimately so vast a circle of the intellectually illustrious of her time."[4]

Furthermore, King differs markedly from that earlier school of American women writers described by Nina Baym, who wrote domestic sentimental novels usually with didactic intent. The "self-conception" of these women, according to Baym, lay in the fact that they "saw themselves not as 'artists' but as professional writers with work to do and a living to be made from satisfactory fulfillment of an obligation to their audience." This emphasis also characterized a great many postbellum women writers, who used writing as little more than a practical means by which to support themselves and their families. Partly because she was never compelled to write to earn her keep, King was more ambitious and more self-consciously an "artist," never responding simply to the demands of her readers or editors but always aware of her critical reputation. Indeed, King viewed herself, and gained critical approval for so doing, as a representative rather than individual voice, as a literary ambassador for the South and for her fellow southern women. She appears to have taken on that "mission of the southern poet," which Henry Timrod implied was to "help a society under great historical stress to make an image of itself and of its meaning in history." Her political project both set her apart from most contemporary women writers, and contradicted orthodox definitions of southern womanhood.[5]

This project drew strength and gained conviction from the rising status of the South in northern letters. The journalist Edward King and the magazine *Scribner's*, as well as other magazines and accounts in the 1870s and 1880s, had helped develop a major market, thus vogue, for Local Color writing. Edward King is best known for discovering and encouraging the writer George W. Cable, as Grace King recounts in her *Memories*. Describing Mr. King's influence on Cable and his help in placing Cable's stories about New Orleans with northern magazines, she notes bitterly,

4. John S. Kendall, "A New Orleans Lady of Letters," *Louisiana Historical Quarterly,* XIX (1936), 28.

5. Nina Baym, *Woman's Fiction: A Guide to Novels By and About Women in America, 1820–1870* (Ithaca, N.Y., 1978), 16, 18; Henry Timrod, "Ethnogenesis," quoted in Lewis P. Simpson, *The Brazen Face of History: Studies in the Literary Consciousness in America* (Baton Rouge, 1980), 78.

"the young author was soon rising steadily in fame and fortune. With him Louisiana stepped also into fictional fame, but not into good fortune."[6] Yet Grace King gives her namesake his due as the "pioneer" of northern magazine commentators, one whose name "will never be forgotten in New Orleans." She recognized the important contribution that Edward King was making to the new romantic construction of her native city.

Edward King's commentary on Louisiana moves between panegyric and censure. Like many northern visitors, he was charmed and seduced by Louisiana, especially New Orleans, and relished its rich history and customs, remarking as others have done on the luxuriance of patio gardens and the bewitching nature of creole girls.[7] But he was also aware of the social injustices on which the apparently easygoing city and state were founded. He points to the "gigantic struggle" taking place in Louisiana: "the battle of race with race, of the picturesque and unjust civilization of the past with the prosaic and leveling civilization of the present." He quotes at length "a prominent historian and gentleman of most honorable Creole descent"—without doubt Charles Gayarré—to show the white establishment's view of blacks: for instance, that the "lazy" ones flocked to the cities from plantations, and that the Negro's "present incapacity" came about because he was "an inferior being . . . devoid of moral consciousness." Although not exactly an egalitarian thinker, Edward King points to the impossibility of racial equality while whites regarded blacks as incapable of voting or legislating. He argues that the white Louisianian "is not more glad to be rid of slavery than he would be to see the last negro vanish from the soil," a sentiment echoed by Grace King in a letter sent North four years later: "If the negroes could only be coaxed or driven North or West!" It is clear that the critical parts of King's articles rankled with Grace King, fueling that defiant patriotism which was to be articulated in her writing. And it is not surprising that Edward King was excited to discover George W. Cable, a white native of the state who was similarly critical of Louisiana's intransigence toward its black population, and that he encouraged Cable to publish in the North.[8]

By 1885, the year she began to write, Cable was a well-known figure nationally as well as in New Orleans, where he was despised for his earlier political campaigning and his fictional advocacy of the black cause. In

6. King, *Memories*, 50.

7. Although the term *creole* can indicate a West Indian Negro or a black or white native of New Orleans, throughout this study it will refer specifically to white descendants of French and Spanish early settlers in Louisiana.

8. Edward King, *The Great South*, 17, 31–32, 33, 89. Grace King records in *Memories*, 50, that Edward King "visited the Gayarrés and had long talks with the Judge on the condition of the country." Grace King to Charles Dudley Warner, May 28, 1889, in King Papers.

1884, Cable had left his home city permanently for Massachusetts, where he was supported and encouraged in his views. Thus he evacuated a space that was quickly filled by the southern apologists. In that same year, 1884, the Virginia writer Thomas Nelson Page's explicitly racist short stories began to appear in *Century* to wide acclaim. Grace King was to write later in her autobiography of the importance of Page to contemporary southerners, with his "stories, short and simple, written in Negro dialect. . . . [portraying] the Negro character, humorous, shrewd, and loyal to his master and his family." At the same time, as Edmund Wilson points out, northerners, desiring to hear of the South's "glamor, of its old-time courtesy and grace . . . took over the Southern myth and themselves began to revel in it."[9]

Thus, in terms of political and literary fashion, with a new conciliatory northern publication policy, Grace King was living in a fashionable city at a time when southern materials were of national interest. To give these promising conditions the necessary boost to get her into print, the Cotton Centennial Exposition, held in New Orleans in 1884 to publicize the city as a great commercial and trading center, attracted northern and foreign visitors. Although the exposition turned out to be a "mighty fiasco . . . an enormous embarrassment to New Orleanians, and attracted few patrons," Grace King enjoyed the stimulation of the club set up by Julia Ward Howe's Woman's Department, and many notable figures were entertained by the hospitable King family. In *Memories,* King recorded why, unlike some others, the journalist Joaquin Miller was an acceptable visitor: "[He] was not troubled, as other Exposition visitors were, about our political problems or our social injustices, as they were termed, to the colored people." She adds that "we wanted commendation at that time from our conquerors, and we needed it," and certainly this kind of "commendation" was forthcoming from some of the visitors to the exposition and the King household.[10]

At this time King was preparing the ground for her project as a writer because of key contacts with prominent male figures who either stimulated her into literary production or provided paradigms that she could emulate or react against. Edward King was one, but of greater personal significance were the Louisiana historian Charles Gayarré, the editors Richard Watson Gilder and Charles Dudley Warner, and Cable (whose importance will be discussed later). These very different men in various ways helped reinforce King's southern apologist and orthodox racial lines.

9. Grace King, *Memories,* 53; Wilson, *Patriotic Gore,* 605.
10. Carolyn E. Delatte, Review of Robert Bush's *Grace King: A Southern Destiny,* in *Journal of Southern History,* LI (February, 1985), 110; King, *Memories,* 53.

But they also represented a range of social and political ideologies through which she could negotiate her own position as a southern woman, departing from and challenging patriarchal models and structures. And from the start of her writing career, these men impressed upon her the importance of the debates around race in the South. So throughout her life questions of race and—because she was a woman—gender and authorship were to form a dialectical pattern in her work.

She was certainly well prepared to become a woman of letters. Charles Gayarré (1805–1895) was a close family friend and encouraged King to engage in the kinds of research he had pioneered in Louisiana. He was a creole lawyer who had become a judge and Louisiana's secretary of state and who, before the war, had undertaken exhaustive research into the state's history in Europe and New Orleans. Fiercely pro-Confederate, he lost his fortune in the war and refused to take the loyalty oath; his political stand and passionate white supremacist views impressed his young protégée. She used many of Gayarré's papers and materials for her own historical and biographical works on Louisiana, and identified herself as legitimate heir(ess) to his position as official state chronicler. But this relationship, and her own ambitions, are considerably obfuscated in the self-dramatizing account of the genesis of her authorship. She recounts in *Memories* her meeting in 1884 with Richard Watson Gilder, editor of *Century* magazine, at a gathering during the New Orleans Cotton Centennial Exposition. One night Gilder asked Grace why the people of the city were inimical to the writer George W. Cable. She explained that it was because Cable, a "well treated" native of the city, had "proclaimed his preference for colored people over white and assumed the inevitable superiority . . . of the quadroons over the Creoles," thus stabbing the city in the back "to please the Northern press." Gilder's reply, according to King, was, "Why, if Cable is so false to you, why do not some of you write better?" The next morning, the story goes, Grace King sat down and wrote "Monsieur Motte." Such a romantic view of the solitary King discovering her métier through a single provocative encounter leaves out of account the groundwork that had already been laid, especially by Gayarré.[11]

At the time Grace King met Gilder in New Orleans, he was the most influential of all the magazine editors, and *Century* (replacing *Scribner's*) the most important magazine. Unlike other Genteel Tradition editors who

11. King, *Memories*, 60–62. It is interesting to compare Margaret Mitchell's response to the editor Harold Latham who was author-searching in Atlanta. He challenged her, "If Southerners want to stand right before the world, why don't they themselves write the truth?" Mitchell then produced her manuscript of "Gone With the Wind" (quoted in Jones, *Tomorrow Is Another Day*, 318).

sought sectional reconciliation during Reconstruction, Gilder was prepared to reopen thorny questions about the war, commissioning a series of
papers on battles and leaders of the war, and arranging for serial publication of a biography of Lincoln. He admired and encouraged Cable, publishing seven of his stories in the mid-1870s. But he was highly moralistic
and authoritarian, and unprepared to touch what he regarded as unpleasant
material. Larzer Ziff claims that Gilder "most clearly epitomized the sup-
pressing tone of the literary establishment"; he critically edited and
emended a whole range of works by Mark Twain, James, Howells, and
Robinson. He rejected Cable's short story "Bibi" because it was concerned
with the notorious *code noir,* and he and his assistant Robert Underwood
Johnson drastically edited Cable's best work, *The Grandissimes.* Gilder
praised Grace King for her "exquisite little dramas" but censured her
indelicacies, asking her, for instance, to drop the word *red* from her description of a priest's nose, on the grounds that Catholic readers "might
think that this was an attack on the priesthood." Gilder was one of three
editors who formed what has been called a "triumvirate of genteel ide-
alism" whose magazines breathed (in Ziff's words) "an air of high-class
mediocrity." These men had a softening or silencing effect on many writers and works; Edmund Wilson calls the "slow strangulation of Cable as an
artist and a serious writer" by his genteel editors "one of the most
gruesome episodes in American literary history." Cable's literary decline
into romantic genteel novelist, paralleled though it was by his growth as a
radical reformer, was directly due to the advice and censorship imposed on
him mainly by Henry Alden of *Harper's* and by Gilder and Johnson.[12]

Grace King responded deferentially to Gilder, as to all her editors. Male
mentors and critics (usually much older than she) were vital to her development, and she welcomed their advice and support. The most important
of these men, and the person who had most impact on the author's early
career, was Charles Dudley Warner, whose friendship, political experience, and contacts were to influence King a great deal and who could have
done much to shake her political, racial, and sexual conservatism. When he
met Grace King during the exposition in early 1885, Warner was a fifty-
six-year-old married, successful author and contributing editor to *Harper's
New Monthly Magazine.* He was also well known by his friends for acting
as literary agent to various young women writers; already among them
were Helen Hunt Jackson, Frances Hodgson Burnett, Annie Fields, and

12. Ziff, *The American 1890s,* 123, 128–29; Richard Watson Gilder to Grace King, September 24, 1891, in King Papers; Rubin, *George W. Cable,* 63; Wilson, *Patriotic Gore,* 579. The
third editor of the "triumvirate," besides Gilder and Alden, was Roger Burlingame of
Scribner's.

Sarah Orne Jewett. Two years later he was to play a similar role in the career of Ruth McEnery Stuart, whom he met on vacation. He was apparently a most appealing man; Mark Twain wrote of "a charm about his spirit, and his ways, and his words, that won all that came within the sphere of its influence." Grace King, herself an attractive, impressionable thirty-four-year-old currently reading about George Eliot and her (married) mentor G. H. Lewes, was by no means immune.[13]

Like Lewes, Charles Warner was invaluable at the outset of his protégée's career. He helped her with an article she was preparing for the *Times-Democrat* and took "Monsieur Motte" in hand, offering it first to *Harper's,* then to William Sloane for *New Princeton Review,* where it was published. He criticized the stories she sent him, while offering generous help as unpaid agent and adviser on everything from how to deal with proof sheets to how to make money and a name out of writing. It was he who advised initial anonymous publication. In the early years, King relied on the presence, or thought, of Warner to keep her writing, and her letters indicate the faith she put in him and the extent to which he acted as confidant of her fears and anxieties about the business of being an author. Undoubtedly adding some spice to this semiprofessional correspondence was the insistence by both of them on their sexual difference. With girlish modesty King refers to herself as "a young lady in a novel" and as "too much of a woman not to dwell more on the sentiment that you cared enough for me to take so much trouble to get Monsieur Motte published," while Warner directly reveals his physical attraction: "I confess, I am so weak minded, that I would rather see you in your new white silk . . . than to read all that your genius can put on paper." Indeed, some of Warner's letters are sexually very provocative; King rapidly learned how to respond with appreciative flirtatiousness.[14]

Ironically, though ideal as a confidence-booster and emotional support for the young writer, Warner was by no means the ideal literary mentor for King in those early years. He never challenged the many inconsistencies, sentimentalities, and irrational fears within King's fictional treatment of blacks. He also discouraged the critical edge in her early work and tried to encourage her to write love stories, which she felt unable and disinclined to do. A third-rate fiction writer himself, imbued with genteel standards, he was a poor prose stylist for her to emulate, and she allowed his moralistic

13. For a fuller account of this relationship, see my article "The Case of Grace King," *Southern Review,* XVIII (1982), 685–702; Kenneth R. Andrews, *Nook Farm: Mark Twain's Hartford Circle* (Cambridge, 1950), 256.

14. Grace King to Charles Dudley Warner, September 17, 1885, October 4, 1885, Charles Dudley Warner to Grace King, November 28, 1885, all in King Papers.

judgments to prevail over the greater tolerance she developed in emotional matters. For example, on her first trip to Europe, she was asked by a friend of Madame Blanc's to translate and publish some letters believed to be by George Sand. Though shocked by them as she translated, King described being "transported by their literary beauty." However, when Warner saw them, his response was such as to indicate the inhibiting force he had on King's timid but pronounced departure from genteel sentiments: "He jumped away from them as from a fire, and wrote me a severe scolding for translating them. No magazine would publish such things . . . and he was ashamed that I should even think of submitting them to an editor. I meekly put them away and said no more about them, although in comparison with what magazines publish at the present time they are mere icicles."[15]

Over political questions about the South, Warner tended to bolster rather than challenge King. In the 1850s and 1860s, he had been a Radical Republican and edited the Republican *Evening Press* in Hartford; but he came staunchly to defend the South during Reconstruction. Like Samuel Clemens (Mark Twain), in the 1870s he began to lose his radical sympathies and his earlier advocacy of universal male suffrage; unlike Twain he became increasingly nostalgic and conservative over many social and political issues. The active presence in Hartford during the 1870s of female suffragists had made Warner uneasy about all reform, especially suffrage, and it is hardly surprising that he became interested in and supportive of a conservative southern lady who was then scornful of blacks' as well as women's rights. In several letters, Grace King argued with Warner's vestigial Republican views of the Negro, and she defended her fictional portrayal of blacks. He tended to make playful, dismissive references to their once major ideological differences: "Didn't you know that I was an abolitionist and prayed seven times a week for the destruction of slavery, and hated rebellious people as much as you did Yankees? Do you forget that I am a Yankee? Ah, well, you are one of the people who have made me love the South." King replied in kind: "You needn't fling your being a Yankee and Abolitionist at me; if you can stand it, I can. That's one of the things that makes you so fascinating—the contradiction of the least Yankee of persons coming from the most Yankee of places."[16] So thoroughly did he, and indeed the whole Hartford community, make light of King's political sensibilities that her views of the Civil War, the postbellum South, and the southern black remained unquestioned and unexamined.

However, although King's contacts with the North reinforced her racial

15. King, *Memories,* 153–54.
16. Charles Dudley Warner to Grace King, October 9, 1885, Grace King to Charles Dudley Warner, October 18, 1885, both in King Papers.

conservatism, they certainly challenged and shifted her views on gender. While Warner and Hartford seemed to confirm her white supremacism, the women she met in the North introduced her to more progressive views of sex roles and male supremacy. And these women began a process of alerting King to her own needs as a woman. She had already come under the influence of a northern feminist during the Cotton Centennial Exposition, when Julia Ward Howe was appointed head of the Woman's Department. Despite her reservations about Howe's political sympathies (she had, after all, written the "Battle Hymn of the Republic"), King eagerly joined the "PanGnostics" literary club that Howe set up in March, 1885. Together with her daughter Maud, Julia Howe became a charismatic central figure in social and cultural life. According to King, she found little to displease her in New Orleans: "she was too tactful to hint at the obnoxious designation of the 'New South' and too intelligent not to ally herself with the 'Old South,' to which, in fact, she was allied by family tradition and social inclination." She delighted the old creole families by inviting them to exhibit miniatures, jewels, laces, documents, and pieces of furniture in her Woman's Department. King reports that the result of this unheard-of idea was "the opening of the past history of the city, not only to strangers, but to the citizens themselves, in whose minds the hard chances of the Civil War and its consequences had effaced the historical traditions of the past."[17]

Besides making the creoles conscious and proud again of their own past, Mrs. Howe became a society hostess for the duration of the exposition. She knew many leading literary figures and brought people together in her house for discussions; she quickly set up a literary club, the "Pan-Gnostics," for local and visiting literati. Grace King took an active role in club meetings, acting as minutes secretary and producing her first essay, "Heroines of Novels," to read at one of the sessions. Thus King had a unique opportunity to meet others interested in literature from many parts of the country, and to hear ideas debated. The "Pans" devoted much attention to women's rights: of fourteen discussions that King listed in her Minute Book between March, 1885, and May, 1886, six were on the subject of women. She met there many strong, intelligent women who were to provide models for her own development as woman of letters, long after everyone had left the city. And when, invited north by Warner, she visited the Hartford community, she was conversant with women's rights issues and eager to meet northern women.

On her first trip to Hartford, by contrast with her experiences in New Orleans, King met and was fascinated by eccentric and unorthodox

17. King, *Memories,* 54, 55.

women. They perhaps allowed her a refreshing taste of the freedoms available to independent "New Women." To begin with, she became familiar with the sight of Harriet Beecher Stowe, now senile and simply tolerated by the Nook Farm community, wandering around talking to herself. King was struck, she says in her *Memories,* by the "pretty apparition" of this once controversial and influential figure who had written *Uncle Tom's Cabin,* that "hideous, black, dragon-like book that hovered on the horizon of every Southern child."[18] She must also have known of the other, more recent scandal in which Stowe was involved, one that conflicted even more with her role as respectable woman of letters—namely her 1869 revelation in *Atlantic* of Byron's incest, disclosed to her by Lady Byron. But Stowe was not the only unorthodox woman King met on that first trip. The other was her sister, Isabella Beecher Hooker, who had just returned to Hartford after an absence abroad. Isabella had supported Victoria Woodhull's publishing the story of her half-brother, Henry Ward Beecher's, alleged adultery with Elizabeth Tilton. Although the scandal and her refusal to side with Beecher had blown over, Hooker was still an outspoken feminist who, under Woodhull's influence, chronicled her belief in the coming of a worldwide matriarchal government that would merge with Christ's kingdom in a great millennial period.

Despite attempts by Charles and Susan Warner to keep them apart, Grace King sought out Isabella Hooker and was fascinated by her. In her autobiography, perhaps with the conservatism or ironic detachment of old age, she dismissed Hooker with a one-line remark as "a tall, handsome woman, who talked to me about 'Woman's Rights' and converted me to her point of view." However, King's letters from Hartford reveal a far deeper interest on her part, and a more serious "conversion." She was well aware of the scandal attached to Hooker—as friend of Victoria Woodhull, feminist, spiritualist, "& all sorts of unorthodox things"—and she was acutely aware that she was breaching etiquette by courting a woman of whom her hosts disapproved. On one occasion, she visited Hooker on a flimsy excuse and was taken to her bedroom where they discussed at length women's rights, spiritualism, and family troubles; it seems that the southerner was charmed and convinced.[19]

On that first visit to Hartford, Grace King also met Olivia Clemens, of whom she soon became a confidante, and an aspiring writer, Warner's current protégée (and possibly mistress), Mrs. Cabell. On her second visit to Nook Farm, she met Mary E. Wilkins (later Freeman), whom she described as having a "dreadfully worn face—no aristocratic glamour—

18. *Ibid,* 77.
19. *Ibid.;* Grace King to May King McDowell, July 7, 1887, in King Papers.

no refinement about her—a clear headed—poetical hearted, little
Yankee." Wilkins was nonetheless a source of fascination to King, especially as she reported that all the American, English, and Continental
publishers were "after her."[20] From these early contacts with northern
feminists and autonomous creative female figures, Grace King appears to
have gone on to meet and actively seek out strong female friends, to read
women's writing, and to focus closely on women authors. Her confidence
in herself and her ideas grew correspondingly stronger.

    She quickly became part of an American-French-British network of
female contacts; when she went to England she was put in touch with
women educationists like Anne Clough of Newnham College, Cambridge, and on her travels in France she was embraced in female literary
circles. Annie Fields introduced her to Madame Blanc, and through this
friendship she came to know Sarah Orne Jewett, Blanc's closest friend;
she became a good friend and admirer of her contemporaries and neighbors, Mollie Moore Davis and Ruth McEnery Stuart; and her letters and
published writings refer to the lives and works of women writers, such as
Jane Carlyle and the Brontë sisters. The wide variety of King's women
acquaintances and her intimacies with a few women involved in the
world of letters helped enhance her sense of herself as a serious writer and
gave assurance and depth to her fictional treatment of women characters.
As a result of her extensive travels and many female friendships, King
was forced radically to review her ideas about woman's role, responsibilities, and practices—legal, economic, and sexual. While deploring
some of Isabella Hooker's views on "free love" and spiritualism, she was
convinced by Hooker's feminist arguments. Shocked at the moral un-
scrupulousness she felt Mrs. Cabell showed by spending hours in Warner's study, she confessed to a confusion over "etiquette" since people in
Hartford were "puritanical about some things and utterly lax about others," and she admitted to being "almost convinced" by George Sand's
pupil Madame Blanc about the desirability of adultery for unhappy
wives. She became increasingly self-conscious about her status (nationally and in a small way internationally) as a female "southern man of
letters." The role has never been an easy one for a woman to play, and the
more formidable the woman the more absurd the title becomes (as when
Sheldon Rothblatt writes, "George Eliot is a particularly happy choice
for illuminating the development of the man of ideas in England"). Like
other women of letters of the period, Grace King published first under
initials, then anonymously, and only after proven success and editorial
pressure did she use her own name. Although she enjoyed using her fem-

20. Grace King to May King McDowell, October 24, 1891, *ibid.*

ininity with male editors and writers (but was disconcerted by Samuel Clemens' patronizing treatment of her and other women, "as if they were nice clever boys"), she valued what she felt to be her ungendered position in the world of letters. And as her own way of life became more distant from that of her southern female contemporaries, she looked increasingly to women friends who had disregarded convention and were living in unorthodox ways.[21]

King made few overt pronouncements on other women's writing, but there is no doubt that she read widely in women's fiction, which influenced her work profoundly. Her repeated use of themes such as women's work, education, family role, position in marriage, and so on echo the work of women she evidently admired, from Madame de Staël and George Sand to Charlotte Brontë and George Eliot, as well as many minor American sentimental writers such as Susan Warner, whom she read in childhood. In her first published article, she outlined what she saw as the differences between men's and women's writing. She praised Charlotte Brontë and George Eliot for creating plain, unexceptional heroines, and criticized Henry James for doing everything possible for each of his heroines "except to let her die or make her speak."[22] Grace King clearly saw part of her project as a *woman* writer to be the necessity to let her heroines speak and act for themselves, rather than simply embodying virtuous and charming qualities; and in this way—like many of her female contemporaries—she drew on other women's writing and departed significantly from her male peers.

Earlier I quoted David Kirby's absurd assertion that Grace King became a "man of action." But this seems a singularly inappropriate label for a woman always acutely aware of being both a southern lady and a woman of letters. From the early years, King was self-conscious about questions of gender and concerned centrally with the nature of women's lives; she was also unashamedly a committed political writer. While admiring assertiveness and strength in women and cultivating those qualities herself, she retained the ambivalences and anxieties of southern women of her time and place, and allowed these to surface constantly in the fiction, mainly through a heavy use of irony. Kirby reads the black Marcélite in "Monsieur Motte" as a "man of action," thus missing the complex series of ironies that King weaves in this story and its sequels about women of both

21. Grace King to Annie Reagan King, June 26, 1887, Grace King to May King McDowell, February 17, 1894, both in King Papers; Sheldon Rothblatt, "George Eliot and the New Intellectuals" (paper read at the George Eliot Centennial Conference, Rutgers University, November 21–23, 1980), 1; Grace King, "Mark Twain, Second Impression," n.d., Notebook, in King Papers.

22. Grace King, "Heroines of Novels," New Orleans *Times-Democrat*, May 31, 1885.

races, of different classes and kinship relations. When he defines King's "paradigmatic community" as one of women "bonded together in a world sadly mismanaged by men," he ignores (as King never does) the class and race separations between the women characters. It is perhaps worth noting that the female bonding Kirby sees as central to King's work rarely occurs between white and black women except in controlled circumstances, and in some cases it is violently rejected.[23] There is a clear distinction between King's move toward a progressive feminist ideology and a conservative adherence to southern racialism. The complexities of her positions on race and gender must be kept in play in any consideration of her work.

From the start, Grace King's project as a writer of fiction was specifically addressed to questions of race. As with earlier white writers, King's fictional treatment of blacks was mainly confined to the mulatto, a familiar type in American national literature. The mulatto is at the center of a whole body of fictional work upon which George W. Cable and King drew.[24] While Cable's writing about the mulatto followed the political example of the antebellum antislavery writers, such as Richard Hildreth and Harriet Beecher Stowe, King made the mulatto *woman* the focus for contradictions and problems around gender.

It is interesting to note that critical discussions of the mulatto (which ignore King's particular contribution) fail to recognize the gender implications within that body of fiction, which makes considerable use of gender stereotypes. This is particularly startling in the most comprehensive review of such fiction by Judith R. Berzon. *Neither White nor Black* is organized around "the concept of marginality" and discusses the "crisis experience" when mulattoes become aware of their racial and social marginality.[25] Although it is an excellent, long-overdue survey of the mulatto character in American fiction, unfortunately the book veers dangerously toward an assumption that the mulatto of history is interchangeable with that of representation. Berzon refers throughout the book to the mulatto and his author as masculine, and gives no special consideration to the

23. Kirby, *Grace King,* 38; for instance, "The Little Convent Girl."

24. For instance, Richard Hildreth, *The Slave: or Memoirs of Archy Moore* (1836; Upper Saddle River, N.J., 1968); Henry Wadsworth Longfellow, "The Quadroon Girl" (1842); Harriet Beecher Stowe, *Uncle Tom's Cabin* (1852; rpr. 2 vols. in 1; Columbus, 1969); Mayne Reid, *The Quadroon* (New York, 1856), later dramatized by Dion Boucicault into a significantly less black *The Octoroon* (London, 1859). Since the Civil War, major American writers such as Mark Twain, Willa Cather, and William Faulkner have made the mulatto a central figure in their work, as have racist writers like Thomas Dixon and Robert Lee Durham.

25. Judith R. Berzon, *Neither White nor Black: The Mulatto Character in American Fiction* (New York, 1978), 13.

question of gender even when discussing special cases or women writers. She does not examine the many ironies of her own organizing principle of marginality, even when it is clear that male and female mulattoes are marginal in different ways: for instance, the "tragic mulatto" is invariably female while the mulatto as "race leader" is invariably male. It is necessary, therefore, to discuss the mulatto in fiction with more specific attention to gender.

Feminist criticism has focused attention on the concept of female marginality to a dominant male culture, as represented in women's writing. Patsy Stoneman argues that in Victorian England, for the first time, the literary type of the outcast/exile (a familiar *male* literary figure from the Seafarer onwards) was definitely associated with *women,* and this must dramatically affect the way in which the Brontë sisters' female characters are interpreted as outcasts, window gazers, and rebels. She demonstrates, in discussions of *Wuthering Heights* and *Jane Eyre,* how physical freedom and mobility that take women out of the home and family into the "outside" and into places and realms of being in which they are not definable by orthodox social terms lead them to be "fallen women" and outcasts. If one examines the marginality of the mulatto woman from the point of view of gender and class determinants as well as those of race, the contradictions and overdetermination of her historical and representational positions become clearer.[26]

Jules Zanger provides a useful summary of the features of a literary type, the "tragic octoroon" (which also apply to the quadroon). She is "a beautiful young girl who possesses only the slightest evidences of Negro blood, who speaks with no trace of dialect, who was raised and educated as a white child and as a lady. . . . In her sensibility and her vulnerability she resembles . . . the conventional ingenue 'victim' of sentimental romance." He goes on to summarize the customary plot: at her father's sudden death, she is discovered to be still a slave and is thus sold into slavery by her father's creditors and victimized by a slave dealer or overseer (often a Yankee) who wants to sexually abuse her; a goodly northerner or European wishes to marry her and sometimes does so; more often, though, she dies of shame or suicide. Zanger argues that the tragic octoroon type appears in at least a dozen works between 1836 and 1861, and Judith R. Berzon (identifying the "tragic mulatto") names several more written between 1861 and 1933, pointing out that the formula was used as late as 1950 in Elizabeth Coker's *Daughter of Strangers.* This type of heroine clearly appealed to antebellum northern readers because she approximated

26. P. M. Stoneman, "The Brontës and Death: Alternatives to Revolution," in Francis Barker *et al.* (eds.), *1848: The Sociology of Literature* (Colchester, 1978), 79–96.

to the ideal sentimental heroine of popular fiction, and because the sympathy of those readers could be "aroused less because they are colored than because they are nearly white." The heroine's virtue, gentility, and sexual vulnerability were all associated particularly with her white blood, while her octoroon status made her a particularly effective focus for analysis and criticism of the institution of slavery. In postbellum works, this heroine was used to present dramatic case studies of marginality and of class, caste, and race confusion exacerbated by the war. Berzon points out that for many white writers "the all-but-white, usually female and beautiful, often tormented character is titillating and effectively meets the specifications for successful melodrama."[27]

The two texts featuring quadroon/octoroon figures that were best known to Cable and King are of considerable historical interest. For the purposes of the present discussion, it is instructive to examine the female mulatto characters in *The Octoroon* and *Uncle Tom's Cabin*. Zoe, the octoroon of the play's title, fulfills all the requirements of the standard literary type as described by Jules Zanger, while Stowe features two more distinctive mulatto women who are both survivors, Simon Legree's quadroon mistress Cassy and fugitive slave Eliza Harris, called quadroon by Stowe but "technically" octoroon. In *The Octoroon*, Zoe is contrasted with a white heiress, Dora, fair-haired and of little sexual appeal to George. This is the very contrast Leslie Fiedler points to in Cooper's *The Last of the Mohicans*, between Cora and Alice Munro, that "pattern of female Dark and Light that is to become the standard form in which American writers project their ambivalence toward women." When Fiedler talks of Cora's death as "Cooper's admission of American society's inability to provide a meaningful position for Cora and those like her," he is pinpointing something important about the nature of women slaves and miscegenation. For a *female* quadroon/octoroon, there is no "place" in American society in terms of sexuality and the family; raised as white, she inevitably identifies herself as part of white society and sees herself as pure, white, and innocent—*not* the dark outcast/wanderer who is rejected by fear, hatred, and/or envy by whites and blacks. The destiny she might hope for is illusory within her culture; marriage with a white man or recuperation into a white family is illegal, therefore evil. As Patsy Stoneman argues for

27. Jules Zanger, "The 'Tragic Octoroon' in Pre-Civil War Fiction," *American Quarterly*, XVIII (Spring, 1966), 63; Robert A. Bone, *The Negro Novel in America* (Rev. ed.; New Haven, 1965), 23; Berzon, *Neither White nor Black*, 13; and see, for instance, Henry Wadsworth Longfellow's sentimental poem "The Quadroon Girl," in *Poems on Slavery*, 1843, in *The Poetical Works of Henry Wadsworth Longfellow* (London, 1893), 71.

Cathy in *Wuthering Heights,* death or permanent exile is the only solution, and death by a woman's own hand preferable.[28]

Stowe's quadroon figures, on the other hand, are strong, and they survive. They are beautiful and sexually prized; like her white women, they live through their children for whom they take huge risks; and they demonstrate superhuman courage and tenacity that are ultimately rewarded. Their natural superiority to others is recognized by many. Because part of the novel's explicit project is to highlight and deplore the "public and shameless sale of beautiful mulatto and quadroon girls," their eventual fate is intended to reward their Christian virtue and loyalty and to counter the tragic fate of other slaves, notably Uncle Tom himself.[29] But the conclusion is forced, and Cassy's discovery of her daughter and son seems gratuitous and falsely sentimental. Cassy's history, as told to Uncle Tom, contains the tragic elements that were to be used intertextually by many subsequent writers, anti- and proslavery. For Stowe's predominantly female readers (and later Genteel Tradition audiences), the attraction of Cassy's story lay in its foregrounding of the "sudden reversals of fortune" which marriage, motherhood, family illness, bereavement, and poverty had brought so many women, white as well as black, and which the Civil War was to bring devastatingly. Many bourgeois white women readers were well able to identify if not with her enslavement at least with the perilous marital and sexual experiences of a woman who loses a beloved "husband," has her children taken from her, and has to prostitute herself in order to stay alive. The fate of the women slaves in the novel appeals to women readers both through the discourses of planters' wives and daughters through the text, but also because the women slaves are firmly located in familiar familial contexts—caring for and wishing to provide adequately for their families, and identifying themselves centrally as *mothers* rather than as sexual beings, workers, or outcasts. For George W. Cable and Grace King, the point about the marginal quadroon is that she cannot be recuperated into orthodox social and family structures; her isolation and anomie arise out of the social formation that institutionalizes racial difference and disadvantage.

28. Boucicault, *The Octoroon;* Sidney Kaplan, "*The Octoroon:* Early History of the Drama of Miscegenation," *Journal of Negro Education* (Fall, 1951), 554, 556; Stowe, *Uncle Tom's Cabin;* Leslie Fiedler, *Love and Death in the American Novel* (Rev. ed.; New York, 1966), 200–201. There is no evidence that King read *Uncle Tom's Cabin,* but I find it unlikely she had not done so, given her vehement denunciation. She would have been well aware of the story, even had she refused to read it.

29. Stowe, *Uncle Tom's Cabin,* II, 311–12.

Of course, Cable and King departed from Stowe's version of the quadroon for very different political reasons. While King had seen *Uncle Tom's Cabin* as "hideous" and "dragon-like," Cable wrote in 1882, "blessings on the day when Harriet Beecher Stowe was born." Indeed, Stowe's courageous attack on the slave system and hypocrisy of southern society was something Cable built on and went beyond in his condemnation of the racist creole caste system in his native New Orleans. The modern psychoanalytic writer Julia Kristeva argues that in certain cases "a text works by absorbing and destroying at the same time the other texts of the intertextual space." Although she is talking specifically of the poetic text, this seems an apt description of Cable's absorption and destruction of the sentimental *Uncle Tom's Cabin* in his *The Grandissimes*; whereas Grace King's early work (especially *Monsieur Motte*) is an example of work produced (in Kristeva's words) "in the complex movement of a simultaneous affirmation and negation of another text." Cable certainly became the authoritative patriarchal figure set up by King's editors, mentors, and southern contemporaries as a challenge for critical intertextual response. There were many similarities between the lives and careers of these two writers of the same generation, and since they both regarded themselves as political writers (albeit with different politics) their common experiences and their divergent responses to them are of relevance to the study of southern letters.[30]

Both Cable and King came from noncreole stock and were born in New Orleans, he in 1844, she in 1852. Both were on the Confederate side during the Civil War and had families who refused to take the loyalty oath after the city's occupation. Both were Presbyterian in a mainly Catholic community. They began to write for local newspapers and were "discovered" by northern writer/editors who arranged for publication of their stories in northern journals (Cable by Edward King in 1873, King by Gilder and Warner in 1884); they had considerable success with Local Color fiction and were associated with the same editors. They visited the North early in their careers and were entertained in Hartford by Samuel Clemens and Warner, who befriended both. They became professional writers in the early 1880s, and were acclaimed particularly for their contribution to southern regionalist literature (they both published a history of Louisiana creoles). After 1900 they were regarded by most readers and editors as passé, and they resorted to publishing nostalgic fiction for a residually genteel public while still drawing audiences for their lectures. All their

30. George W. Cable, *Boston Evening Transcript,* June 15, 1882, quoted in Philip Butcher, *George W. Cable* (New York, 1962), 54; Julia Kristeva, *Semiotiké* (Paris, 1969), quoted in Jonathan Culler, *The Pursuit of Signs* (London, 1981), 107.

lives, the two writers saw themselves first and foremost as political writers, contributing to contemporary debates about the South.[31]

But there are significant differences that are crucial in the development of these two writers. First, Cable's family never enjoyed the King family's economic and social status and security: Cable always had to work to support his widowed mother and siblings, as well as his wife and children, while Grace King was supported by her family investments and income, and used her literary earnings for personal luxuries. Cable's fictional, though not political, capitulation to Genteel Tradition pressures was due mainly to financial obligations. And in political terms, Cable's experiences as a soldier, supplemented by his later work with the census and mixed-race education, made him reject altogether that Confederate jingoism to which King adhered all her life. While for some southern men, battle experiences hardened their white supremacism and Confederate loyalties, Cable was horrified at the futility of, and suffering caused by the war. His daily contacts with blacks in the army and the racism he witnessed among the troops led him to question the validity of secession and the justice of slavery. His subsequent courageous stands against racial prejudice and discrimination led to permanent exile in the North, where initial editorial enthusiasm for his critical fiction gave way to censorship and pressures for romantic fiction celebrating a South these editors were now helping to construct. Away from his native city, Cable's political fervor was eventually softened, so that by the end of his career he had taken his place as a relatively subdued successful minor romantic novelist and liberal public speaker.

Cable certainly made Louisiana "step into fictional fame," emphasizing and romanticizing its non–Anglo Saxon Protestant elements to the fascination of a largely northern reading public. The fact that he spent a fair amount of time in his fiction describing the sights, sounds, and different peoples of the state, familiarizing his northern readers with the cosmopolitan character and the regional differences within the state and especially in New Orleans, allowed subsequent writers to use a kind of descriptive shorthand (as Chopin does in her short stories about northwest Louisiana, already described in Cable's *Bonaventure*). His New Orleans white creoles are made to speak a kind of *patois* to distinguish them from the Anglo-Saxons; this confused many non-Louisianian readers into believing they were of mixed black and white blood, and enraged the French creoles themselves. This was a salutary warning to Grace King and other Louisiana writers to avoid any attempt at capturing the creole dialect, and in

31. See Arlin Turner, *George W. Cable: A Biography* (Durham, N.C., 1956); Rubin, *George W. Cable;* Butcher, *George W. Cable;* Wilson, *Patriotic Gore.*

fiction it was almost certainly never attempted again. Grace King's correspondence makes clear the many ways in which Cable's example and ideas influenced her own career and sharpened her ideas about the South and southern blacks. Her comments on her famous contemporary range from the spiteful (in the 1880s) to the generous (in the 1920s). Early in her career, the correspondence points to her anger at Cable's success in the Northeast and her desire to use her writing to repudiate his versions of "the situation of whites and blacks after the war" and especially of the Louisiana quadroons; her only published reference to her rival in *Memories* is a bitter one.[32] She paid verbal tribute to him in an interview late in life (probably 1923), presumably at a time when she could afford to be generous— Cable's radicalism was by then forgotten and virtually silenced in both North and South.

King's fictional works can thus be read as antitexts to Cable's, most notably in terms of their approach to the women of Louisiana, especially mulattoes. Cable was locked into the sentimental, chivalric tradition of heroines, and his innovations in fiction do not apply to women characters. Gender is problematized throughout his work only in relation to beauty and love. He sees *all* women as mute victims of systems they do not understand and cannot challenge. It was these heroines and minor female characters against whom King was to create her own, using his as models to rewrite with irony.

Louis D. Rubin was the first critic to point out Cable's stereotyping of women characters as primarily objects of male desire. Certainly, close examination of *The Grandissimes* reveals considerable stereotyping and idealization of the women characters, and (as Rubin says) all are characterized in emotional and sexual, rather than political or intellectual terms. There is a symmetrical neatness about the typification of the women that is probably derived from Cable's intertextual derivations: he includes a wronged creole beauty (Aurore Nancanou), an innocent lovelorn daughter (Clotilde Nancanou), a wild voodoo quadroon artist (Palmyre), and a canny entrepreneurial black (Clemence). The blacker the women are, the more fully realized and active. Clemence, whose fate is the most tragic, is most sympathetically portrayed as a figure whom the slave system has dehumanized and destroyed. The quadroon Palmyre, however, is the most fascinating, and sexual, of the women characters. She is a spell-maker and dabbler in supernatural arts, and like other classic quadroons is seen constantly in terms of a wild, free nature: "That barbaric beauty . . . feline . . . a creature that one would want to find chained." Palmyre is one version of the marginal quadroon; the opposite of Longfellow's lovely

32. Grace King to May King McDowell, June 10, 1886, in King Papers.

innocent prostituted, Palmyre represents the sensual, sexually mature woman who is almost designed to bear out Cable's contemporary white readers' worst fantasies about black female sexuality. But the articulation of Palmyre's plight is given, like all other social comment in the novel, to its narrator Joseph Frowenfeld—mirroring his author, a white, male German Protestant. Thus, as in other mulatto fiction, the female quadroon is given no voice; following Stowe and Boucicault, Cable makes Palmyre the wounded victim of an oppressive system that others (including the white author/narrators) articulate and criticize for her. Like other women characters in Cable's fiction, she suffers from the evils of manmade caste laws, male pride, and male legislation forbidding mixed marriage. Cable's women can only operate through "witchery," voodoo, and trickery. Unlike Grace King, he sees no autonomous life or communication between women; his women direct their attention to men, or to each other simply for protection, envy, or amusement. Furthermore, none of his women characters is placed in an active or powerful position regarding interracial marriage choice, something that (as Eugene Genovese demonstrates) is not historically accurate. Philip Butcher points out that, although there are many mixed alliances in the fiction, Cable's pattern is always the same: "Always the male partner belongs to a race commonly regarded by Americans at the same time as superior to the race of the woman. A beautiful Creole girl may win the love of an Anglo-Saxon, or an octoroon may capture a male Creole but the coin is never reversed."[33]

There are two important stories by Cable that secure marriage for his heroines who, because of caste laws, have no hope of any future kinship structure beyond their mothers. In one, the woman is recuperated into a kinship structure though a surprise revelation; in the other, through deceit. In "Tite Poulette," once the Dutch/German Kristian Koppig has demonstrated that he will marry Poulette regardless of her color (though she is conveniently as white as a magnolia), her "mother" Zalli reveals that Poulette is not her daughter and is indeed white. In the other, "Madame Delphine," the mother lies about her daughter in order to secure her marriage; after the wedding, she reveals to the priest that Olive is in fact her daughter (thus raising difficult questions for southern readers about the "whiteness" of the creole race). Perhaps partly because of the sensitivity of this whole subject, Grace King avoided such a shock dénouement (as did

33. Rubin, *George W. Cable*, 58; George W. Cable, *The Grandissimes* (London, 1898), 76; Eugene D. Genovese, *Roll, Jordan, Roll: The World the Slaves Made* (New York, 1976), 422 ("Despite the legend, white women of all classes had black lovers and sometimes husbands in all parts of the South, especially in the towns and cities"); Butcher, *George W. Cable*, 40. *Dr. Sevier* and one short story are the only exceptions to this.

Cable after "Madame Delphine"). Both King and Kate Chopin used the surprise ending, but never to a woman's advantage, and certainly not to secure for her a social position. Edmund Wilson briefly compares Cable's "Delphine" with King's "The Little Convent Girl" and Chopin's "Désirée's Baby," but he does not notice that the *women* writers use their stories as demonstrations of the destructive effects of revelations about race and the impossibility of magical or surprise social recuperation. Perhaps partly for racist reasons and to avoid suggestions of mixed blood in the Louisiana community, but partly to emphasize the impossibility of transformation from social outcast to happy bride, King and Chopin make the revelation of color drive the heroines to suicide, since they cannot cope with social ostracism and their necessarily marginal social position. Heavily influenced by sentimental and genteel traditions, Cable made his women find a kind of safety in marriage or in the convent but, in King's work, both these institutions have their perils and traps for women. Death is sometimes safer than a marriage based on perilous assumptions, or on caste and race uncertainties.

As I have suggested, crucial to King's intertextual and oppositional response is her emphasis on gender. King makes far heavier use of irony than Cable, especially in relation to her women characters (black and white). She wrote no story that idealized or celebrated passive femininity and innocent beauty, qualities that are seen as invariably dangerous and undesirable. Although she never emulates Cable in creating as sensual and sexually active a black woman as his quadroon Palmyre, she does create autonomous black and mulatto women and allows them a voice of their own unmediated through a patronizing and/or male narrator. She also provides a richer variety of female types than Cable; several of her stories and novels feature women workers, and by avoiding the conventional love story in most of her work she was able to create women with problems and concerns that would have been inappropriate to Cable's romantic and limited female protagonists.[34]

THE FICTION

"Monsieur Motte" was written at great speed, as a conscious response to the immediate challenges of Gilder and Cable, and, I would suggest, to the

34. Examples of women workers are a seamstress in "One Woman's Story," *Harper's Bazaar,* XXIV (March 21, 1891), 218–19, and "Making Progress," *Harper's Magazine,* CII (February, 1901), 423–30; a railroad charge-hand in "The Flitting of 'Sister,'" *The Youth's Companion,* LXXVII (June 25, 1903), 305–306; a black fieldworker in "The Clodhopper," *McClure's Magazine,* XXVIII (March, 1907), 487–91; and a "New Woman" editor in *A Splendid Offer: A Comedy for Women,* in *The Drama,* XVI (March, 1926), 213–15, 235–37.

less pressing but nagging irritants of Stowe and Edward King. It was written out of Grace King's buoyant sense of confidence in her own class, race, and gender, and was so successful that it drew the attention of several northern editors, including William Sloane who commissioned sequels to the story. In *Memories*, King is frank about expressing to Gilder her view that Cable was a traitor to his race and native city, and that he believed in the superiority of blacks in general, especially of quadroons to white creoles. But when trying to place "Monsieur Motte," she expressed herself in more guarded terms. Sending her manuscript (already rejected by Gilder) to Charles Dudley Warner, she wrote that her intention was "to call attention at least to some of those relations brought on by slavery, honorable to all concerned. It seems to me, white as well as black women have a sad showing in what some people call romance . . . one of these days my stories may prove a pleasant record and serve to bring us all nearer together blacks and whites." In a later letter, she makes her project even clearer:

> The friend I showed it to here wanted me to give a cause such as saving her [Marcélite] from the auction block, but I feel this was gross and untrue to my own conception. Great instances of devotion were found among even the worst treated slaves. I love to dwell on this, what I would call holy passion of the Negro women, for it serves to cancel those other grosser ones, with which they are really victimised by their blood. And besides, I think it highly honorable to the Southern women that they could be so served and loved by slaves.

Thus, Grace King's conscious project was to write conciliatory fiction that focused on the social relations of southern women, black and white. But in terms of race, her confident white supremacist assumptions are clear: the black woman's inferior, "grosser" sexualized nature is saved by the loyalty and respect she shows in abundance to her white superiors. Thus Marcélite's "natural" bestiality is assuaged by her "holy passion" for Marie: the story's intention is to celebrate the sacramental nature of a black woman's love for a white girl.[35]

"Monsieur Motte" is an ironic title, since it names the one figure who never appears. He is the fictitious uncle of Marie Modeste Motte, herself the daughter of a wealthy plantation owner and his wife who died during

35. Grace King, "Monsieur Motte," *New Princeton Review*, I (January, 1886), 91–133, later published in book form as *Monsieur Motte* (New York, 1888), with three sequel stories, "On the Plantation," "The Drama of an Evening," and "Marriage of Marie Modeste." All page references given parenthetically in the text will be to the London, 1888, edition, except for references to "Monsieur Motte," which are taken from Bush, *Grace King of New Orleans*. The Bush edition will be noted in the text. Grace King to Charles Dudley Warner, September 17, 1885, October 4, 1885, both in King Papers.

the Civil War. The orphan Marie was taken from the plantation by her quadroon nurse Marcélite, who paid out of her earnings as hairdresser to send her charge to the Institut St. Denis in New Orleans. The story is set in the convent school and describes the events of the last two days of the school year, the final history examination and graduation day when Marie anticipates beginning her new life in the home of her uncle Motte. As graduation day dawns, all the boarders and teachers await the arrival of Marcélite to fix their hair. When she fails to turn up, there is chaos, and the Institut's formidable principal, Eugénie Lareveillère, has to attend the ceremony somewhat dishevelled. Afterwards, Marie alone of the girls is collected by no one, since her uncle cannot appear; she weeps herself to sleep. As Madame Lareveillère tries to find Monsieur Motte through her friend and attorney Monsieur Goupilleau, a disturbed and bedraggled Marcélite suddenly arrives and confesses she has invented Marie's uncle. Admitting that *she* is Marie's lifelong benefactor, she begs forgiveness. Eugénie and Monsieur Goupilleau acknowledge their affection for each other, offer to be Marie's parents, and Marcélite is forgiven by all. A transitional passage linking this first story with its three sequels describes the emptiness of the school during the summer vacation and Marie's desolation at the discovery of her orphan state. Her dejection is matched by the reduction of Marcélite to a "crouching, cringing, trembling" creature who cannot look her mistress in the face and is in pain "like some wild animal." Marie's would-be parents discuss her and her nurse, and Eugénie decides to take them for the summer to the plantation of her old school friend Aurore Angely.

"On the Plantation" takes place in early autumn on the Bel Angely plantation. A letter from Goupilleau declaring his love for Eugénie has been inadvertently lost, and there is some tension between her and Aurore, a stern, hardworking Catholic and plantation manager. Aurore has persuaded Marie to become a devout practitioner of religious exercises. Marie enjoys her stay, communing with nature and the black plantation workers, while Marcélite is wretched at losing the girl's trust and holds herself aloof from those workers to whom she considers herself superior. Goupilleau arrives to propose to Eugénie, who is dressed for the occasion by Marcélite. Aurore generously offers to hold the ceremony on the plantation and to look after Marie during the honeymoon.

"The Drama of an Evening" is set in carnival time in New Orleans, at the first *soirée* of the season, a debutante's ball. Marcélite dresses all the ladies' hair, while poor blacks from the city, though uninvited, enter by the back door and stand round the dance floor and in corners observing events. Marie is a guest, invited to dance by Charles, stepson of the French Madame Montyon, who fled to Paris during the war and is now back to reclaim outstanding debts and a huge legacy. She insults the creole community, and so Charles is challenged to a duel. Meanwhile, the once-beloved nurse of the child Charles has arrived at the *soirée* and recognizes him. Nourrice is dirty and homeless, but Charles, recognizing her, takes her away and arranges a home and finances for her—to his stepmother's consternation. Charles reminds her, however, that Nourrice was given to him by his mother, but sold by her, his *step*mother. He leaves in anger for the duel, a fact that Marcélite reveals to Madame Montyon, then deep in financial talks. Chastened, she writes a note of apology to prevent the duel. Marcélite, pitying her, accompanies her home.

The final part of the novel, "Marriage of Marie Modeste," details the marriage arrangements of Charles Montyon and Marie. The story begins with Eugénie's discovery of the pair avowing love and agreeing to marry; she is annoyed that her permission has not been asked. Charles tells his stepmother he intends to marry a penniless girl, and she is so angry that love is his sole reason that she arranges a spiteful marriage contract. The wedding day arrives, and Marcélite gives Marie the wedding gift she has held since the girl's mother's death. It is a small workbox with a secret compartment containing gold dollars, giving her (as Marcélite says) "some picayunes of your own." The final part of the story reveals that Marie is rightful heir to the lucrative Sainte Marie plantation and its earnings since the war, so her wealth easily outmatches that of her husband and mother-in-law. It is Marcélite, not Eugénie, who accompanies Marie on her wedding day, performing all a mother's tasks. The novel ends with a happy marriage, Marcélite's place on the plantation fully assured.

Monsieur Motte is organized around broken families, surrogate parenthood, adoptive relations, and orphanhood. No major character is situated within a stable family: the central figures, Marie, Marcélite, and Charles, are orphans; Madame is a motherless widow; and Goupilleau a bachelor. All these characters act as surrogate kin to one another: Marcélite and Eugénie act as mother to Marie, who in turn plays their daughter and that of Goupilleau. Marie's plantation mistress grandmother treated Marcélite as a daughter when her own mother had been sold out of the parish. Goupilleau, before declaring himself as lover, is seen by Eugénie as a father figure. Charles rejects his stepmother Montyon in favor of his devoted nurse with the maternal name Nourrice. All four stories that comprise *Monsieur Motte* revolve around issues of key importance to Louisiana and the South in the first decades after a war that had rendered all economic and social relations unstable and precarious, and that had led to redefinitions of class, race, and gender. The carnage caused by the war and the common phenomenon of orphans, widows, and unmarried female workers of both races allowed King much fictional scope. As a result, the work is full of these female types (and to a lesser extent male figures) of dubious parentage and marital and family status. *Monsieur Motte* thus gives a very different version of southern social relations from that of contemporary male writers such as Thomas Nelson Page and Cable. As a southern woman, King placed at the center of her fiction those postbellum female alliances within, and in opposition to, male-dominated society, as well as using motifs common in earlier women's writing—Catholicism, education and economy, and female sexuality.

The main foci of the stories are women undergoing major changes in social and familial relations. For Marie and Marcélite, whose names echo each other and whose crises of subjectivity ironically mirror each other's, the contradictions are greatest. It is through their transformed relationship that King introduces the discussion of the larger crises and compromises in southern society that she was to make the subject of most of her fiction. Marcélite behaves, as everyone acknowledges, like a real mother; she is crucial to Marie's notion of herself as part of a social and familial structure that is kept alive by Marcélite's tales of the girl's dead parents and her imaginative creation of Monsieur Motte. Marie is obsessed with the blood relations she has never known, clinging to Marcélite only as a poor substitute for a real white mother. Indeed, the white Eugénie and Goupilleau—an unorthodox pair of "parents" since they adopt her initially as two single people—are at first shown to be privileged over the quadroon, whose revelation of deceit casts her into temporary obscurity.

The first story of the novel derives its dramatic interest from the threatened betrayal of vulnerable white southern womanhood by newly hostile, autonomous quadroon/black women, the very group that had "so served and loved" their mistresses as slaves. This fear of a breakdown of relations between the races and thus of the social order, because of the rising power and resistance of freed blacks in New Orleans, was a common nightmare of Reconstruction and the early 1880s, when racial tension was high and whites were organizing their own backlash. Thus, however comically King describes the desertion of a schoolfull of women helplessly awaiting their hairdresser, she nonetheless demonstrates the extraordinary power the servant Marcélite has over her paymistresses. Not that this is seen unironically; indeed, part of the story's considerable subtlety lies in this scene, which reveals how narrow the line is between bestiality and civilization, a demarcation that Marcélite is expected to reproduce with absolute loyalty to her own sex, if not race. The teacher Madame Joubert, deprived of Marcélite's skills, has to comb her hair in "that most primitive and innocent way . . . called *la sauvagesse*" (Bush, 78), while one schoolgirl complains, " 'The more I brush, the more like a *nègre* I look' " (Bush, 81). It is thus the woman who is herself neither white nor black whose art distinguishes the two races and sexes from each other—a *"nègre"* is after all *male*—and whose nonappearance reveals how fragile is the construct of femininity, and indeed of whiteness. Madame Lareveillère feels Marcélite's desertion "[approaches] tragic seriousness" (Bush, 82), an exaggeration that King undoubtedly makes comic, but which also underlines the necessity of preserving white femininity, as the novel goes on to elaborate. Just as Eugénie gives Marcélite a final message for the fictitious Monsieur Motte, the author refers to the school principal's predecessor (whom she resembles) as "the aristocratic old *réfugiée* from the Island of St. Domingo" (Bush, 75). Historical treachery is hinted at perhaps to unsettle the reader's faith in the hitherto trusty Marcélite; even if King did not intend it, the reference would have been enough to alert contemporary southern readers to the potential destructiveness of all blacks. Racial distrust and fear are activated in the (white) reader when it is disclosed that not only has Marcélite lied to Marie about her uncle, but by her actions has almost lost Marie her wealth. The harmonious closure cannot remove the disgrace of the servant's selfish and wayward actions.

In the third story, "The Drama of an Evening," the *soirée*/ball testifies to the desperate attempts of a diminished white creole ruling class to re-establish itself and restore its position in postbellum New Orleans. The room in which the reinstated debutante season begins bears testimony to the class's straitened circumstances: "The antique gilt chandeliers festooned with crystal drops lighted up the faded, as they had once lighted up the fresh glories of the spacious rooms. . . . Old magnificences, luxuries, and extravagances, hovered about the furniture, or seemed to creep in, like the old slaves at the back gate" (115–16). Thus the creole ruling class is reviving both its old pursuits, and also its antebellum social relations; the "old magnificences" are concomitant with and dependent on the presence of the "old slaves," who emulate their role under slavery, slipping into the back gate while the white guests enter the wide front door. Although one black woman, Nourrice, emerges from the dark corners to claim her Charles, this is from no defiant position. She merely wants a time-honored show of protection from her old master. In general, the nameless, statusless blacks are described in terms of a passive, subordinate function in the lives of their white superiors:

> What did they not know of the world in which destiny had placed them in the best of all possible positions for observation? . . . From their memory or experience, as they sat there, what private archives of their city might not have been gathered, . . . the crossings and counter-crossings of intrigue, the romances

dipped in guilt, the guilt gilded with romance. . . . Understanding the problems of the heart better than those of the head, they translated them into the
unveiled terms of their intimate language, giving free vent to their versions and
theories, but aggressively in their loyal partisanship and their obstinate servility
to family and name. (124–25)

Thus King justifies the exclusion of black women from full participation in society on the flimsy grounds that (as slaves first and now as
freedwomen) they have access to a special knowledge about their white
superiors and actively enjoy their own marginality. "Destiny" rather than a
racist hierarchical social structure placed them on the periphery; their
snoopings at critical moments in white people's lives are dignified by the
author's suggestion that these might constitute "private archives" of a city
assumed to be the proper province of whites. Elsewhere, King talks of
white women in similar terms, also referring to their "destiny." Her somewhat idealized picture of black and white women maintaining separate
underground cultures subordinate to, but also independent of, the dominant white male culture can be seen to draw on contemporary discourses
of white woman suffrage and women's fiction that suggested analogies
between disfranchised male blacks and white women.

It is interesting that the most bitter overt critique of the creole city
comes not from a black, but from the appalling Madame Montyon. She is
contemptuous of the profligacy of the city's creole society, holding balls
while failing to honor bills and claiming to found its families on romantic
love. She, whose stepson despises her for her mercenary attitude toward
debt recovery and toward his own choice of wife, criticizes everything
from the standpoint of Paris, her adopted home. King condemns her in
every way: she fled her native state and country during the war (something
King's family and friends resolutely refused to do), and she is contrasted in
her avarice and miserliness with the carefree, generous dignity of the
creole society that King so celebrates in *New Orleans: The Place and the
People*. She is judged severely for being untrue to her own sex—her
boudoir likened to "a soldier's quarters" (159), her thoughtlessness almost
leading to her son's duel, and her cruelty to Nourrice and Marie exposed
by the more noble Charles.

However, the most damning critique of this society comes not from
Madame Montyon but from Marcélite, even though that critique is weakened and finally dissipated because of her very structural subordination.
Marcélite is neither Longfellow's nor Boucicault's tragic mulatto whose
mixed blood marginalizes and isolates her, nor Cable's destructive, sensual, but mute "barbaric beauty" Palmyre. She is possibly the first literary
quadroon with neither youth nor beauty, but in possession of considerable

wealth and legal information. She is potentially a deeply tragic figure, since she has known all along that Marie's discovery of her uncle's nonexistence would alienate the girl's affections. But Marcélite's fate is entirely happy; her lies are forgiven, and her role as Marie's only "real" mother confirmed at the marriage. The sequence of stories does indeed bear out the "holy passion" of the quadroon for her white charge, and the conclusion appears to reward the resourceful and determined quadroon for her loyalty. So closely does the writer seem to identify with and compel sympathy for Marcélite that a critic such as Anne Goodwyn Jones can argue King herself is speaking through the "mask" of the quadroon, using her to "[represent] in the extreme the condition of the *white* southern woman" (my emphasis).[36] But this is to ignore both the historical and literary contexts in which King created Marcélite, and especially to ignore the fact that at no point does King forget this character is black. Although there is only one reference to Marcélite's quadroon status (not, as Goodwyn Jones says, from Eugénie, but from the hostile white Gasconne servant Jeanne), nonetheless there are emphatic, repeated references to her blackness—most of them by Marcélite herself, full of self-hatred and contempt. For King, there is no ambivalence about Marcélite's race, nor do her good qualities derive from her white elements. It is the creation of the virtuous, pure Marie that saves Marcélite, providing the quadroon both with an appropriate object of passion and also (most ironically) with an opportunity to reinforce an ideal white femininity fit for social recuperation into bourgeois marriage and property ownership.

The novel is constructed around recurrent metaphors and metonymies relating to the economic, spiritual, and sexual—with Marcélite fusing all three in her outrageous actions and her dramatic changes of state throughout the book. It is she who both condones and condemns the idea of women's "saving" their money and their love; who blames the Catholic church and its educational system for their effects on women; and who demonstrates both the positive power and the destructive potential of uncontrolled sexual love. Before the secret of Monsieur Motte emerges, Marcélite is characterized largely in terms of her physical presence and her passionate sensuous relationship with the orphan Marie. When trying her graduation costume on the girl, she pats and kisses her, gazing with "desperate, passionate, caressing eyes, 'savoring' her like the lips of an eager dog," and—like a black female Prince Charming—pulls on Marie's satin boots by "straining, pulling, smoothing the satin, coaxing, urging, drawing the foot" (Bush, 64). She and Marie relate to each other in secret by the girl's bedside, and exchange the most intimate memories, feelings, and

36. Jones, *Tomorrow Is Another Day*, 105.

caresses. Marcélite's sexual vitality is contrasted repeatedly with her charge's weakness and small stature, and with Eugénie's declining charms. Both white women admire and rely on Marcélite's "strong, full maturity" (Bush, 62) and her "superb physical strength" (Bush, 71), and these are set against the pusillanimity and furtive practices of the convent school and of Catholicism itself:

> Her untamed African blood was in rebellion against the religion and civilization whose symbols were all about her. . . . She felt a crushing desire to tear down, split, destroy, to surround herself with ruins, to annihilate the miserable little weak devices of intelligence, and reassert the proud supremacy of brute force. She longed to humiliate that meek Virgin Mother; and if the form on the crucifix had been alive she would have gloated over his blood and agony. (Bush, 72)

Like the powerful quadroons of Cable's *The Grandissimes,* male and female, Marcélite becomes here almost a caricature of pagan primitive negritude, presented by King as both splendid and dangerously destructive.

But unlike Cable's quadroons, Marcélite has material and ideological functions in white women's lives, demonstrating most effectively how they may "save" themselves and their own, albeit through forms of deceit and dissimulation. Not only does the narrative play on the notion of Marcélite's skill as hairdresser being vital to make the most of women's natural resources; it also emphasizes the economic skills that have enabled the quadroon to finance Marie *and* save her a dowry. For the white characters, economy is related consistently to the holding back of sexual expression and experience, with the infantilism of the Institut making a mockery of female sensuality and capacity to give love openly. The young women's activities are seen strictly in terms of "labor invested," "net profit," and so on; learning is engaged in only as a means of eventual escape beyond the school walls. Madame Lareveillère, sorting out the delicate business of prize-giving, asks herself, "Why could not the rich girls study more, or the poor less?" (Bush, p. 69). She expresses a hope to Marcélite that Marie will "repay" her affection, the love that "money can never pay for" (72–73). Investment in feminine beauty is to be made with the ultimate promise of gratified desire: in the case of the Catholic aesthete, appropriately named Aurore Angely, "economical Nature seemed stealthily recalling one by one charms which had proved a useless, unprofitable investment," in favor of religion's offering "a crucifix and Golgotha" and the "extinction of desire" (75).

Sexuality itself is seen constantly in terms of secrecy, surprise, and containment. In "On the Plantation," Eugénie tells Aurore, "Yes, our lives are surprise-boxes to us women; we never know what is going to come out of them" (93), and King notes that whereas at the age of sixteen the two had exchanged "deep mysteries and experiences," those confidences "ceased as soon as there was really something to confide" (78)—clearly the area of sexual feelings and relationships. The enclosed box or casket becomes a metonymic signifier for a female sexuality suppressed or hidden with the collusion or direction of the Catholic faith, and constrained by women's social and family positions. The small container (associated at some point with each female character) is linked most persistently with Marcélite, bearer and user of secret compartments and baskets. She, the schoolgirls' main link with the city and thus with adult social and sexual life, bears cosmetics and "implicative missives" (59) across the convent school walls; and in her first appearance in the novel Marcélite brings two baskets, a large one carrying the tools of her hairdressing trade, and a small one "invested with . . . preternatural importance," containing "delightful mysteries" into which her charge is eager to be initiated. She makes Marie await its contents and tantalizes her as if in love play: the girl "twisted and turned ceaselessly on the bed during the ordeal of assumed procrastination" (Bush, 61–62). After revealing the clothes she has brought for Marie's graduation, Marcélite hides all away in the "*armoire*," that repository of feminine treasures. Similarly, the widow Eugénie Lareveillère has a bureau that inspires awe in her pupils but reflects her still-vital sensuality: "The bureau with its laces and ribbons, its cushions, essence-botttes, jewel-cases, *vide-poches*, and little galleried étagères full of gay reflections for the mirror underneath" (71–72). These, together with her dark, gloomy bedroom dominated by a majestic "crimson-housed bedstead" in several details recall Mrs. Reed's red-room in *Jane Eyre*, and Elaine Showalter's observation that its "Freudian wealth of secret compartments, wardrobes, drawers, and jewel chest [give it] strong associations with the adult female body; Mrs. Reed, of course, is a widow in her prime."[37]

The most sexually suggestive box in the novel is the workbox with the secret compartment containing gold dollars with which Marcélite provides Marie the dowry she cannot receive from any other source. It is significant that this, the most furtive and valuable gift Marcélite has ever given her—assuring her an independence of her husband's charity and her mother-in-law's contempt—is the one gift Marie initially refuses to take. King spells out explicitly why she refuses: "She was to take this, acquiesce in what conscience, tradition forbade, receive money from a negro woman

37. Elaine Showalter, *A Literature of Their Own: British Women Novelists from Brontë to Lessing* (London, 1978), 114–15.

rather than her husband" (175). Marcélite is offering her symbolically her own life, her own sexual freedom, and it is the alliance between black and white women overriding proprieties of race and class (with its disturbing anarchic sexual implications) that Marie feels she must refuse. That alliance is saved, however, once Marie is awarded a fortune of her own white inheritance; she is then free to accord Marcélite a place in her heart as desexualized mother, and a home on her plantation.

It might help to understand King's serious narrative flaws if one considers as significant absences and omissions the author's failure to explain or justify crucial elements in Marcélite's behavior, such as why she invents Marie's uncle, and what happens to her during graduation day to bring her shuffling in transformed from "*their own* clean, neat, brave, honest, handsome Marcélite" to "*this* panting, tottering, bedraggled wretch" (Bush, 91; my emphases). The shift from being "their own" to "this" speaks Marcélite's punishment by exclusion from white acceptance, something she has to earn back through the three sequels. Not to be owned (with its double meaning of acceptance and the idealized relations of slavery) is Marcélite's potential tragedy, and her physical derangement and subsequent diminishment (in terms of physical stature and mobility) are a necessary process before she is rewarded with her role as black Virgin Mary/holy mother. The author's inability to explain Marcélite's personal crisis and transformation can only be interpreted by extrinsic evidence. King's gendered identification with and understanding of Marcélite allow her finally to treat the quadroon sympathetically, but her race and class positions compel a thorough humiliation and confirmation that the servant's self-hatred is justified and that the whites who trusted her require a new humility and respect.

Anne Jones argues that the novel's conclusion gathers together all those characters embodying "the good 'heart'—the androgynous values that King would like so much to see prevail" without regard to race, sex, or class.[38] But if the novel is read within its contemporary political context, bearing in mind the impact of Stowe and Cable, it is impossible to read the conclusion as other than a crude attempt at a sentimental closure appropriate to southern fiction of the period. Marcélite is the bride's mother because she has suppressed and then conquered her race's particular claims and desire for revolt, while Marie—given the key to economic and sexual autonomy with the quadroon's box of secret gold—is installed victorious as romantic heroine and plantation mistress, almost as if the Civil War had never occurred. Aurore describes Marcélite's behavior as "heroic" and "sublime" (103); in the New Orleans of the mid-1880s, this highly politi-

38. Jones, *Tomorrow Is Another Day,* 117.

cally motivated writer created an original version of the quadroon story with Marcélite neither tragic nor rendered marginal, but rewarded with surrogate white kinship relations so long as she controls her own power and lowers her voice. Through King, the white Bourbon ruling class of Louisiana spoke its warning to the northern public as well as to its own people: in future, the physical and emotional damage that it is implied were self-inflicted in Marcélite's dark night of the soul will come from organized whites. The interdependence of white and black must prevail, especially between women, so long as the latter accepts its own subordination.

The next collection of Grace King's stories to be published in book form differed from *Monsieur Motte* in bringing together a heterogeneous group of stories, already published in magazines, under the curious title *Tales of a Time and Place*.[39] The stories are concerned neither with one time nor one place, as the title implies, though they all share King's preoccupations outlined in *Motte* and continued through her work: the past; social change during and after the Civil War; the relationships between different ethnic groups in New Orleans; and most of all, the developing roles and problems of women as a result of the war.

In the first story, "Bayou L'Ombre," Grace King writes a satirical and bitter explosion of the notion of romance, which, as "Monsieur Motte" demonstrates, was a difficult genre for her to handle. This story is ideologically more transparent, and is a considerably less sympathetic study of black women's relationship to their white mistresses. It is significant that this more hostile picture is set, not in contemporary New Orleans, but in the more safely distant past, on a remote plantation during the war. Once again, Grace King used her childhood as material for fiction; although the episode related almost certainly never occurred, her descriptions of the plantation itself, the three sisters, the guerilla cousin, and black slaves are directly drawn from the author's family experiences when they fled from newly occupied New Orleans to their plantation. Family letters written to Grace King in Hartford where she was staying when the story appeared in *Harper's* all praise the accuracy of her depiction of the plantation and the family's time there.[40]

"Bayou L'Ombre" is a curious blend of frontier tall-tale, antiromance, and black comedy. The story concerns three sisters, Christine, Régina, and

39. Grace King, *Tales of a Time and Place* (New York, 1892). All page references will be to this edition.

40. Mimi King to Grace King, June 23, 1887, Annie Reagan King to Grace King, June 25, 1887, May King McDowell to Grace King, June 25, 1887, all in King Papers.

Lolotte, left on the plantation by their parents under the guardianship of a trusted black slave, "Uncle John." Because of the plantation's isolation the slaves know nothing of the Emancipation Proclamation, nor do any of them realize until the very end that Lee has surrendered and the war is over. The girls' cousin Beau, a Confederate guerilla leader, arrives on the plantation posing as a Federal captain escorting Confederate prisoners. He locks them in the smokehouse and orders dinner for his men. The girls and a few loyal slaves release the imprisoned soldiers and give them a gun, provisions, and boat in which to escape. Régina and one of the men tenderly kiss goodbye. Meanwhile, a group of women slaves, washing clothes in the bayou, hear of the Yankees' arrival and are led by "Dead-arm Harriet" to abandon their washing and babies and wait to be taken North to freedom and to " 'git white gentlemen to marry 'em' " (59). Beau confesses that he has played a trick on them. The story ends with the steadfast "Uncle John" expressing anger at Beau's tasteless joke, at the loss to the plantation of valuable provisions and clothing, and scornful amusement at the beatings the black women will get that night when their husbands come home. Beau's final gesture is to write a note to his uncle telling him the war is over.

The story is evidently intended to set up a series of contrasts between the reactions of the white and the black women, and between those of the loyal and trusty slaves and the dishonorable and treacherous ones. The three sisters feel useless and excluded from what they imagine to be the heroics and excitements of war. This was a common experience, one that (as I argued earlier) the women war diarists discuss repeatedly. Like the diarists, the girls' childhood reading had given them a notion of what war was: "soldiers, flags, music, generals on horseback brandishing swords, knights in armor escalading walls, cannons booming through clouds of smoke" (3). But after four years of exile on the plantation, they had seen nothing of the war and were forced to create it imaginatively—writing journals, learning war songs, and showing heroism simply by going to bed in the dark. Like the diarists, too, they fantasize about being soldiers: " 'Ah, if we were only men!' But no! They who could grip daggers and shed blood, they who teemed with all the possibilities of romance or poetry, they were selected for a passive, paltry contest against their own necessities" (12). Forced into inactivity for so long, they jump eagerly into their first opportunity to show heroic mettle, but of course are made to seem and feel foolish.

The trick played by Beau, lightly though it appears to be treated, is clearly meant to be a paradigm of the betrayal by men, northern as well as southern, of the hopes and ideals of their women. No wonder Beau gazes at Titine and thinks histrionically, "if he could kiss her feet, if he could beg pardon in the dust—he, a man for all men, of her, a woman for all women" (53). But Beau is rendered comic, treated indulgently by his author. The main focus of King's attack is the betrayal of white women, not by inadequate men, but by their loyal and loving women slaves. As discussed earlier, black loyalty to whites (especially white women) was a recurrent subject of King's discourses (correspondence, nonfiction, and fiction) throughout the 1880s. In May, 1886, around the time she was writing this story, she described her brother Will's accompaniment of the visiting William Hamilton Gibson to the Teche country settlement of slaves who had worked on the King plantation. Proudly she reports that "Gibson was rather surprised that slaves should be so delighted to greet former masters and tyrants." This loyalty, as the defensive letter suggests, could no longer be relied on, nor indeed had it ever been unanimous. In a scene of appalling caricatures and grotesque racist exaggerations (incidentally praised for its strength and humanity by her editor Henry Mills Alden and later by William Dean Howells), King develops the ambivalent and contradictory image of black women that she began in *Monsieur Motte* and that articulates the fears of her class during Reconstruction.[41] Two loyal black women— Aunt Mary and Black Maria—are set against the rest of the "gang" led by Dead-arm Harriet, whose arm had been raised to curse the plantation overseer then paralyzed by a falling tree branch (thus presumably demonstrating that God was on the planters' side). At first the scene is idyllic enough, an Arcadia similar to Bel Angely in *Monsieur Motte*. The female slaves embody both nostalgic pastoral ideals and the timelessness of myth—as long as they accept their own subordination and exploitation. Once this haven is disturbed by the ugly reality of the Yankees' arrival and the promise of freedom, the ungrateful and unpleasantly unmythic slaves leap at the chance to escape.

Having described at some length the simple joys of the slaves' daily tasks, King now unleashes a stream of vituperative rhetorical questions that reveal her contempt for blacks' ingratitude and for that sensuality which (as in *Monsieur Motte*) seems so threatening: "What did the war mean to them? . . . Could their rude minds draw no inferences from the gradual loosening of authority and relaxing of discipline? . . . Had they, indeed, no gratifications beyond the physical, no yearnings, no secret burden of a secret prayer to God, these bonded wives and mothers?" (24– 25). It is the older black women (in King's terms mature enough, presum-

41. Grace King to May King McDowell, May 18, 1886, in King Papers; letters to King, quoted in Robert Bush, "Grace King," *American Literary Realism 1870–1910,* VIII (Winter, 1975), 44.

ably, to appreciate the blessings of servitude) who scorn the Yankees: Aunt Mary returns to her cabin, while Black Maria attempts to knife her fleeing daughter-in-law. The younger women abandon babies and children to follow Harriet, "the worst worker and most violent tongue of the gang" (28), and the most sensual and emotional: with her "half-nude body," "moist lips," "sleepy eyes, looking with languid passion," she would urge them at revival meetings to "rave in religious inebriation" (26–27). For King's white readers, Harriet embodies all the most feared and loathed attributes of blacks; the paradigmatically sensual black woman's danger to whites lies in her incapacity for reason, thus her lack of a sense of duty or gratitude. Though Harriet and her followers express exuberance and bravado, King's judgment is crushing: the noble Maria's outrage, Harriet's immoderate insurrectionary fervor, and the baby wrested from its mother's breast and dropped so that she can marry a white Yankee—all pronounce the guilty verdict that is confirmed by the conclusion.

Later in the story, the sisters' profound sense of betrayal emphatically reinforces the author's censure: "These were *their* servants, their *possessions!* From generation to generation their lives had been woven together by the shuttle of destiny. . . . What a farce, what a lying, disgusting farce it had all been! . . . After this there was no return, no reconciliation possible!" (37; my emphases). Just as for the white women at the Institut, Marcélite is transformed from being "their own" to "this" bedraggled stranger, so for the sisters there is no forgiveness once the relations of ownership are broken. While the girls reminisce sentimentally about "little episodes of their pastoral existence together" (38), the black women are condemned through the words of a sage patriarchal figure, Uncle John (almost "Tom"), who laughs at the thought of " 'dem fool nigger wimen a-sittin' on de brink o' de byer . . . a-waitin' for freedom!' " (59) while revealing that he advised "Marse John" long ago to " 'git shet o' ' " Harriet. It is interesting that John's words are given in black dialect, which Grace King rarely used; she may have chosen it here to soften the harshness of her own final verdict to northern editors, and also to maintain the ironic tone that allowed her often to make bitter political points about race and gender that could be smiled away. As Catherine Belsey argues, "irony . . . guarantees still more effectively than overt authorial omniscience the subjectivity of the reader as a source of meaning."[42] By this stage of her career, King was sure of a sympathetic reader, northern as well as southern; the treachery of disloyal slaves could be judged with more severity than in her first stories.

42. Catherine Belsey, *Critical Practice* (London, 1980), 79.

The second story in *Tales of a Time and Place* is very different in tone from the first, indeed very similar to a Local Color story of the New England writers Sarah Orne Jewett and Mary Wilkins Freeman. "Bonne Maman" is about isolated, recently impoverished genteel women clinging together after the Civil War. At the center of the household is an old creole aristocrat who, having lost her plantation and wealth, came to live in a slave cabin in New Orleans. She lies on her deathbed reflecting on the glorious past and southern women's bravery, while her granddaughter Claire and their black servant Betsy sew clothes to make ends meet. The closely observed details of economic survival anticipate the New England writers and conform to the definition of "female realism" that Ellen Moers notes in many nineteenth-century women's writing, and which is a recurrent theme in Grace King's.[43] While her grandmother recalls the work done by women on plantations before the war, Claire of the new generation has no fantasies about labor and sets her sights lower, sewing for women of both races. Betsy is outraged that the white girl sews for wealthier black women, and Claire keeps this fact from her proud grandmother; though King does suggest strongly how foolish the old woman's backward-looking punctiliousness is in the face of hard economic realities.

When *bonne maman* dies, Aza, the quadroon slave she cared for as her own child but who had run away with stolen goods, visits the house and recognizes her mistress' body. Betsy remembers Aza as the madam of the brothel where she has worked as floor-scrubber. In an encounter reminiscent of the most powerful scenes in *Monsieur Motte,* the two black women are set against each other as they argue over who should take care of Claire, although Betsy has been entrusted with the child by the dying woman. But this time the conclusion is less conciliatory than that of *Motte.* At Madame Nénaine's funeral, her long-lost relatives arrive, expressing horror that they knew nothing of her impoverished state in the city (assuming her to be safe in France), and they embrace Claire who "clung to them as indeed to the successors of bonne maman" (115). Betsy is not mentioned in the joyous conclusion: for King, any wealthy, white creole group of anonymous relatives is to be preferred above a poor black adoptive mother. Admittedly, Betsy has no fat dowry to give to Claire, but the economic arguments are superseded in this story by those of racial precedence.

Grace King's next collection of stories proved her most critically successful and popular publication. *Balcony Stories* brought together thirteen stories

43. Ellen Moers, *Literary Women* (London, 1978), chapter 4.

and one sketch published in *Century* magazine under the editorship of Richard Watson Gilder who, since rejecting "Monsieur Motte," had become an enthusiast of King's work. The collection, with a preface entitled "The Balcony," went into three editions.[44] Gilder was generally enthusiastic about the manuscript, though his editorial criticisms reflect the pressures of the Genteel Tradition on the direction of King's work. He was anxious about the tone of some of the stories, and it was he who suggested a preface that would signal to readers the fact that some were "perhaps too strong meat . . . for public ears."[45] The preface King wrote made clear both the source of the stories, and also the nature of her implied reader:

> Experiences, reminiscences, episodes, picked up as only women know how to pick them up from other women's lives,—or other women's destinies, as they prefer to call them,—and told as only women know how to relate them; what God has done or is doing with some other woman whom they have known— that is what interests women once embarked on their own lives,—the embarkation takes place at marriage, or after the marriageable time,—or, rather, that is what interests the women who sit of summer nights on balconies. For in those long-moon countries life is open and accessible, and romances seem to be furnished real and gratis. (2–3)

"The Balcony" thus exploits northern stereotypes of hot sultry southern nights and the intimate anti-intellectual sensuality of its fiction-making. It also makes clear that these stories are told by women for women; the author justifies her female narrative voice, which more than earlier works predominates in this collection. While men, who "are not balcony sitters" (1), and sleeping children are excluded from these fictions, women narrators tell stories from "mother-knowledge" with "mother-voices" (2), anticipating Kate Chopin's "mother-women" on Grand Isle who also transform their sisters' lives into "destinies." King undoubtedly saw herself as a balcony-sitter; as she relates in her autobiography, the stories came largely from the experiences of her uncle Tom and her mother, who had "an appreciation of the romantic and picturesque in life that I had never seen equalled." Indeed, the author seems to have found an ideal popular female voice in these stories, as first-person narrator/eavesdropper (justified by a role as protagonist's niece, friend, and so on). *Balcony Stories* was written at the height of national interest in the South, especially in the exotic and romantic reputation of New Orleans, as well as in fiction by women about their own sex. The stories' fluency and economy are thus a reflection of the author's confidence in her material and herself, a confi-

44. Grace King, *Balcony Stories* (New York, Century, 1893; New Orleans, 1914; and New York, Macmillan, 1925). My page references will be to the last edition.
45. Richard Watson Gilder to Grace King, July 2, 1891, in King Papers.

dence reinforced by the enthusiastic letters she received after publication from friends such as Rose de Bury and Olivia Clemens, and admiring editors like Alden and Hamilton Wright Mabie.[46]

Of the thirteen stories published in the first two editions of *Balcony Stories,* eleven are concerned with a female central character, the others with a blind boy and a creole couple. The two stories included in the 1925 edition also describe a woman's experiences as wife and widow. Since with few exceptions the stories are presumably contemporaneous, they reflect the nature of postwar Louisiana life: women characters have experienced loss, deprivation, and/or social deracination. Five of the stories have an orphan as protagonist; six feature widows; there are tales featuring a woman unhappily married to a tyrannical husband, and a reluctantly childless unmarried woman. Once more King is exploring the theme of kinship relations as inflected in class, race, and gender terms, though these stories—shorter than other works—have a surface brilliance rather than the ambitious complexity of less apparently successful works. Nonetheless, the obsessive way in which King plays with these themes is of considerable interest.

"La Grande Demoiselle" is the story of sudden orphanhood and classlessness: the family of Idalie Sainte Foy Mortemart des Islets loses its considerable wealth and status during the war, and she, the sole survivor, is rescued from the humiliating job of teaching in a colored public school by a fellow creole *nouveau pauvre,* who marries her out of pity. "Mimi's Marriage" describes a happy and successful class transition: when a proud creole's family is reduced to indigence after his death, Mimi is initially dismayed at having to accept as husband her *nouveau riche* "American" neighbor, then delighted at how well it turns out. "A Crippled Hope" concerns race, class, and surrogate parenthood: at an antebellum slave auction-mart, a crippled black girl, known as "Little Mammy," unattractive to buyers, acts as nurse mother to the other black children, then after the war ends her days as a nurse mother to white soldiers' distressed wives and widows. The white *"dugazon manquée"* of the opera troupe, as charmless and isolated as "Little Mammy," also satisfies her frustrated maternal instinct by abandoning the opera in favor of caring for children in the city's poorest orphan asylum. "The Little Convent Girl" relates the story of a girl brought by steamer to New Orleans after her father's death to live with her mother; discovering her mother (and thus herself) to be black, she silently jumps into the Mississippi. "A Delicate Affair" is concerned with intense female friendship and the divisions that men can drive through it:

46. Kate Chopin, *The Awakening,* in Per Seyersted (ed.), *The Complete Works of Kate Chopin* (Baton Rouge, 1969), 888; King, *Memories,* 99.

an old widow who had sworn never to forgive her childhood friend for being her husband's real love is persuaded by a mutual (male) friend to visit the friend's deathbed. The women are passionately reunited. Pupasse, the protagonist of the final story in the first two editions, is an orphan whose grandmother dies leaving her with no home or family other than the convent school at which she is an academic and social failure. The principal attempts to force her to leave, for she is far older than the other girls (having repeated each year several times), but she begs to return and is allowed back, as this is her only security. "Joe," the last story in the 1925 edition, is Grace King's final comment on racial feelings in antebellum Louisiana: Joe, the slave of a widow who is in dire financial straits, begs her to sell him because the family badly needs the money. She finally agrees, with great reluctance, and he immediately runs away from his new master once the money reaches the family. He sends fond messages to the family from Montreal where he lives and dies, asking his doctor to send his prayer book back to "Miss Polly" who gave it to him, with assurances that he has read it and prayed daily as she taught him. Like "Little Mammy," Joe proves his devotion to the white race by ending his days ministering to white southerners (this time in exile).

In *Balcony Stories* Grace King's characters are unusually anonymous and their fates have a somewhat schematic neatness. Few of the protagonists have names; the author has presented a range of characteristic female types who are made to symbolize social and racial changes within their society: "la grande demoiselle," "Little Mammy," the "dugazon," "the little convent girl," "the old lady." Almost all the stories take place in New Orleans, and we are constantly reminded of the city's changed circumstances and character since the war; comparisons between ante- and postbellum New Orleans are drawn constantly. Two examples will suffice. In "La Grande Demoiselle," the first part of the story recalls the New Orleans of 1859 when it "was not, as it is now, a one-heiress place . . . one could find heiresses then as one finds type-writing girls now" (23). The author describes the great wealth and pampered leisure of the des Islets family before it is devastated by the war: Mortemart des Islets is killed in his first battle; their plantation is used by a colored company of soldiers, then looted and burned; and the spoiled daughter who had once given her costly, hardly worn dresses to her negro slaves reappears ten years or so later teaching for pitiful wages at a colored public school. The humiliation of another girl of professional family is recorded in "Mimi's Marriage," with the creole girls humbling themselves socially to take in darning from the neighboring American family whose head was a clerk. The daughters have to learn that the old social codes no longer apply in a more fluid, less class-conscious commercial society.

As the author promised in her preface, the stories are overwhelmingly concerned with the experiences of women, and especially with women proudly affirming their relationships or making the best of altered, usually worsened circumstances. As usual, Grace King's attitude to her female protagonists is clear, except when questions of gender and race come into conflict. In "The Old Lady's Restoration," the author obviously approves of her protagonist's proud rejection of fair-weather rich friends in favor of the proletarian poor who remained loyal through her lean years. It is also clear that for her a woman's desire for a surrogate family should be satisfied, even if this means her acceptance into an institution ("One of Us" and "Pupasse"). Not that she idealizes women or creates an homogeneous collection of admirable types; several of her characters are willful, tactless, and cruel. But on the whole they are life-affirming and find their satisfaction in family rather than sexual relationships. As in the rest of her work, Grace King avoids choosing women characters who are seeking sexual love. The conclusion of "Mimi's Marriage" implies sexual happiness, but this is an unexpected result of a virtually arranged marriage; "La Grande Demoiselle" ends with a joyless marriage made from class pity. The most passionate emotional relationship described in the collection is that between two *women* friends in "A Delicate Affair." The women, reunited after years of separation because they were loved by the same man, fall into each other's arms on the deathbed of one, calling each other as in the past " 'Mon Amour! . . . Ma Divine!' " In their "murmuring" on the pillow, they completely forget the men in their lives, especially the man who separated them for so long (218–19). Grace King's white women characters tend to be loyal to their class, race, family, husbands, slaves, and servants, and especially each other; they are courageous, independent, and infinitely adaptable.

There is, however, one notable exception. This is the little convent girl. She, above all other female protagonists, is an exaggerated example of the ideal southern belle: passive, timid, silent, and submissive, she presents a challenge to the crew of the steamboat that brings her from school in Cincinnati to live with her mother in New Orleans. Grace King makes it clear that she is unable to do anything for herself and simply responds obediently to the initiative and commands of others. The title is an ironic description of what she is. The author says of her:

> She was the beau-ideal of the little convent girl. She never raised her eyes except when spoken to. Of course she never spoke first . . . and when she did speak it was in the wee, shy, furtive voice one might imagine a just-budding violet to have. . . . She would sit all day in the cabin, in the same place, crocheting lace. . . . Never leaning back—oh, no! always straight and stiff, as if the conventual back board were there within call. (144, 147, 148)

The girl's terror of the world outside the convent is absolute; she is a grotesque parody of the feminine ideal. King cannot resist satirizing this version of femininity with its dangerous dependence, which she knew from her own experience and that of her class to be of little value when times and circumstances change. Thus, with her characteristic jibe at Catholic education, she satirizes the sheltered conditioning that reduces a girl to such helpless terror that she imagines every shout and whistle on board ship to signal a shipwreck, and has to be protected from the roughness of ship life by the crew's avoidance of swearing in her hearing.

However, as the story develops, the girl responds to the captain's gentle interest and support, loses her passivity, and begins to move and look around with enthusiasm; the reader anticipates a cheerful outcome. In New Orleans the mother arrives to collect her daughter, and everyone on board gasps because she is black. A month later, when the two reappear at the quayside where the captain encounters them, the girl's mother reports that her daughter has reverted to utter passivity: " 'she is so quiet, so still, all the time' " (160). The conclusion is startling in terms of King's habitual pattern of kinship restitution: since the captain does not invite the girl to become his "daughter" (a solution both mother and daughter hint would be ideal) the little convent girl jumps into the river. Rejecting her natural mother and deprived of an adoptive father, she denies her own heritage and jumps into the river to absorb herself into the "great mother-stream" (155), which, the captain has told her, is the source of all the others.

This is the only story in which a woman character directly rejects natural kinship ties, and the girl's action is not directly linked by the author to race. But the fact that the ship's passengers and crew express horrified astonishment at the mother's race and the pale complexion and tightly drawn lips of the girl a month later indicate that there is no way in which *natural* ties can be formed. Even a white ship's captain of very brief acquaintance is regarded as a more promising parent, and as a last resort the mythic mother river is chosen as eternal parent. The conclusion is abrupt and uncompromising; the girl's most assertive action, coming as it does from timidity and passive silence (she has never spoken a word), shocks the reader in a way no other story in *Balcony Stories* even attempts. The rejection of racial equality and the repudiation of mixed-race alliances is here most powerful; like Marcélite, the girl hates and punishes herself for a society's racial intolerance, but unlike Marcélite she is given no salvation through vicarious social status. The story was published in 1893, five years later than the complete *Monsieur Motte*; racial differences were fast becoming institutionalized, and by the early 1890s the relatively conciliatory attitude toward the mulatto (for which the state and New Orleans had been renowned) was fast disappearing behind the bigotry and violence of White League rhetoric and harassment.

The most autobiographical of Grace King's works is the collection of stories (usually referred to as a novel), *The Pleasant Ways of St. Médard,* published in 1916, based once again in Reconstruction New Orleans. Though commissioned by Macmillan's, it was rejected, and was only published by Holt after an enthusiastic review by the English writer Edward Garnett, who had read the manuscript and assumed it was published in the United States. Publishers had been shrewd in deciding against publication; despite excellent reviews, few copies were sold. Robert Underwood Johnson's rejection letter to the author said it all: the vogue for Local Color and Civil War fiction was now over, and " 'all [your] sources are in N O—& the past.' "[47]

In correspondence, King admitted the strongly autobiographical nature of this work, punning on her own literary production as "working at reconstructions—more as a wife and mother than a politician." A measure of her personal involvement is the fact that she collapsed after completing the novel; Hamilton Mabie later wrote her, "I fear you put your blood into it." She was praised by two nostalgic southern writers, Thomas Nelson Page and Lyle Saxon, for her ability to recapture their own feelings about the period: Saxon wrote of some quality "that catches at the throat . . . that goes down into you on the inside of your skin." The introduction to *The Pleasant Ways* is unashamedly nostalgic and has a mawkish air that the detachment and irony of the stories generally do not share (with one notable exception, "Jerry"). Addressing a sympathetic southern reader, King recalls the idyllic antebellum days when men were noble and women beautiful, and the children revelled in stories of colonial Louisiana. She bemoans the disappearance of the stable patriarchal family unit, with men and women alike now reduced to poverty and degrading circumstances. Her capacity for a light, ironic touch, which pervades the earlier nonfiction and fiction, is lacking here as her class and race élitist bias, hardened by middle age and literary success, is given naked expression.[48]

The Pleasant Ways of St. Médard is a fictional discussion of the problems facing white women after the war. Deprived (however temporarily) of

47. Grace King, *The Pleasant Ways of St. Médard* (New York, 1916); quoted in Grace King to Robert Underwood Johnson, March 10, 1913, in Century Collection, New York Public Library.

48. Grace King to Robert Underwood Johnson, March 30, 1909 (unreliable date—this must be 1912), in Century Collection; Hamilton W. Mabie to Grace King, June 22(?), 1914, Lyle Saxon to Grace King, September 13, 1917, both in King Papers.

their class status, homes, and other forms of security, they are forced to face life in the absence of the old support networks of extended families, women friends, and slaves. The book demonstrates how the past and future of women have been taken "as a spoil of war." As in King's earlier fiction, in order to survive women must abandon their orthodox expectations of southern womanhood, family life, and the loyalties and courtesies they had grown to expect. The real survivors among their contemporaries are the opportunists or collaborators and the black women who make their living from paid domestic labor for white families. But the novel sustains the argument that it was the majority of white women Confederacy supporters who suffered most from the war. Significantly, the most overt expression of this view is given to a benevolent doctor, paradigmatic male figure of authority: "There are no fortunes of war for women and children. It is all misfortunes for them, they are the sufferers" (231). Although there is no evidence of the extent to which King revised her manuscript over the years, it is known that she was reading the proofs of Sarah Dawson's war diary in 1913; the strong emphasis on women's wartime sufferings in that diary may have encouraged King to insert passages of comment and set speeches in *The Pleasant Ways*.[49]

The first story of the collection/novel, "A Journey into a Far Country," begins by describing the return of the Talbot family from the plantation to which they had fled after the 1862 occupation of New Orleans, to a small, humble home on the outskirts of the city. The family name is given only late in the story, so their journey and situation are clearly meant to be emblematic of the "American family" of their class borne "like so many barks of Charon from a past to a future"—though significantly their story is identical with the King family's experience.[50] Wartime adventures fill the eyes of the head of the family with "heroic fire," while his wife is a sadly pathetic figure, thinking "thoughts . . . other than the ones that lighted his dark eyes" (212) and embodying in her physical appearance the grotesque nature of this "journey into a far land" of poverty and new humiliations. She, whom the children have become accustomed to seeing in homespun dress and alligator shoes on the plantation, is adorned in her old, now unfashionable "city bonnet" trimmed, incongruously, with great pink roses and broad blue ribbons (210).

The father's role is to describe the dramatic devastation of the city and the reversals of class and social order that the war and Federal occupation have brought to New Orleans. The loss of social and economic power and

49. Joseph Conrad to Grace King, July 23, 1913, in King Papers.
50. Bush (ed.), *Grace King of New Orleans*, 209. All quotations from this story and "Jerry" will be taken from this edition. Page references to the other stories will be to the Holt edition.

prestige of the old professional class to which Talbot belonged is exemplified by the new invisibility and dispensability of men like him: he describes the city as being full of "*ci-devant* fine gentlemen" being "dodged or refused" by old friends, pockets "buttoned up at the sight of a poor Confederate" (212); the sign on his office door has been replaced by that of his former office boy, Tommy Cook; and the family name has been removed from their old church pew. Mr. Talbot is, however, undaunted and enthusiastically outlines their new future and his plans to recover his wealth.

Mrs. Talbot, like other women of her class after the war, remains uncertain of her role or indeed her feelings about this new life. While her husband, the loyal Confederate, reviews their plans in militaristic terms ("he unfolded the map of the future . . . as if it were a campaign to be fought again" [215]), she is reduced to silent anxiety: "She let her mind follow his with her characteristic docility, embracing his views, adopting his conclusions, conceding that the great future was his, the husband's, the man's affair; the little future of daily life, hers, the woman's, according to the traditions of conjugal life in which she had been raised. But . . . she had presentiments—they were all she ever had to oppose to his clear reasoning" (215).

Not only is her postbellum experience analogous to her dependent role as southern wife and mother, consistent with the ideology of southern womanhood, but it is also parallel in Mrs. Talbot's mind with the changed circumstances of her own ex-slaves: "Somewhat like her freed negro servants she was not sure of what she was riding into and she could have murmured with Milly: 'My God! My God!' without knowing what she was calling on Him for" (215). In the introduction, Grace King said that the *children* of antebellum gentlemen saw their fathers cut down to human size after the war; here the postbellum *wife* of such a man notices her husband's decline from "that aristocratic gentleman with classic features and noble expression of countenance" to "a coarse, plain, common man substituted as her lord and master" (216)—one whom, moreover, she blames bitterly for sending his family not to safety in Europe but to the unhealthy swamp of the plantation where her daughter contracts fever. As in many of the women's war diaries and fiction, the very term "lord and master" is mocked; the authority that the husband holds has yielded little but bitter fruit.

The depiction of female survivors is very revealing. Mrs. Talbot, who was forced out of female passive dependence in her time alone on the plantation in her husband's absence, settles uneasily back into a dependent, though altered role as homemaker. But there is a whole community of other women, widowed or deprived of the opportunity to marry by the war, who are shown as adapting to the fortunes of war. For instance, Mademoiselle Mimi, whom Mrs. Talbot engages to teach her daughters, is a classic female type who survives only because of education and her matter-of-fact approach to her own single, financially perilous state. The author informs us that, poor and ugly, she "had become poor at the very time when her money, so to speak, might have floated her ugliness into society," while Mrs. Talbot tactlessly reinforces Mimi's deviant position by quoting her husband's opinion of "learned ladies," namely that they are "simply, ladies with big feet" (48). She is, however, made to swallow her words when she hears Mimi's story of her existence as both breadwinner and housekeeper for her spendthrift father, who sits at home brooding and reading Voltaire. In a later story, King ironically comments on Monsieur Pinseau's feebleness by giving him the instruction of Mimi's pupils in those feminine skills that Mimi (and indeed, King herself) disdains—piano, dance, curtsying, and so on.

Working women are always presented in King's fiction as deserving of respect and admiration. Mrs. Talbot, who had worked and seen herself as productive on the plantation, is nostalgic for that sense of worth she felt in those difficult years. Restored to her primary role as consumer in Reconstruction New Orleans, she reflects on the relative merits of the new stockings she can buy her children at the New Orleans shoeshop, and the rough ones she had knitted on the plantation: "the soft lisle thread ones . . . were merely a purchase, the others an achievement" (89). She is angry when a shopkeeper assumes that she has spent the war idly in Paris, "the Paradise of the ladies" (92). The story "Peace, Perfect Peace" is an ironic journey to past shopping haunts, where Mrs. Talbot has to come to terms with the material changes in the city, but more significantly with her own changed attitudes to the frivolous, extravagant life she had accepted as natural before the war. The city is made strange to her, and thus to the reader: the shoe-shopkeeper's patronizing attitude to her children's home-spun footwear, of which she is the proud producer, and his annoyance over her concern at prices; the clerk Volant's indulgent treatment of ladies as irresponsible children, and his view that what distinguished his "ladies" (customers) from the "woman" typified by his own "coarse mother" was precisely their "easy, careless extravagance, their utter indifference to their money and to the trouble they gave" (95). The final visit to her favorite cakeshop brings the most poignant estrangement: its customers are now Yankee soldiers rather than the old friends to whom she was accustomed, and among them is her treasured former employee Coralie, who snubs her.

The radical transformation in relations of production and social relations is reinforced in the story "Walking the Rainbow," in which Mr. Talbot discusses with his wife the education of his daughters and sons. While planning to set up his sons in the law practice he hopes to reestablish, he fears that the lack of dowries will reduce his daughters' chances of marrying and wonders how they will survive. Waxing lyrical about women's "spiritual" as opposed to men's "intellectual" force (108), he delights in the choice of Mademoiselle Mimi to teach his daughters, as any girl taught by a man "would end up by trying to imitate him and the result would be a hobbledehoy" (107). This is especially ironic in view of Mimi's contempt for orthodox female education; indeed, Talbot's words are followed by the arrival of a nephew who describes his sister's changed position. Since her husband was wounded in the war, she and her mother have taken over the work of the family plantation, earning gold by spinning, planting, and so on. With relish he describes Elizabeth's "skirts up to her knees . . . a pistol stuck in her belt. . . . And the more of a man she is, the better her husband likes it" (121). King's final ironic comment on the inappropriateness of Talbot's Rousseau-like definitions of gender-specific education comes from the description (in "Tommy Cook") of his sons being trained each afternoon in oratory, while the girls sit sewing, silently imitating the speeches.

At the heart of *The Pleasant Ways* is King's most reactionary and racist story, "Jerry." It relates the disintegration of the black family who had worked as slaves on the Talbot plantation and now live in New Orleans working as employees of their former master. The story describes Jerry's attempts to keep his family together, engaged in respectable work, but he loses his three daughters and wife to petty theft and finally to the black "Settlement," where he reluctantly joins them. Jerry is a stock literary character—a virtuous, loyal, and obsequious Uncle Tom very familiar to King's readers. More than any other, this story interpellates its reader as affluent white female New Orleanian with the wisdom of historical hindsight, which King implies (without irony) is shared and confirmed by blacks. Jerry has been instructed in his postbellum role and manner by his old master: "all he had to do now to fulfill his duty to God and man was to continue living in the future as he had done in the past. A good slave was bound to make a good free man" (244). Jerry colludes happily with this, listening solemnly to Mr. Talbot's ironic words, " 'You know you are your own overseer and master now' " (245). He humbly accepts Talbot's injunction that he continue to identify with his white masters rather than his black peers: "When you see a crowd of lazy negroes, herding together like sheep as they are doing in that old warehouse or on the Levee, you may be sure they are doing no good to themselves or to any one else. Keep away from them" (245).

The (white) implied reader is reminded of "old ladies still living in the city who, sitting in their quiet rooms, said that they knew all about revolutions: their mothers had related to them what had taken place in the French revolution," as well as "other old ladies . . . [whose] mothers had fled from the insurrection of the slaves in Santo Domingo and . . . [who] predicted something worse" (247). As in *Monsieur Motte,* Santo Domingo and (by implication) all the race riots and violence since the war in New Orleans are a crucial race memory for white women.

Jerry represents the "good" ex-slave, one of a group of older blacks whom King identifies as incapable of adjusting to freedom: "Freedom from slavery meant freedom from work or it meant nothing to the negroes. . . . Inured to chains, perhaps more at their ease with them than without (even if the chains were forged of sentiment and affection as some of them seem to have been), they still remained in servitude when servitude grew harder and harder under the changed conditions" (246). The obsessive repetition of images of slavery/servitude, as well as the sly parenthetical authorial comment, represent King's compulsion to write polemically about emancipation and also to subvert the very historical meaning of the slave system itself. Thus "freedom" is redefined as idleness, "prison" and "chains" as benevolent protection, and antebellum "slavery" as relative liberty in comparison with present hardships. King's customary irony here becomes bitter peevishness toward the younger generation of blacks who have, as she sees it, rejected the compulsion ("discipline") of slavery: "There was nothing to bind them or to constrain them. . . . They even could be impudent with impunity now to the whites; to those sacred whites against whom to raise a hand was once a capital crime for a slave. . . . They could now curse white men, aye and even white women, to their faces. . . . They, the negroes, had been freed and exalted—so their preachers preached to them—their owners conquered and abased" (Bush, 246–47).

At first Jerry's family scorns such attitudes and behavior, calling such blacks "city niggers" (247) while clinging to their old plantation loyalties, attitudes, and dress. But within three months the two daughters have symbolically discarded plantation homespun in favor of fancy city clothes and deferred the gratification of Canaan after death to the immediate pleasures of New Orleans life. Jerry shortly learns they have been stealing clothes, have left their jobs in service, and are living dissipated lives in the "Settlement"—a discovery that provokes a violent fight between wife and husband, which the latter calls upon his former master and mistress to resolve.

Jerry, constructed as childlike and still helplessly dependent, has to turn to Talbot for practical advice over his daughters' behavior and also—significantly—for general observations on his race. He consults his former master on his race's unreliability, lack of self-discipline, and even the responsibility of African blacks in making the slave trade possible. Jerry's bewilderment about the social and moral depravity of his own race is presented entirely without irony, and Jerry is shown—like Marcélite—increasingly facing a crisis of his own subjectivity, judging his family in white racist terms and attempting to counter the more anarchic or militant black influences on his wife and daughters. While he attempts to follow "the future that his master had planned for him, and that he knew God approved of" (255), his wife and last daughter run away to the Settlement, and he recognizes that he must follow.

Significantly, he runs to Mrs. Talbot to break the news; and just as the stern patriarch shared his thoughts, so the warmhearted mistress shares his tears. The final tableau is of the two weeping for the loss of a shared companionship and memories that so many sentimental writers (from antislavery Stowe to white apologist Page) were to repeat in their fiction. Like a lovers' parting, the mingled tears and unspoken words conceal crucial feelings that white slave-owning women often shared not with their absent or remote husbands but with male and female slaves. King's recording of their feelings, conventional as it is, speaks again the loss and betrayal that white affluent or once-affluent women felt as old loyalties with slaves hardened in postwar years into distrust and hatred. Mrs. Talbot's cry reflects the self-concerned panic of her class and sex: "Her friend and servant who had stood by her during the war . . . many a time her only help! He alone of all the plantation knew the hard path she had been set to walk in. . . . She did not have to tell him. He knew . . . Ah! That dreadful future! worse; worse than the war!" (256). In an unconscious recognition of the gender ambivalence of the women who had run plantations without men in the war and commanded slaves of both sexes, Jerry buries his head in Mrs. Talbot's skirt and sobs, " 'Master, Mistress, Master, Mistress' " (256). This uncharacteristically sentimental, overtly patronizing conclusion relies far more than King's other black stories on the clichés and stereotypes of the plantation novel and her contemporary Thomas Nelson Page. But it is also a bitter class and gender outrage at the betrayal by blacks of white women at their most vulnerable. For King, as for other women of her generation, the very *family* structure that for them

embraced their slaves and servants (albeit in a subordinate role) was ruptured by emancipation. "Jerry" is a reminder of this, and the story's lack of
irony betrays its political force, reminding the reader that for some women
this story must obsessively be retold to keep alive that white female intransigence which nothing could ever appease.

The most poignant story in *The Pleasant Ways of St. Médard* about the
fate of women after the war is "Mademoiselle Coralie." Mrs. Talbot,
reduced to absolute penury initially by the war itself, then by her husband's lack of practical money sense, has explored all financial avenues,
including asking old friends for loans. In desperation, she seeks out her
former governess Coralie, to whom—as she fled to the plantation—she
gave the keys of her house shortly before its occupation by Federal troops.
The reader is taken back to the night in 1862 when Coralie went to the
Talbot home and recognized how *she* could survive the occupation. Coralie is a typical New Orleans proletarian woman: with an invalid father and
an alcoholic brother (types familiar to readers of ante- and postbellum
literature), she has no means to "catch a husband" (her best route out of
economic dependence and poverty) except through "art and good luck,"
which King wryly dubs "notoriously poor servitors of the poor." It takes
Coralie only a short while to seize her opportunity to recognize "her
plunder" as "the fulcrum she needed" (278), and then to pack as many of
the Talbots' clothes and fripperies into trunks as she can get carted away.
With new confidence and shrewdness, she discovers the way to ensure her
financial future. King sees this transition in terms of a journey: Mrs.
Talbot's fall to dependency and degradation begins with a flight; Coralie's
new fortunes are seen in terms of class mobility:

> it may only have been her five minutes' interview with the young officer who
> received the keys from her that revealed to her that it rested with no one but
> herself to change her lot from being governess of children to governess of men.
> She very soon *traveled up* from that young officer to the supreme peak of military
> state and authority . . . and before her borrowed plumes had received their
> second wearing out, she was fledged in feathers of her own growing. (278–79;
> my emphasis)

This comic description contrasts the shrewd Coralie with the pitiable Mrs.
Talbot, who also made journeys to try to repair her losses but refused to
make her way via sexual means and relied, to no avail, on past loyalties and
good nature for help.

English and American literature abounds with women characters of
contrasted fortunes, especially contrasts between women who, in the face
of adversity, retain their "purity" and those who sacrifice their principles

and/or bodies to get out of trouble. The war subject and ironic tone of this story recall especially the satirical contrast in Thackeray's *Vanity Fair* between Amelia Sedley and Becky Sharp, both of whom "travel" from one kind of fortune to another. The theme of journeying, and the swift shift from minor deception to elaborate lie, echo the journeying women of earlier fiction who must live on their wits: Coralie's fake "flight from San Domingo, escape from massacre, faithful slaves, etc., etc., etc." (279) suggest the wanderings and fictional constructions of Moll Flanders, Jane Eyre, Eliza (*Uncle Tom's Cabin*), and Lyndall (*The Story of an African Farm*). And like many of theirs, Coralie's sexual career isolates her from other women. The independence and self-protectiveness that the hardships of war have taught the women who survived are shown to have toughened them and thus destroyed the reciprocal practical and emotional support systems by which women had been accustomed to live. Thus Coralie makes her brother turn Mrs. Talbot away from the house with a lie that the family long ago moved away.

And symbolically, the families *have* moved irrevocably apart. The division in 1862 between white prostitutes and "respectable" women had been thrown violently into question by the challenge of normally modest southern matrons to the Yankee soldiers of General "Beast" Butler. One of the earliest incidents recorded in Grace King's *Memories* is her mother's humiliating visit to the "Prince of Darkness" who apparently treated her with misogynist contempt. Butler became famous for his "Woman Order"—an exasperated gesture toward New Orleans women who expressed disdain for his troops by refusing to acknowledge or abusing the Union flag and Federal soldiers. The Woman Order decreed that "when any female shall by mere gesture or movement, insult, or show contempt for any officers or soldiers of the United States, she shall be regarded and held liable to be treated as a woman about town plying her avocation." This order shocked the Victorian world and won much sympathy for the Confederate cause from Britain, Europe, and some northerners. The city's women, meanwhile, resorted to more subtle means of defying Butler, placing his portrait in the bottom of their chamber pots and writing parodies of him. In June, 1862, *Harper's* published "The Ballad of Crescent City," which suggests that the white woman's

> spotless soul joys doubtless, soft her modest bosom beats
> That she so has aped the harlot in her city's public streets!

The ladies of New Orleans were certainly exhilarated to challenge notions of femininity that conflicted with their vocal loyalty to the Confederate cause, and angered at being described as whores simply because of their

political protests. I would suggest that this story makes a (possibly unconscious) allusion to the questions of women's sexual definition around this
time. Coralie's decision to survive the war through sexual exploitation at
the expense of loyalty to and eventual intimacy with her friend, added to
Mrs. Talbot's own refusal to resort to sexual means to pay the family's bills
during Reconstruction, are used as further examples of the humiliation
enforced on the South and southern women by the occupying troops. The
proletarian Coralie's sexual appropriation by each rank of the Federal army
and her subsequent brutal rejection of her friend are used in a deliberately
emotive way to express the sexual and emotional violence that King argued consistently had been perpetrated on her class, race, and especially
sex.[51]

The story of Coralie's hardheartedness is sandwiched between two
stories about the rapacious Italian family the San Antonios, who profit
enormously from the war and who exploit and feed on the miseries of
others. Like Coralie, the San Antonios are *nouveaux riches;* they have hardened their hearts to the sufferings of previously wealthy established families and ruthlessly set about acquiring the commodities and status symbols
of the New Orleans establishment, with their daughters' private music
lessons and attendance at the St. Ursulines convent school and the acquisition of a beautiful house recently vacated by a fleeing creole family. Grace
King shared fellow New Orleanian prejudices against "dagos," and Tony
and his wife are obnoxious examples of those business people who made
fortunes corruptly out of the confusions of war and the ruin of other
citizens. The San Antonio daughters, like Coralie, see their physical attributes as a means rather than an end. King refers twice to their "capital of
beauty" and to the ways in which it could be "profitably increased"; like
the women of the Institut (*Monsieur Motte*) and like Coralie, they learn that
it is a matter of "vigilance here, enterprise there" (268).

In the final story of the collection, the Talbots get their just deserts after
the death of Tony, when Mr. Talbot is given the task of dealing with the
dead man's estate, now locked in "the armoire of litigation" (294). Mr.

51. King, *Memories,* 8. The title given to Butler presumably alludes both to his misogyny
and also to his celebrated support for the city's blacks. It is significant that the only contemporary woman who publicly celebrated Butler is the *black* writer Alice Dunbar-Nelson, who
recalled his achievements—abolishing whipping-posts and star cars (early Jim Crow cars), as
well as bringing sick and starving freed blacks into camps. See Alice Dunbar-Nelson, "People
of Color in Louisiana, Part II," *Journal of Negro History,* II (January, 1917), 67–68. The Woman
Order is quoted in Schuler, "Women in Public Affairs in Louisiana During Reconstruction,"
16. "The Ballad of Crescent City," *Harper's Weekly,* June 14, 1862, p. 370, describes the
behavior of the New Orleans "haughty Creole matron" with her "foul and meretricious
taunts" at northern soldiers.

Talbot is restored to his former position as important city lawyer largely through the machinations of Tommy Cook, who believes that the rise of his patron and the fall of the San Antonios indicate "now, the country *is* safe" (294). This "safety" that Tommy Cook celebrates is King's final show of triumph of the white Bourbons over what her class defined as corrupt Reconstruction carpetbag governments led by illiterate, irresponsible blacks. At Tony's deathbed there is a conspiracy of all the white patriarchal figures who control the St. Médard society and oppose the new regime—priest, doctor, and lawyer—to keep Tony's dubiously acquired wealth away from the public administrator to whom it belongs. The doctor explains why this is desirable: "you know who the public administrator is! A negro! . . . But in addition there is a politician, a white carpet-bagger, behind the negro . . . negro, carpet-bagger; carpet-bagger, negro; that is what our government is from governor down" (286–87).

The Pleasant Ways of St. Médard is a story of the restored fortunes and status of a defeated and humiliated white professional class, orchestrated through patriarchal old-boy networks so that Mr. Talbot, its representative, can be restored as proud family head and breadwinner. The fate of Mrs. Talbot is not clear; she is not mentioned in the final story. Her last appearance is at her husband's sickbed, reflecting sentimentally on the past and preparing for his possible death; her last poignant independent action was her visit to Coralie, from whose door disappointedly she moved "slowly away, on tired feet" (280). These stories, like King's other collections, focus on white men far more than on blacks or men of other ethnic groups (who are always caricatured as heroic martyrs or villains), and on white women more insistently and passionately than on men. What King created in this, her final sustained fictional comment on postwar New Orleans, was an expression of nostalgia for a bourgeois white hegemony which, restored though it was to power, had been badly dented and demoralized. The reader is made to feel strongly for the Talbot family by the use of various conventional literary devices such as a child's sickbed, a father's near-death, the final leave-taking of a loving freed slave. But most of all, the reader is compelled to feel for the silent suffering of a woman who endures and weeps, and whose ultimate fate lies in the hands of male machinations and legal finesse.

A novel roughly contemporary with *The Pleasant Ways,* Ellen Glasgow's *Virginia* (1913)—which takes an emblematic heroine who represents (as her name suggests) both the victimized South and defeated southern women as a result of the war and social changes that followed it—has a more optimistic conclusion than this. Ellen Glasgow implies that the emotional strength and resilience of southern women are eventually given their due, since in her moment of deepest despair Virginia receives a telegram saying that her beloved son is returning to her from Europe. Like Margaret Mitchell in the later *Gone With the Wind* (1936), Glasgow suggests that female endurance is rewarded perhaps because of its very centrality and indispensability to southern life and experience. Although King expresses some of this buoyancy and confidence in earlier works, and throughout her work argues that this *should* be so, in *The Pleasant Ways* her optimism for southern womanhood is much muted. The women all disappear: Coralie vanishes behind a closed door; Madame San Antonio and her daughters must now fend for themselves and their future is unresolved; Mrs. Talbot makes no appearance in the final scene. While Mr. Talbot is restored to his old network of friends and legal contacts, his wife is turned away from her ex-governess's house. Powerless women are shown as having too much to lose and too perilous a foothold on life to be able to offer generosity or friendship across class barriers.

It is significant that in old age Grace King selected a remote historical subject. For her last full-length novel, *La Dame de Sainte Hermine,* she returned to her youthful passion for the early colonial history of Louisiana in a strong indictment of the eighteenth-century "lottery" system that shipped French girls to Louisiana to be colonists' wives.[52] To the end, she chose feminist themes, but she must have realized that her obsession with the Civil War and Reconstruction was no longer shared by her contemporaries and editors, and that another war had long overshadowed it. It is likely that her decision to write her memoirs came from a strong need to rehearse all those preoccupations she had still failed to resolve in her writings, this time through yet another discourse.

The portrait used to illustrate both the Robert Bush selection and the David Kirby book is of a very young, demure Grace King, in a softly frilled gown, the epitome of southern womanhood. However, in her papers there are many more photographs of the older King, very assured, rather imperious and arrogant, usually surrounded by friends and colleagues in the Historical Society and other city clubs. These convey a different impression: not the solitary, thoughtful writer of the early portrait, but of a sociable, busy woman much admired and cosseted in her native city, whose parochial politics were reinforced by her influential peers. Because her work was so successful for many years and because she received little adverse criticism on her trips to the North and Europe, King's limited political analysis was never really tried or challenged. Thus her historical and biographical work reflects an unquestioned loyalty to the

52. Grace King, *La Dame de Sainte Hermine* (New York, 1924).

Lost Cause, and a certainty of the absolute rights of the white ruling class to reassert itself, especially over the freedman / woman.

Of all her contemporaries, Grace King experimented with the greatest number of discourses, almost as if she were determined to write the truth of her region, class, and sex in each possible nuance and tone of voice. But apart from the occasional personal note, the nonfiction work was clearly intended to speak in the public, masculine discourses of objectivity and authority. It is in the fiction that the contradictions and fragmentation of her own private voice can be felt. Because of her clear move toward feminism, King used conventional themes and characters in new ways, often unconsciously subverting her own political project in the texture of her stories and novels. In fiction, King indulged far more in consciously feminine voices in order to express and work out the many contradictory feelings that women of her generation shared. Her work is possibly the most comprehensive attempt to probe the meanings of the Civil War and emancipation for southern white bourgeois women (and, less fully felt, for some black and proletarian women). By focusing mainly on women's postbellum sufferings, it explored more fully than her male contemporaries could do the nature of the radical shifts in class, race, and gender in the South and in the lived experience of southern women.

II

Ruth McEnery Stuart

Of the three writers in this study, Ruth McEnery Stuart (1849–1917) has been most completely erased from literary history. All her work is out of print, and most of it is unobtainable outside the U.S.A. The few critical references to Stuart dismiss her as a minor Local Colorist, a specialist in southern dialects, following a "sentimental, optimistic formula."[1] She is the subject of serious consideration by one group only, the Ruth McEnery Stuart Clan of New Orleans, which takes an uncritical, hagiographic approach to all her writings.

My concern with Stuart's work derives from its considerable significance in the history and historical application of southern women's writing. This chapter will focus on the ideological impact of her very popular and critically successful writing about southern blacks, which to a modern liberal reader is exceptionally patronizing and racist, and her less fêted but (for a modern critic) more important focus on gender issues and tentative forays into feminist fiction. A southerner who moved to New York City and made a career out of southern materials, she served well as a spokesperson for that crucial imaginative construct, a hegemonic national culture from which regional conflict and difference had been erased. The atrocities of Reconstruction and the violent repression of blacks in the *real* South were forgotten as Stuart's humorous and pathetic black characters spoke garbled truths in dialect on behalf of a silenced and forgotten race. Therefore this chapter will focus on the ideological and political function of her writing, and the ways she both accepted and mediated the role of southern spokesperson. And it will discuss the indications, which emerge in fragmentary and often confused ways in her works, that Stuart, an

1. This typical quotation is from Robert Bain, Joseph M. Flora, and Louis D. Rubin, Jr. (eds.), *Southern Writers: A Biographical Dictionary* (Baton Rouge, 1979), 438.

active supporter of women's movements, was able to challenge orthodox positions on gender, and might have developed as an iconoclastic writer on feminist issues. But since her position on race was politically at odds with her feminism, it is important to examine the writer's contradictory politics as they emerge in, and are worked out, through the fiction.

Early in her career, Stuart found a formula of writing about blacks that she repeated—with various significant variations—throughout her literary career. Arriving in New York at the moment when southern material was being sought and welcomed relatively uncritically by editors and readers alike as a boost to a new sense of national unity, Stuart succeeded too easily for her own good. As a result, much of her work on blacks caters to a reading public already cultivated by Sherwood Bonner, Joel Chandler Harris, Thomas Nelson Page, and others for sentimental, comic versions of black experience. But her works featuring blacks need to be examined in the light of the historical period at which they were published; for unlike those earlier writers, Stuart reveals a certain self-consciousness about her project as white female interpreter of southern black lived experience at a time when blacks were losing power and ground significantly in the South. And this apparently clear, fairly consistent literary project relating to blacks reveals, or confirms, a great deal about national editorial publication policy toward the South and race matters during the final decades of the century.

In terms of Stuart's feminism, however, there is no such clear project, and the writer's progressive views and writings about (white) women contrast strongly with her repeatedly reactionary and racist constructions of blacks of both sexes. In the last years of her life, it seems she intended to abandon black themes in favor of specifically feminist subjects. A journalist records that in 1913 she was contemplating a novel "along the lines which Miss Mary Johnston and Miss Ellen Glasgow have followed recently . . . the story of a girl in modern times, meeting problems in the light of 'feminism' as it flourishes to-day," a novel about a southern girl in New York. The report also notes that Stuart found it "striking, but not remarkable, that she, Miss Glasgow, and Miss Johnston, Miss Sarah Barnwell Elliott, and so many of the Southern writers, despite the traditional conservatism of their action, should be so unhesitatingly champions of the feministic movement."[2] It seems, from these quotations, that Stuart experienced feminism as an area of conflict and difficulty for all southern women, and that her interest in fictional treatment of the subject stemmed

2. New York *Post,* December 6, 1913, in the Ruth McEnery Stuart Collection, Special Collections Division, Tulane University Library, New Orleans, hereinafter referred to as RMSC.

from personal experiences of the tensions inherent in seriously engaging with feminist issues. Indeed, writing about such issues was bound to involve a far more personal involvement than the earlier work; it is perhaps no coincidence that this reserved, conservative writer featured more *male* black characters than female, and avoided creating a female protagonist who would speak for and about her. As a southern woman of letters living and publishing in New York while drawing her materials from her native and adopted southern states, Stuart must have experienced considerable contradictions in her life as a writer. Some of those conflicts are inevitably felt in the works that foreground problems of gender, lacking as they do the stylistic coherence and homogeneous comic tone of most of the black stories. A handful of stories come close to expressing the real implications and complexity of the determinants race and gender, and of the author's racism and feminism. There are also occasional fragmented recognitions throughout the work of the nature of race and gender difference, especially in relation to the family, domestic life, and sexuality.

As a Louisiana woman writer, Ruth McEnery Stuart was unusual in several ways, and her career trajectory is significantly different from that of King or Chopin. She moved to New York at the beginning of her career and made her permanent home there; she became a committed feminist and supported woman suffrage and women's rights; she made the southern black rather than the white bourgeois woman the main focus of her fiction and verse; and her main genre was the comic dialect tale and verse rather than the sentimental or gothic romance of the war and Reconstruction. She was highly regarded in her adopted New York; the most prestigious editors and writers admired her and featured her work in their magazines. Her first publication, "Uncle Mingo's 'Speculatioms,'" appeared in *New Princeton Review* in 1888, and she was in demand thereafter. All her fiction and verse was published in the North. Like Grace King, she was fêted by Henry Mills Alden and Charles Dudley Warner of *Harper's* and Richard Watson Gilder of *Century*; between them, they published the lion's share of her seven short novels, eleven story collections, one "burlesque," and two anthologies of "plantation verse." The majority of this work focuses on the blacks of New Orleans and unspecified plantations, and makes heavy use of black dialect and speech patterns. There are also a few collections of stories about whites in Arkansas and Italians in New Orleans, and one of the novels, set in a sanitarium for women, is concerned specifically with feminist issues. Her predominant tone is humorous, and her mode of writing usually comic; there are few tragic endings.

The most crucial difference between Stuart and the other two subjects of this study lies in her extensive and repeated use of dialect. As I have discussed earlier, this was a feature of much Local Color fiction from the mid-1870s, and Stuart's most successful contemporaries (Page, Harris, Twain) made reputations and fortunes out of it. Like Mark Twain and George W. Cable, Stuart made a fair income out of touring the country and reading aloud to captive audiences her dialect stories, imitating black voices. In major ways, she was a central figure in the construction and dissemination of a mythic South that rapidly became the received version. Apart from Cable and Twain, most Local Colorists have been evaluated according to their degree of success in capturing the quality of particular regional dialects and speech patterns, and Stuart has always been regarded as a faithful recorder of black and Italian *patois*. There has been little or no critical attempt to analyze the social and political implications of American dialect fiction in relation to standard English, as it mediates class, race, and gender relations. Henry Nash Smith is typical of the serious rather than dismissive attitude to regional and dialect fiction when he argues that dialect, used by Fenimore Cooper and sentimental antebellum fiction to indicate low social status, became transformed by key writers such as Edward Eggleston and Mark Twain into the elements of an American literary vernacular prose. But this argument provides no tools for analysis of dialect fiction in general.

One of the Oxford English Dictionary's main definitions of the word *dialect* emphasizes its linguistic function as peripheral and subordinate: "One of the subordinate forms or varieties of a language arising from local peculiarities of vocabulary, pronunciation, and idiom. . . . A variety of speech differing from the standard or literary 'language'; a provincial method of speech." In order to examine the implications of linguistic difference within a country with a national language, and its relevance for literary study, it is necessary to turn to recent European criticism; three studies have clarified the relevant issues. In *The Country and the City*, Raymond Williams discusses the ability of Thomas Hardy's *Tess of the d'Urbervilles* to speak "two languages"—dialect at home and "ordinary English" learned at school to "persons of quality" and outside the home. Williams uses this example of bilingualism to argue against the standard version of Hardy's "timeless" rural life, with figures like Tess as mythic English peasants. While not discussing dialect in detail, Williams suggests that in social and educational terms this clear division between standard English and Wessex dialect is something the observer/writer foregrounds to emphasize the very provincialism and stagnation of those economically obsolescent rural communities. Renée Balibar's discussion of George Sand's "La Mare au Diable" is also useful in its historical location of the post–French Revolution construction of a "national language common to all citizens" related as it was to a national education system's attempt to eradicate linguistic differences between social classes and disparate provinces of France. Calling the normative expression of Sand's peasants a radical break with class-inflected linguistic forms, she points to the phonetic and syntactic "faults" and simplicities of Balzac's agricultural workers (in *The Peasants*, 1844), who are thus "excluded, imaginarily, from the republican linguistic network." Finally, discussing *Wuthering Heights*, David Musselwhite uses the notion of Pierre Macherey and Etienne Balibar that literature is "an ideological 'opérateur' because it has as its condition of existence a 'standard language' established by the bourgeoisie for the purposes of maintaining its cultural hegemony." In the novel, Musselwhite argues, Joseph is placed in structural opposition to the "standard English" Nelly; he is constructed as completely marginal to and invisible from the family history, representing a past and now irrelevant language and morality.[3]

Although all these writers focus on class and region rather than race and gender, their relevance for this study is clear. A standard national language must define dialect as provincial and subordinate, and can thus construct particular groups (a race, class, sex, etc.) as obsolescent, marginal, even irrelevant. Using a "hierarchy of discourses," writers can either reinforce and naturalize, or foreground and challenge a hegemonic national culture.[4]

In the case of Ruth McEnery Stuart, the hegemonic culture being reinforced and condoned is bourgeois white supremacy, which marginalizes and renders anachronistic black language and thus black social reality. The use of dialect in her stories about blacks and white New Orleans Italians served to exclude two troublesome, militant ethnic groups from the national language, and thus to marginalize or render them safely ineffectual through a controlling "standard language" that resolved conflicts and disguised or glossed over political and social contradictions. This was the literary language of New England and New York literary culture still strongly dominated by English letters, a language that any southern woman of letters in exile had to learn to use effectively, exploiting the vernacular speech of her region in order to gain recognition. By the time

3. Raymond Williams, *The Country and the City* (London, 1973), 243; Renée Balibar, "An Example of Literary Work in France: George Sand's 'La Mare au Diable'/'The Devil's Pool' of 1846," in Barker *et al.* (eds.), *1848: The Sociology of Literature*, 27–46, 30, 44; P. Macherey and E. Balibar, "Sur la littérature comme forme idéologique," *Littérature*, XVIII (1974), 30, quoted in David Musselwhite, "*Wuthering Heights*: The Unacceptable Text," in Francis Barker *et al.* (eds.), *Literature, Society and the Sociology of Literature* (Colchester, 1977), 155.
   4. See Belsey, *Critical Practice*, 70.

Stuart began to achieve national success, southern Local Color was helping prepare the nation for black disfranchisement and the most violent suppression since emancipation; in every way, as Louis Rubin argues, "in the eyes of the nation the image of Uncle Remus replaced that of Uncle Tom."[5] Stuart played along with the trend, though with a certain degree of self-consciousness, and made a good living out of it.

Although she departed from her female contemporaries in significant ways, Ruth Stuart shared with many of them key experiences, especially in terms of her decision to make a living as a writer.[6] Like Grace King and Kate Chopin, she was born approximately a decade before the Civil War; she published her first work in the late 1880s and wrote the bulk of her fiction before the turn of the century. She drew her literary material exclusively from Louisiana and her adopted state through marriage, Arkansas; and she was celebrated both in the North and in her native state. She was born Mary Routh McEnery, and adopted the simpler "Ruth" for her pen name. Her birth date, like that of many southern women, is a subject of speculation; it is variously given as 1849, 1852, and 1860, though the earliest date is the most probable. She was the first of eight children born into a wealthy, well-connected family; of Irish and Scots ancestry, her parents both came from plantation-owning families with a long tradition of professional, commercial, and political involvement in Louisiana. The Stirlings (her mother's family) and the McEnerys represented Louisiana in Congress regularly during the nineteenth century, and five of Ruth's kinsmen were governors of the state. One of her relatives, Mary Ann Dorsey, helped Jefferson Davis in the writing of *The Rise and Fall of the Confederate Government* (1881). Her father, a cotton commission merchant as well as planter, was a key figure in the Customs House, and this was the reason the family moved, when Routh was three, from Marksville, Avoyelles Parish, to New Orleans, though they regularly visited the plantation thereafter.

The young Routh attended both public and private schools in New

5. Louis D. Rubin, Jr., *The Writer in the South: Studies in a Literary Community* (Athens, Ga. 1972), 38. Also see Louis D. Rubin, Jr., *William Elliott Shoots a Bear: Essays on the Southern Literary Imagination* (Baton Rouge, 1975), 61–106.

6. There is no comprehensive biography of Stuart. Biographical information has been taken from the *Dictionary of American Biography;* Mary Frances Fletcher, "A Biographical and Critical Study of Ruth McEnery Stuart" (M.A. thesis, University of Virginia, n.d.); Robert B. Bush, "Louisiana Prose Fiction, 1870–1900" (Ph.D. dissertation, State University of Iowa, 1957); Edwin A. Alderman, Joel C. Harris, and Charles W. Kent (eds.), *Library of Southern Literature,* XI (New Orleans, 1907), 5145–61; Bain *et al.* (eds.), *Southern Writers,* 437–39; *Ruth McEnery Stuart Clan: A Brief History on the Occasion of Its Sixtieth Anniversary* (New Orleans, 1975).

Orleans, but her schooling was cut short by the Civil War, which—as for Grace King—impoverished her family and led Routh to earn a living by teaching for some years in primary grades. In an interview with a northern journalist she gave a rare glimpse into the difficulties of her upbringing. Of her attendance at various schools, she recorded that "parents were then glad to avail themselves of any educational privileges that could be obtained for their children, so demoralized was the condition of the South. . . . The recollections of my childhood . . . are very strange and troubled: it is as if the atmosphere upon my mental canvas were dimmed with the fire and smoke of war." Like many girls of her generation, Stuart was forced to grow up faster than she had anticipated, and during adolescence the absence of slaves meant that she undertook many of the burdens of domestic work for which the family could not afford to pay. One of her biographers, Mary Fletcher, records that she was responsible for the general housekeeping, cooking, and sewing, and that her sisters depended heavily upon her. However, Stuart's health was never good and was probably undermined by these responsibilities; this may explain why she was sent on daily "health walks" in the city. It was while walking that she became aware of ethnic communities different from her own, and she apparently found more to interest her in the Italian traders, poor white creoles, and blacks of New Orleans than she ever did in her scholarly father's library.[7]

Thus Mary Routh McEnery's childhood and young womanhood prepared her quite well for the later, unexpected career she followed. Her family's entrenched position in Louisiana's economic and political life (restored in some measure after the war) meant that she shared a confidence in her class's integrity and right to govern, and a view of all other groups as subordinate, providing the city with picturesque local color and folklore: "I have always felt interested in the common folk."[8] Certainly, her duties as housekeeper and responsible oldest daughter must have taught her a great deal about the lives of women of classes less privileged than her own, and undoubtedly made her especially conscious of the burdens on her sister in later years, when Sarah became *her* housekeeper. Also, as a teacher, she got to know girls of different families and economic positions, and learned much about the socialization and hardships of white middle-class women in the postwar years. Like her, many of them had grown up to expect a certain kind of privileged womanhood and had lived through dramatically changed and reduced circumstances, needing now to adjust to new demands and pressures. An awareness of the fragile notion

7. "A Southern Writer of Note," n.d., in RMSC; Fletcher, "Ruth McEnery Stuart," 19.
8. Ruth M. Stuart, quoted in "A Southern Writer of Note."

of "the southern lady," together with the harsh realities of working for a living and facing a second job at home, undoubtedly gave McEnery a predilection for the feminist arguments she later met and eagerly adopted in New York.

In 1879 she went on vacation to Arkansas where she met—and within a few weeks married—Alfred Oden Stuart, a wealthy cotton planter much older than herself and already thrice widowed. Her family was distraught at the news (perhaps altruistically because of Stuart's age and the haste of the match), but her speedy decision suggests a desperate attempt to escape the heavy demands and trials of home life in New Orleans. Routh McEnery Stuart then settled in Washington, Arkansas, living in her husband's colonial house on his vast plantations, where his family had for many years been politically, socially, and economically prominent land- and slave-owners. Like Kate Chopin in northwest Louisiana, Stuart developed a folklorist's interest in the black and white employees and families on her husband's plantations and commissary. Like Chopin and Joel Chandler Harris, she collected from them stories, anecdotes, and local gossip. Along with those of the blacks and Italians of New Orleans, these people's lives, idealized and romanticized, became a staple of her literary success.

At first it must have seemed as if Routh Stuart had fallen on her feet and was enjoying the kind of life she had virtually ceased to expect since the end of the war; but a year after her son Stirling was born, her husband died. There is no written evidence of the young widow's exact financial position after Alfred Stuart's death, but since he had many children from his three previous marriages, and since he died intestate (possibly in debt), it may be that his wife retired gracefully without hope of any settlement. It is clear that she returned virtually penniless to New Orleans to live with her sister Sarah, principal of Chesnut School, and soon began to write in order to support herself and her son.

There are many gaps in the details of Stuart's biography, and one is her reason for turning to writing rather than returning to her former profession (shared with Sarah), teaching. However, like Grace King, she benefited from the fact that the 1884 Cotton Centennial Exposition was making New Orleans a focus of some national attention and of the interest of northern writers and editors. Though there is no record of Stuart's participation in the women's clubs and other activities during the exposition, it is virtually certain that she visited some events and lectures, and understood the new demand for southern literary materials. Like many women writers, Stuart explained her decision to become a writer in terms of economic pressures. This was perhaps partly an apology for her own ambition, which may have been fueled by the existence of the PanGnostics and the presence of other budding women writers in New Orleans at the time:

> Impending poverty did it. . . . Like the majority of Southern women, I had been brought up to enjoy life and take no thought of its serious complexities, but when the problem confronted me, I knew that I must rise to the emergency, as so many have done before and since. I had never written anything for publication, but decided that I would try. I spent three weeks planning a story, then sat down and wrote it. I was fortunate enough to have it obtain instant recognition.[9]

Both Grace King and Ruth Stuart owe the launching of their writing careers to the same man. While King met and formed a strong attachment to Charles Dudley Warner in New Orleans in 1885, Ruth Stuart came across him soon afterwards on vacation in a North Carolina resort. The womanizing Warner and Stuart were evidently mutually attracted. Mary Fletcher records that Stuart spoke of the " 'lovely, gentle' " man with whom she walked and relaxed. When she returned to New Orleans, she sent two of her stories anonymously to the editor, asking his opinion of "Uncle Mingo's 'Speculatioms' " and "The Lamentations of Jeremiah Johnson." Warner replied (without indicating whether he guessed his correspondent's identity), "I didn't go to bed last night until I had read both of your stories. One I have kept for *Harper's*; the other I have sent to *The Princeton Review.*" "Uncle Mingo" appeared the following year, 1888, in the *New Princeton Review,* the journal that had published Grace King's first story, "Monsieur Motte," two years earlier. It was so successful—providing as it did the kind of southern material currently in vogue—that Ruth Stuart's career was assured from that time. Warner may not at first have known who his anonymous author was, but he soon learned. He then followed her work with interest and enthusiasm until his death, often sending her a note of congratulation when she published a new book and visiting her at least once in New Orleans. Writing in the Hartford *Courant* of her public readings, he praised her "winning personality and lively intelligence" and claimed that "her pictures of Louisiana life, both white and colored, are among the best we have—truthful, humorous, and not seldom pathetic, but never overdrawn or sentimental." As with King, Warner was to provide the worst kind of fawning admiration, which did nothing but harden Stuart's race and class biases.[10]

9. Ruth McEnery Stuart, "American Authors at Home," New York *Mail and Express,* April 28, 1900.

10. Fletcher, "Ruth McEnery Stuart," 24, 25; New Orleans *Picayune*(?), February 23, 1907, in RMSC; Charles Dudley Warner, "What Is Said of Mrs. Stuart's Readings," n.d., in RMSC.

Around 1890, after the success of "Uncle Mingo" and "Lamentations," in response to pressure from northern editors that she produce more southern fiction, Ruth Stuart left her son with Sarah and moved to New York City to be closer to publishers and literary circles. From that time she published regularly, mainly in *Harper's Bazaar* (which she guest-edited occasionally) and *Century*. Possibly due to Charles Dudley Warner's early patronage and skills as unofficial literary agent, she had a relatively easy time getting established as a writer in New York. In a two-part article published in 1904, writer Julia Tutwiler outlined the problem facing a southern woman coming to New York to make a living as writer; she described the slow progression from book reviewing to ingratiating oneself with editors, to obtaining regular work—with many perils of rejection, neglect, and indifference along the way. Tutwiler pointed out that many editors encouraged new talent as a matter of course, but then dropped writers without compunction and discriminated in favor of men, patronizing women and seeing them as minor and/or merely fashion writers. But Ruth Stuart, she claimed, knew "little or nothing of the material side of literary struggle" since her first two stories (published before her arrival) created an audience for her that continued to grow. By the time she wrote this article, Tutwiler claimed, "there is no woman whose work is more widely known and loved, and whose personality has a further reaching influence."[11]

Tutwiler made no reference to the importance of a woman's lifestyle and general demeanor on her New York success, though Ruth Stuart learned fast how vital it was to present a respectable front and to attract no adverse criticism for one's way of life and relationships. By the time she moved to New York there already existed an example of a southern woman writer who had moved North and eventually been driven home in a humiliating way. Katharine Bonner McDowell (1849–1883), better known by her pseudonym Sherwood Bonner, had come from Holly Springs, Mississippi, and acquired a notorious reputation besides minor national fame as a Local Colorist and romance writer. Though the fiction was soon forgotten after her early death from cancer (and she is not mentioned in Stuart's writings), her biographer claims Sherwood Bonner had emerged as "a hauntingly enigmatic and possibly scandalous figure in literary New England's Indian summer."[12] She came from a planter's family very similar to Stuart's own, and like the New Orleanian had her

11. Julia R. Tutwiler, "The Southern Woman in New York," *Bookman*, XVIII (February, 1904), 633.

12. Hubert Horton McAlexander, *The Prodigal Daughter: A Biography of Sherwood Bonner* (Baton Rouge, 1981), 209.

childhood and education disrupted by the war. She married and had one child, but unlike her widowed contemporary, had an embarrassing and difficult separation. She began to write fiction and, encouraged by male mentors, moved to Boston where she lived a semibohemian life as writer/ hostess and became a vigorous defender of woman suffrage. In 1878 she published one of the first strongly feminist American novels, *Like Unto Like*. She was a close friend of influential writers, especially Longfellow, who helped her financially, employed her as secretary, and encouraged her writing. Their relationship led, however, to rumors of a sexual scandal, and in her last years in Boston, polite society inexorably closed ranks against her. The case of Sherwood Bonner demonstrates the limits of emancipated behavior permissible for an outsider, and for all southern women living without men, in the North in the early postbellum decades; her unhappy experiences in Boston were an indication of the resistance that faced feminists who were careless about their public image. She was a literary pioneer of Local Color and dialect fiction, preparing the ground for later southern writers, but her notoriety as a "New Woman" and feminist writer must have been a salutary warning to Stuart as she embarked on a New York life of letters.

Stuart played safe, then, to her advantage as writer and representative figure of her region in New York City. She worked hard, lived modestly, and gained a reputation for wit, charm, and good southern cooking. Encouraged by her early success, she brought to New York her son and sister Sarah, who gave up her New Orleans school post to become full-time housekeeper, child-minder, and amanuensis. Like Grace King, Ruth Stuart was fortunate in having a self-abnegating sister available to play the traditional roles of wife and hostess, so that she could both write uninterruptedly and also leave her son for long periods to undergo national reading tours—in churches, women's clubs, and hotels, with such writers as Mary Wilkins and Frances Hodgson Burnett. Sarah McEnery's support, like Annie Reagan King's, was invaluable as the pressures of free-lance writing, guest editorships, public readings, and relentless entertaining took their toll on Ruth Stuart.

By the early twentieth century Stuart was established as one of the best known and most admired of all the southern women who had come north to make their literary reputations and fortunes, and she was making a fairly comfortable living. She got to know many writers and became well known as a salon hostess; she was a central figure in three of New York's prominent cultural clubs—the Barnard, MacDowell, and Wednesday Afternoon. Apart from Charles Dudley Warner, Stuart befriended New York editors and literary men and women, and old friends from Louisiana sent encomiastic letters. William Dean Howells was an admirer, sending her a book and publishing her work; Hamlin Garland inscribed a copy of *Main-Travelled Roads* to her in 1895. Henry Mills Alden, one of Grace King's admirers, evidently thought a great deal of Ruth Stuart: she describes a "nice letter" he wrote asking for material and "saying some things which make me feel that I must prove worthy of the faith they put in me, for good work." George W. Cable, *bête noir* of most New Orleanians, became a friend and clearly a southern ally: in 1894 he sent her a copy of his Louisiana stories *Bonaventure* with a greeting, and a year later a copy of *The Grandissimes,* inscribing it: "Dear Ruth: Let me hope that these few ink marks may make to both of us a little sweeter and dearer our far-away homeland of magnolias and mocking birds."[13] Stuart, for her part, wrote him a couple of letters in black dialect inviting him to visit, and referred affectionately to *The Grandissimes* in a letter to another friend.

With Cable and another fellow writer-in-exile, Hamlin Garland, Stuart shared a peripheral relationship to the northeastern world of letters and co-option by Genteel Tradition editors and journals. All came to live in the East to make their living as writers and to be at the center of national cultural life, and to varying degrees they were tamed by that experience—though Garland moved back to the Midwest in 1893 to escape Boston's influence and remake contacts with his own region. In the case of the two New Orleanians, I suspect their very success and easy assimilation into northern literary life account for the orthodoxy of their writings in the 1890s. Cable's best work was produced when he was radically at odds with his native state but passionately involved in and committed to it. Ruth McEnery Stuart's smooth transition to becoming a southern woman of letters in New York meant that she colluded (albeit unintentionally) with an increasingly sterile version of regionalist literature. Her Local Color fiction encouraged a reading of Louisiana regional identity (in all its forms) as marginal and subordinate to an unchallenged hegemonic national literary culture.

There are, however, signs that the ostensible ease of her assimilation and acceptance as a writer placed considerable strains on Stuart. By 1904 she was exhausted and in a state of "near nervous prostration." The constant hard work involved in writing and public reading, together with social and family duties, meant there was little time for relaxation or vacations. Her son Stirling had always caused her great anxiety; letters to friends refer constantly to his irresponsible and childish behavior. In 1904, through a characteristically reckless act, he fell while climbing into their house and

13. Ruth McEnery Stuart to Dr. Pope, January 27, 1907, in RMSC; George W. Cable, quoted in Fletcher, "Ruth McEnery Stuart," 62.

broke his back; after months of suffering (and attendance by the renowned
Dr. Weir Mitchell) he died. Sarah McEnery suffered a complete breakdown as a result, and Ruth Stuart described her own emotional state as
near to "insanity." Stirling's death coincided with the declining demand by
northern editors for regional fiction and a loss of national interest in the
South and its writers; this combination of circumstances may well have
precipitated Stuart's decision to return for the first time to her home state.
She visited New Orleans in 1907 and was welcomed as a great celebrity;
she was presented in and read at Newcomb Hall and got to know the
lawyer Judith Hyams Douglas, who set up the Ruth McEnery Stuart Clan.
Grace King was a member of the Clan; it became (and still is) an exclusive
literary club. Stuart herself enjoyed her visit and during this stay followed
her New York practice of attending meetings of many of the city's wom-
en's clubs. She made a second visit in 1915, to receive (along with Grace
King) a doctorate of letters from Tulane University and to find herself
greatly fêted. When she died two years later, her body was taken to New
Orleans where it lies with that of her son, and there was much mourning
among her friends and admirers. Tulane organized a memorial service in
May, 1917, attended among others by Grace King.[14]

In view of her reception, it is perhaps not surprising that Stuart visited
New Orleans twice in the last decade of her life; the adulation poured upon
her must have helped heal recent wounds. Like her admirer Grace King,
she was celebrated as a prophet in her native state. In her lifetime she was
called "a sort of very Southern Goddess," and one of many appreciations
after her death described Stuart thus:

> . . . In her wide range of feeling, everywhere,
> The Southern heart beat true and, there,
> Its varied harmonies ring vast and free.
> . . . we rejoice
> That this leal [sic] lady wreathed with her dear hand
> Unfading laurels and our Dixie crowned.

New Orleanians thus recognized her as an unequivocal cheerleader for
southern pride and chauvinism, and for them her major achievement lay in
interpreting the "true" nature of the southern black and southern race
relations to a previously unsympathetic northern readership. Belle M'Cormick's posthumous tribute to the writer best illustrates this: "Ruth McEnery Stuart reveals the relation between the southern master and the south-

14. Ruth McEnery Stuart to friends, June 30, 1904, quoted in Fletcher, "Ruth McEnery
Stuart," 124. The doctorate was given "in recognition of her exalted character, her eminent
attainments in Arts and Letters, her constant devotion to the advancement of Truth, and the
welfare of Society," Tulane University, June 2, 1915, in RMSC.

ern darky, which was one of affection and friendliness without familiarity. That relation is something the northerner has never been able to understand."[15]

By the 1890s, Louisiana was regarded as one of the most interesting literary settings, its writers some of the most acclaimed. A "New Orleans school" of writers was identified, and in 1894 Stuart was included in this as the "latest light illuminating the already brilliant constellation of Southern writers." This tribute came shortly after her second published story appeared, and from that time she was celebrated (like Thomas Nelson Page and Joel Chandler Harris) as a writer who was delighting northern audiences with the "truthfulness and charm" of her stories about southern blacks and poor whites. Ruth Stuart's reviewers and admirers agreed that she wrote of the South through humor, pathos, and "the roseate glow of sentiment and romance," seeing good rather than evil in her characters and situations. Furthermore, there is a general agreement that Stuart never attempted "to outline the industrial and economic side of the life of either white or black." She was seen mainly as a storyteller who depicted the "faithful negro" and other impoverished minorities in a sympathetic, amusing light, with considerable use of accurate dialect—the latter of which was the popular feature of her public readings. Typical of her highly favorable critical reception is this observation: "She did not deal with that portion of human society in which the base and ignoble must be emphasized. . . . She sought rather to find the best there was in life and present it to her readers. . . . The effect was elevating and wholesome. . . . It was her mission to treasure the sunshine, the laughter and song of the simple life about her and give it joyously to mankind."[16]

When one reads batches of cuttings relating to Stuart's work, the overwhelming impression is one of critical relief and delight at her palatable light-heartedly conceived southern (especially black) characters. Her humor is repeatedly emphasized, and its rarity in a woman writer referred to several times. The vocabulary used in describing her stories denotes the lightness of touch that critics loved: called a "master of dialects," she was praised for creating work that was "exquisite," "cheering as sunshine," "light/delicate in touch," "full of humor and pathos," superb at capturing "the picturesque in negro life," and producing in the

15. A New Orleans journalist, n.d. (probably 1907 or 1915), Jane Grey Rogers, New Orleans *Picayune,* May 27, 1917(?), Belle M'Cormick New Orleans *Picayune,* May 27, 1917, all in RMSC.
16. No title, n.d., in RMSC; Boston *Courier,* July 8, 1894; Alderman *et al.* (eds.), *Library of Southern Literature,* XI, 5148, 5147; Dixon Merritt, "The South Window," n.d., in RMSC.

reader "laughter and tears."[17] All of these terms reinforce my hypothesis that northern editors and readers welcomed such a writer's construction of the South in terms of what they wished to believe was southern reality: harmonious ethnic relations, pathetic and comic character types, and Arcadian communities. The emphasis on humor and "quaint" dialect especially demonstrates Stuart's role as conservative and celebratory regionalist figure.

Stuart colluded with northern ideological reconstructions of the South, of which she spoke as lyrically as Edward King and other northern visitors. Writing in 1914 of Arkansas and Louisiana, she enthused over the dreamy, soporific atmosphere in summer and New Orleans as "the seething centre of Romance of the Gulf country," as well as "the hospitality of the old South with its unreckoning lavishness and mirth." Earlier, in the 1890s, she furnished romantic local color descriptions and anecdotes about Louisianians whom she called "a People who live amid romance," conjuring up for her readers a colorful, exotic, and harmonious view of the various ethnic groups of the state. A few months earlier that year, she replied to an interviewer over the question of realism in art. Denying that she was a "romanticist," she said that, although "fidelity to life" should be a writer's first aim, "it too often seems to be taken to mean bald and photographic fidelity to pain and helplessness. . . . An artist may paint garbage so that, in looking at the picture, one feels like using smelling-salts. . . . Isn't it better to take hopeful views of life?" Thus, her depictions of her native state and the people she represents in fiction and poetry were deliberately selected for their pleasing, amusing, and colorful qualities. The dark sides of southern life were smoothed over or made light of, especially as these related to New Orleans and Arkansas blacks and New Orleans Italians—both groups Stuart knew to be the subject of violence and hostility throughout and after Reconstruction.[18]

By the time Stuart began to write, black dialect fiction written by whites had become something of a vogue. The Mississippi writers Sherwood Bonner and Irwin Russell had introduced it to northern editors, and by the early 1880s the Georgia writer Joel Chandler Harris had become a national celebrity with his Uncle Remus: His Songs and His Sayings (1880). This was a best-seller as soon as it appeared, and Harris had published three sequels before Stuart's first story, "Uncle Mingo's 'Speculatioms,'"

17. Selections from RMSC.
18. Ruth McEnery Stuart, "American Backgrounds for Fiction, VI—Arkansas, Louisiana and the Gulf Country," Bookman, XXXIX (August, 1914), 623, 627; Ruth McEnery Stuart, "A People Who Live Amid Romance," Ladies' Home Journal (December, 1896), 7–8; John D. Barry, "A Chat with Ruth McEnery Stuart," Illustrated American, June 6, 1896, in RMSC.

came out—with its title's obvious reference to her famous predecessor's collection *Mingo and Other Sketches in Black and White* (1884). Harris' stories were hailed by critics as the first "genuine" pictures of blacks in the South, while Harris himself modestly disclaimed authorship, calling himself a "compiler" and "journalist" who had simply recorded stories told him by ex-slaves on Turnwold Plantation in Georgia. The Uncle Remus figure that replaced the legendary Uncle Tom in popular imagination was an idealized loyal retainer, symbol of the sectional harmony and national unity that northern readers were eager to believe now existed. As Robert Hemenway suggests, "Uncle Remus promised the North that Southerners could see the Negro's virtues and could even celebrate them, which was proof that rehabilitation had occurred."[19]

Stuart used the Uncle Remus type in several stories, though more frequently she spoke through a white narrator figure (usually male), emphasizing more strongly than Harris ever did the close ties between and mutual respect and love of blacks and whites. Only in her last collections of plantation verse and jingles did she use Harris' compilation technique, and then with a clearly stated project of recuperation of the "loyal darky" for white celebratory publication. In the "Foreword" to *Daddy Do-Funny's Wisdom Jingles,* she wrote that her intention in "presenting a loyal and venerable ex-slave" lay in "not composing an individual so truly as individualizing a composite."[20] This is as direct a statement as Stuart ever made about her intentions in writing black dialect fiction, pointing unconsciously to the typification and idealization that pervade her works.

And her use of dialect was clearly intended to bring to life those ethnic groups that northerners found picturesque and curious: in a defensive response to a book reviewer she met on a visit to Chicago in 1895, she said, "I fancy I dislike dialect just as much as you do, and that is why I am emboldened to ask your advice. Now, what am I to do? I detest dialect, and yet the people I write about talk just that way." These words illuminate a major contradiction in Stuart's position: a patronizing and even antipathetic attitude to the people who were the subject of her fiction, while at the same time a strong claim to her first-hand knowledge of blacks (and other southern peoples) and the verisimilitude of her "individualized composites." Though Harris denied his own claim to authorship (while enjoying considerable financial benefits from *Uncle Remus*), Stuart always claimed for herself a special imaginative understanding of blacks. Indeed, a few months before his death, Harris must have compounded Stuart's faith

19. Robert Hemenway, "Introduction," in Joel Chandler Harris, *Uncle Remus: His Songs and His Sayings,* ed. Robert Hemenway (Harmondsworth, 1982), 20.
20. Ruth McEnery Stuart, *Daddy Do-Funny's Wisdom Jingles* (New York, 1913).

in her abilities when he wrote her, "You have got nearer the heart of the negro than any of us." It is perhaps significant that in all the tributes to Ruth Stuart, the quotation most frequently taken from her work is her dedication to *Daddy Do-Funny,* recalling the qualities of Uncle Remus:

> To the memory of those faithful brown slave men of the plantations throughout the South, Daddy's contemporaries all, who during the war while their masters were fighting in a cause opposed to the emancipation, brought their blankets and slept outside their mistresses' doors, thus keeping nightwatch over otherwise unprotected women and children—a faithful guardianship of which the annals of those troublous times record no instance of betrayal.[21]

Other tales of faithful slaves and loyal mammies in postbellum years are the kinds of anecdote with which Ruth Stuart frequently furnished reporters and audiences. Of her verses, two are quoted frequently—about a terrapin and a mockingbird, both strongly reminiscent of the Brer Rabbit sketches.

But although like Harris she used animal and bird allegories drawn from plantation lore in her verses, in the fiction she followed Cable and King in dealing with human characters—albeit within careful limits of subject and tone. One cautious decision she clearly took consciously was to make all her black characters unequivocally black; although in her nonfiction she hints at the blood connections between creoles and blacks, no mulattoes appear in the fiction. There is no story comparable with Cable's "Madame Delphine," Grace King's "Monsieur Motte" and "The Little Convent Girl," or Kate Chopin's "Désirée's Baby." Nor is any drama created out of the association of or conflict between whites and blacks. Unlike Cable, Stuart did not focus on the *problems* of black/white relations and black identity; as I have already suggested, the works emphasize the vivacity and humor of blacks and plantation life, playing into the orthodox white supremacist version of harmonious and loving antebellum race relations. Robert Bush says Stuart's writing about blacks can be classified with what Ellen Glasgow termed "the literature of commemoration, the fiction that shows a regret for the past and in particular pays tribute to the fidelity of the Negro race to the white masters even after the Emancipation Proclamation."[22] However, modern readers are bound to see Stuart's writing about blacks not primarily as commemorative but as distorting and at best naïvely unrepresentative.

Ruth Stuart appears to have shared with other white once-prosperous southerners a view of blacks which dictated that one distrusted and sus-

21. Ruth M. Stuart, Chicago *Record,* April 2, 1895, in RMSC; Ruth McEnery Stuart, quoted in Alderman *et al.* (eds.), *Library of Southern Literature,* XI, 5146.
22. Bush, "Louisiana Prose Fiction," 338.

pected them but expected no better. However, presumably influenced by her northern friends and mentors (perhaps including Cable), she was concerned, however superficially, about blacks' education and work opportunities. In an interview in New Orleans probably during her 1907 visit, Stuart was asked euphemistically about "the servant question." She answered that Booker T. Washington was working on the right lines, and that the answer to the problems of Negroes and European immigrants lay in "industrial education" and "industrial lines of work." This, her most polemical overt statement on the subject, was clearly a safe remark, reassuring as Booker T. Washington's ideas were to whites and offering as they did a liberal appearance to covert white racism. But Stuart's racist stereotyping of blacks emerges most clearly in her frequent remarks about their childlike nature, wisdom, fidelity, and generosity; interviews and letters, and especially her jingles and verses, reiterate these qualities. One of her most quoted poems, "Beauty-land," celebrates the fact that while "white mamma" leaves her child to go the ball,

> Black mammy, nigger mammy, ain't a-gwine away,
> Never leave 'er sleepin' baby 't all.

Contemporary critical reception of Stuart's black stories was remarkably homogeneous in tone: in review after review she is praised for capturing "African nature," black "lovableness," with that "dialect . . . of thick-lipped utterance." Napoleon Jackson, one of her protagonists, was seen as the epitome of the southern Negro: "Slothful, good-tempered, unambitious, ingenuous, a child mentally and emotionally." In a revealing choice of words, a reviewer of *The Second Wooing of Salina Sue* describes Stuart's comic stories as having "much of pathos and true *national* beauty" (my emphasis). The construction of a postbellum national culture required myths of blacks who—though emancipated—were controlled, tamed, and feminized. The light touch, humor, and pathos of Stuart's black characters fitted the bill.[23]

Although Stuart conformed to orthodox racial stereotypes, she was certainly prepared to experiment and risk more in relation to gender. Gender is not problematized only around white women, and while her texts move toward conservative, harmonious closure, there are transgressive feminist elements that open up questions within the fiction. For a southern woman in New York, there was considerable conflict between a conditioned defi-

23. "Distinguished Louisiana Authoress Talks of Work, Women and the Servant Question," New Orleans *Picayune,* November 16, 1907, in RMSC; Ruth McEnery Stuart, *Plantation Songs and Other Verse* (New York, 1916), 3; Troy (N.Y.) *Press,* April 22, 1905, in RMSC.

nition of southern femininity and the new liberating possibilities for women available in the more progressive Northeast. Stuart featured this conflict in her fiction, relating questions of gender to those of regionalism and ethnicity, and to the act of writing itself. But in some of her work the writer's feminism and racism collide and produce reactionary conclusions. Because of Stuart's repeated use of a black male character who is economically powerless, dependent, and often sick or dying, her work demonstrates the mutual sympathy and thus (by implication) the identification between weak white women and feminized black men. It is particularly in those stories that foreground gender in relation to black families and communities that the politically untenable contradictions of Stuart's work can be seen most clearly.

Of the three writers on whom I am focusing, and indeed of all the southern women writers in New York in the late nineteenth century, Stuart was one of the most directly committed to women's rights and to suffrage. In an interview for a New Orleans newspaper (probably in 1907) she stated this emphatically: "I do not remember the time . . . that I was not a believer in woman suffrage. With me it is a principle [she recalls signing a petition for woman suffrage when seventeen]. . . . One of the reasons why I am in favor of suffrage . . . is because it will help the working women; it will certainly mean equal pay for equal work." In this article she stresses the great importance of child welfare (something she believed would be helped if women obtained the vote and equal pay), and in an undated and probably unpublished typescript she writes a poem called "We Speak as Mothers" in which she argues the necessity for women's rights to prevent child prostitution and to give women a voice in national and civic affairs. Indeed, the final stanza pleads a special relationship between femininity and reconciliation:

> With the dove upon our banners and our toddling sons beside us,
> We'll charge the temple at the Hague - - - let sonless ones deride us! - - -
> Depositing our VOTES for PEACE! Let motherful endeavor
> Starve out the yelping dogs of war and silence them forever!
> . . . .
>
> In the name of the song we'd sing again
> Of "Peace on earth, good will to men,"
> We reverently demand to bear
> In the fate of our sons, an equal share.

The rhetoric of this poem, crude as it is in some ways, nonetheless suggests that the author was fully engaged in debates around the nature of femininity and its relationship with general structures of power, as well as the function of the family and woman's role within it.[24]

Of course, New York was a feminist center, and Stuart cannot have escaped discussions about the Woman Question in clubs, salons, and among friends. This was, among other things, the period of futurist and cooperative experiments in apartment hotels for professional women; also Charlotte Perkins Gilman was propounding her view of "kitchenless homes" for working mothers. In an interview for the New York *Mail and Express,* Stuart hinted at her interest in these experiments, though I suspect her domestic arrangement with her sister Sarah prevented her from moving into such a hotel. Arguing that under "ideal conditions" (namely, with reliable servants) a woman should be able to write and keep house simultaneously, she said: "I love home life, and it is almost impossible for me to contemplate giving it up, but I am considering the idea. When you board there is but one bill to settle, and no worries over household affairs, but in keeping house there are thirty bills. No one ought to attempt literary or artistic work and at the same time superintend the details of living."[25] These are identical with the sentiments of Charlotte Perkins Gilman, and though there is no reference to the famous writer in Stuart's papers, it is possible they met at a women's club. Stuart belonged to several such clubs in New York and in 1904 applied for membership in the newly opened Lyceum Club in London (along with other American women including Julia Ward Howe, Sarah Orne Jewett, Harriet Monroe, and Mary Wilkins Freeman). When she visited New Orleans she went straight to the clubs, and in 1897 she traveled to Denver for a meeting of the Federation of Women's Clubs.

Like Grace King, Stuart was impressed and heartened by the dignity of creole women making the most of postbellum adversity. In an article for the *Ladies' Home Journal* in 1896, she praised the creoles of New Orleans especially for their "noble patience and a fine forbearance under misfortune" and described women from "the proudest of . . . proud families, patiently accepting the decree of Fate, and doing her humble bidding, even though it sometimes be to 'measure tape,' or even to fit gloves to the hands of the women of her own class behind shop-counters." She also records the fact that several creole women—in New Orleans and New York—had achieved considerable literary and artistic success. In 1914, writing of the

24. Ruth M. Stuart, n.d., in RMSC.
25. Dolores Hayden, *The Grand Domestic Revolution: A History of Feminist Designs for American Homes, Neighborhoods, and Cities* (Cambridge, 1981); Ruth M. Stuart, December 23, 1899, in RMSC.

settings of her fiction, Stuart referred to the "conceded aristocracy" of the Old South, with its conservatism and resistance to the passing of the old regime. Stuart captures the spirit of both Old and New South in female terms: the New South is characterized as "this or that vulgarian [who] has honked herself into society," and then as "My lady Nouveaux of High Fling."[26]

She describes the New South in pejorative Lost Cause terms as "slashing away at the traditions of the elders, drowning out any possible low, cultured voice of protest." But while conceding that "My lady Nouveaux" and her ilk have appropriated the wealth and social standing of old southern families, she discusses the "secret wires of communication" that exist between the "so-called 'decayed,' the down-and-out, the inarticulate"— and these links are between *women*. According to Stuart, then, the Old South's values and social relations are kept alive by the "submerged" dispossessed woman who has formed her own networks to "get her vote" and ensure that her minority representatives "legislate against innovations." Stuart saw the Old South primarily in feminine terms, and its female representatives as silenced victims of a New South that it had nonetheless managed—in classically female ways—to subvert, undermine, and in some ways control. This metaphoric and metonymic association of Louisiana and the South in general with the feminine is consistent with her continual awareness and problematization of gender in other areas of her life and work, including her self-definition as a writer.

Like other women writers, Stuart thought of her writing in terms of a long, painful childbirth. In a letter to a friend, she wrote of being "in the throes of labour!! over a story that's so long a-borning that I fear either mother or child must succumb," and a month later she wrote of sending out letters (probably containing stories) "conceived and born within the last few weeks." But also like other women, she saw her writing as an activity incompatible with her very identity as a woman. Writing to Dr. Pope in 1903, she described moving home in order to live a "semi-placid life. . . . I hope to be able to work there as a *workman* not as a woman of the world, trying in dilletante [*sic*] fashion to do a few things." The frustrations of her life as a single parent and writer clearly depressed her, and occasionally her notes give clues of the tensions of being a hospitable hostess. In a jotting in 1899, she wrote, "Oh, I wish I'd been brought up to swear! If I had an adequately vocabulated husband to do it for me, I wouldn't mind. But a lone woman [?] really needs it." In her papers, there is a fragment that draws a whimsical analogy between women and or-

26. Stuart, "A People Who Live Amid Romance," 8; and Stuart, "American Backgrounds for Fiction," 629–30.

chids, revealing how hard Stuart felt the demands were on contemporary women writers:

> The orchid answers to no one for where, when, or how it chooses to throw out a petal, nor for the color, shape, or contortions of the same. Its leaves are its own. It is the orchid's affair. . . .
>
> There is an idea afloat that the Ladye Orchid abounds especially among literary women. . . .
>
> It takes character, independence, individuality, and, with an underlying confidence in one's self, a delicious unconsciousness of incongruities to be an Orchid.[27]

Given the numerous references to questions of gender in relation to women's writing and to southern literary materials, one might perhaps expect a considerable number of direct references to other women's novels within Stuart's work. But it is not there; Stuart was a far less self-consciously literary writer than either Grace King or Kate Chopin. She remembers reading hardly at all when a child, and there is little evidence of rereadings or revisions of earlier writers in the fiction. Her use of the short story is conventional, and there are formal parallels with the stories of George W. Cable, Joel Chandler Harris, Paul Dunbar, Thomas Hardy, Guy de Maupassant, and the Tennyson and Browning of the dramatic monologues. But most critics discuss her in terms of other *women* writers, and Mary Fletcher finds in the fiction specific echoes of Louisa Alcott (*Little Women*), Mary E. Wilkins Freeman ("Louisa"), and (absurdly) Willa Cather's *My Ántonia,* published in 1918, a year after Stuart's death. Wilkins Freeman is the woman writer most often compared with Stuart. Robert Bush makes an apt point when he argues that Stuart's mythical Arkansas village "Simpkinsville" seems closer to the New England villages of Sarah Orne Jewett and Wilkins Freeman than to those of Old South fiction.[28] Wilkins Freeman was a fellow circuit-lecturer, and Stuart showed considerable interest in her personal life—writing familiarly in 1900 to her friend Emily Pope about her broken engagement and an interview with a medium. A few critics, including Herbert Spencer, compared her work with that of George Eliot, a comparison Stuart herself found very pleasing. And in her correspondence and articles she makes frequent general references to other southern women writers; Grace King was clearly a fellow New Orleanian whom she admired, though she never mentions her own admirer Kate Chopin. Her novel *The Story of Babette* owes a certain amount to Charlotte Brontë, with its (apparently) orphaned female protagonist,

27. Ruth M. Stuart to Dr. C. Augusta Pope, June 24 and July 13, 1897, July 24, 1903, "Notes and Memorands" (1899), and "Ye Ladye Orchid," n.d., all in RMSC.

28. Bush, "Louisiana Prose Fiction," 312.

who searches relentlessly for kinships ties that she eventually finds, helped along the way by a tutor/mentor figure whom she marries. But the novel has little of the symbolic or metaphoric complexity of its probable models, *Jane Eyre* and *Villette,* and is in no way a conscious response to Brontë.

THE FICTION

In examining Ruth McEnery Stuart's fiction I shall discuss selected works around the two key issues with which her work is concerned: race and gender. This is no artificial distinction, since there is a clear difference of political position, form, and tone between the two kinds. There are the stories that keep within the terms of a national consensus of indulgent reconciliation with the South's postbellum racial attitudes, focusing on problems of language, postbellum anomie, and black/white loyalties. Then there are fictions that challenge and open up those positions on gender and woman's role held by the hegemonic northern male establishment, which was already being threatened by contemporary women's movements. In a few works, both issues come together—but in a way that reveals Stuart's confusions and inability to reconcile her different positions within her work.

The two minority groups that furnish material for most of Stuart's fiction are the blacks of New Orleans and (presumably Arkansas) plantations, and—in a small number of works—the Italians and Sicilians of New Orleans. Stuart's significant departure from Harris' technique in *Uncle Remus* is the centrality she gives to whites as narrator/interpreter figures, constructed both as sympathetic listeners but also as providers of material resources and advice about worldly matters. These white narrators are usually male, perhaps partly so that Stuart can distance herself from them, but also to point up the childlike nature of the male black who turns to his patriarchal, powerful, but reassuring narrator/ex-master/employer. These narrators provide food, shelter, even wedding dresses for their employees/dependents, and in significant ways serve to legitimize those blacks' activities and lives. This legitimation takes two main forms. First, the white narrator recuperates his/her blacks into bourgeois family structures, either through "adoption" into his own or other surrogate families, or by assisting the marriages of blacks for whom he is responsible. Second, he or she saves the lives and/or improves the conditions of blacks in order to record and celebrate those lives in fiction; like Stuart herself, several of the storytellers are engaged in the production of Local Color.

In most cases, the blacks are old, sick, and dying, so (it is argued) the record must be put straight for posterity; in one story, however, the dying man is white, the narrator his ex-slave who will tell his master's history to white audiences. But in all cases, the narration is one upon which both black and white agree; memories of antebellum life and social relations are identical. The white characters regret the loss of their secure, dominant position surrounded by loving slaves, while the freedmen/women are nostalgic for their subordinate and dependent bondage. Both races are presented as heartbroken because of the rupture of those relations of slavery, which white supremacists defined as a kind of glorious extended family, with the bonds between black and white those of love and fidelity rather than of hatred and repression.

In the Introduction, I pointed out the very different interests and needs of the white and black races before and especially after the war, and argued that the "loyal darky" figure, reluctant to let go of his/her chains, existed almost exclusively in the imaginations of and fiction written by southern whites. But given the function of dialect in confirming to a northern critical and reading public the subordination of blacks in the postbellum South, it can be demonstrated that Stuart's success played a crucial ideological role in allowing the North to turn its back on the real sufferings and new forms of repression that were facing blacks in the Reconstruction and Redemption South. Stuart's repeated use of the white narrator—ironic, uneasily guilty, and emotionally responsive as s/he is—suggests an unease about this literary exploitation of peoples she had both literally and metaphorically left behind. It also suggests that (unlike Harris, who is entirely absent from his own texts) the writer felt some need to foreground her own role in the construction of an idealized black and a mythic plantation history. Stuart's first story, "Uncle Mingo," alludes to this, but it seems that in "Blink" (her only story to feature a woman writer like herself) she comes close to parodying and even condemning her own literary practice.

The Italians and Sicilians of New Orleans are presented in a somewhat different light. While Stuart constructs the city's key Italian families as subordinate to the white creole and Anglo-Saxon ruling class, she makes a pointed attack on the patriarchal methods and attitudes of the Mafia. Just as her black fiction can be said to speak for the white race in the South, so her unsympathetic portrayal of the Italian community can be seen to voice the deep hostility of the city's bourgeois whites toward the New Orleans "dagos" during the 1880s and later. There had certainly been many tensions within the Sicilian/Italian community from the 1870s, when the fruit and vegetable trader Giuseppe Esposito, fleeing from arrest in Europe, organized a formidable Mafia cell within the city. After Esposito was arrested and deported, the Italian colony was stirred and members of the community engaged in so many fights and shootings among themselves that Decatur Street became known as Vendetta Alley. There were at least two powerful rich families who competed for business and feuded constantly, and the unease of New Orleans citizens erupted in 1890 when the superintendent of police, David Hennessey, who had tried to curb gang warfare, was shot dead. Ten Italians were charged with murder, then acquitted but detained in jail—and on March 14, 1891, encouraged by inflammatory newspaper editorials, a mob of non-Italian citizens gathered in Canal Street and broke down the jail doors, killing or lynching the prisoners. The incident led to a crisis in U.S.-Italian diplomatic relations and the possibility of war, though an indemnity was eventually paid to Italy.[29]

Since these events occurred at the very time Ruth Stuart was leaving her son and sister in New Orleans to work in New York City, she must have known about and probably shared the general distrust and dislike of the Italian community. In her stories "Camelia Riccardo," *The Story of Babette,* and *Carlotta's Intended,* Stuart writes of the conflicts, feuds, and interracial rivalries between Italian speakers and other races, creating for northern editors and readers a sense of the dangers, excitement, and evils of what they already saw to be an exotic multiracial city. But in gender terms, the stories all undermine the very rigid divisions between the sexes within the Italian/Sicilian family and point to the destructiveness of the Mafia's patriarchal codes and vendettas. Stuart's fiction repeatedly confirms a version of black family life that mirrors that of whites in its warmth, concern, and flexibility for both sexes; by contrast, her Italian families are cold, austere, and heavily male-dominated. It is this aspect of that community which is foregrounded by Stuart and which makes her overt and implied authorial judgments on the Italians far harsher than any on blacks.

Ruth Stuart's first story, "Uncle Mingo's 'Speculatioms,'" sets the tone for her whole career as writer about southern blacks.[30] And it uses the monologue form that she was to employ in many later stories, framed by a silent white narrator who records, interprets, and in some ways intervenes in the black characters' lives. Set in Carrollton, a suburb of New Orleans, it begins with "Uncle Mingo" describing his particular form of "going to market" to an unseen first-person narrator, whose identity as a young white man is gradually revealed as the story progresses. Uncle Mingo's "markitin'" consists of taking scraps from rich whites' garbage bins; he

29. For information about the Mafia and Italian community, see John S. Kendall, "Who Killa de Chief?" *Louisiana Historical Quarterly,* XXII (1939), 498–512; and John Wilds, *Afternoon Story: A Century of the New Orleans 'States-Item'* (Baton Rouge, 1976), chapter 5.

30. In Ruth McEnery Stuart, *A Golden Wedding and Other Tales* (New York, 1893), 69–91. The story was first published in *New Princeton Review,* 1888.

assures the narrator humorously that he can tell the social status of his white providers by the quality of food he plunders. In the course of his monologue, prompted as he is by the narrator's concerned questions, Mingo reveals that he is old and poor, living alone in a cabin on a riverbank notorious for its subsidence, while his daughter lives with his old white mistress "back o' town" in New Orleans. He is more concerned about his old mistress and her mother than his own poverty; more worried about these distressed gentlewomen having to work for a living, making cakes for the Christian Women's Exchange and pralines that his daughter sells in the city. He feels it right that Caroline should stay with the women, and he refuses to spend the money his old mistress sends. The narrator, realizing Mingo is ill and half-deranged by starvation and senility, gives him money, sends him food, and offers him a cabin and token caretaker job on his farm/plantation. Mingo dies the same night as his mistress' mother and is buried at the corner of her family lot—as the narrator says, sleeping as in the old days at her door, now "at her feet." Realizing that he had fought in the war with the dead husband of Mingo's mistress, the narrator determines to help her—with the implicit suggestion he will marry the distressed widow.

In terms of standard and subordinate forms of language, this story is more transparent than many of Stuart's later works, though it sets a tone she was to use consistently later. The very title announces a disruption between the narrator's "correct" use of English and Mingo's comic attempts to formulate ideas. " 'Speculatioms' " not only speaks Mingo's inability to pronounce (and thus "master") standard English, it is also a word he uses inaccurately within the story. His one conversational use of the word demonstrates that he believes this abstract noun to mean "nostalgic memories" or "sentimental thoughts about the past," and Stuart gives him the plural form to add comic effect. The whole story alternates between Mingo's comic dialect and the white narrator's standard English, an English he admits is literary—his interest in Mingo derives from his (the narrator's) role as a writer. Later in the story, he admits the origin of his interest in the ex-slave he has met casually on the levee—"I had cultivated the old negro to put him into a book"—and regrets that this necessitates moving him "bodily into my *yard*" in order to "deal" with "this antiquated bunch of aristocratic recollections."[31] Although the narrator recognizes early on that Mingo enjoyed talking to "an interested listener" (71), he quickly establishes a transactional and dependent relationship with the old man. This is clearly necessary to satisfy the narrator's

31. " 'Ter teck comfort out o' speculatioms, yer has ter know which een ter start at!,' " "Uncle Mingo's 'Speculatioms,' " 79, 84–85.

guilt about objectifying the man's pitiful sufferings, but it also allows him to use Mingo imaginatively as he sees fit, without any awkward residual sense of obligation to him as an individual. Referring to Mingo as "a picture" (80) and "a perfect unit of grace" (83), he constructs the old man as ideal fictional subject, indeed as fictional rather than historically real. Like Harriet Beecher Stowe, Stuart makes her narrator see the old man not in historical or political but in quasi-mystical terms, like Uncle Tom, his dying self illuminated by inner spiritual light. As Balzac's peasants speak "incorrectly" and in simple sentences while the bourgeoisie speak standard French and use complex structures and thus ideas, so Stuart's black Christian Uncle Tom figure uses a black dialect that is naïve, simple, and riddled with grammatical errors. He apologizes for his own subordinate relationship to standard literary English. Trying to explain his instinctive knowledge of the difference between Old and New Southerners, he exclaims, " 'hit's de—hit's de—boss, I wisht I had de book words ter splain it de way I knows it in heah!' He tapped his breast" (71). He later reiterates this point when he says, " 'My min' is do onies' book I's got' " (84).

After his death, the narrator acknowledges his debt to Mingo for informing him of the poor, proud white mistress waiting to be helped, and enabling him to live up to the chivalric ideal of his race: "Had he not made known to me the silent suffering of two Southern gentlewomen? And inasmuch as every true Southern man feels himself to be the personal champion and friend of every needy Southern woman, I might now become . . . a friend to the lonely lady" (90). And in his last days, Mingo is the celebrant of antebellum black-white relations, recalling as he does his happy slave duties—his "departed glory" when he drove the white folks' carriage to church and sat on the " 'silver-mounted ca'ge . . . dat puffed out wid stuck-up-ishness!' " (76). Mingo defends the Old South against the New, privileging members of the white planter class over New Southerners whose "cornsciousness" is of an inferior kind: "De outside cornsciousness, hit bristles an' swishes an' wags termenjus; but de inside cornsciousness, hit jis lay low an' keep still, an' hit's gentle in de high places, an' when de waters o' tribulatiom runs ag' in it, hit keeps a stiff upper lip an' don't meck no sign" (71). Furthermore, he regards his own degrading circumstances as considerably superior to the socially downward mobility of his old mistress, and without irony (though *Stuart* may have intended some) pities her for living among a " 'mixtry o' Gascons an' Dagos an' Lord knows what!' " (73).

Thus in a variety of ways Mingo is made to celebrate the conditions of his own subordination and, by identifying his own fate so completely with his mistress', to erase the real differences between his own history and that of "his" folks. His naïvely conciliatory attitudes and Christian saintliness disguise the dire economic position and ill health he suffers, and the repeated emphasis on his "chil'ishness" emphasizes the helplessness that Stuart's class believed was the nature of emancipated (and, in their view, displaced) blacks. The success of this first story, mediated through its male white narrator, was a triumph for that other narrator, Stuart herself, whose project as spokesperson for southern black experience was now given national approval and confirmation. The ambition of her male narrator was her own; she was now given *carte blanche* to repeat and refine the formula.

In "Crazy Abe," Ruth Stuart creates a figure similar to Uncle Mingo, though this time he is both dying *and* defined as insane by the plantation dwellers around. Living entirely in the past, he alone immediately recognizes the journalist narrator as the grandson of his old master. The narrator relishes the peace and repose of the plantation to which he has escaped for a while from the pressures of a busy life, seeing it as he does in Arcadian terms as a haven innocent of its role in "transforming . . . juices into the bone and sinew of the natural body of a giant king of commerce."[32] And like Uncle Mingo's narrator, he describes the freed blacks on whom he gazes from the plantation house as a colorful spectacle: "Even the gleaming plaids of the blacks, in whose costumes we look always for a pronounced bit of color, were subdued into soft tints by nearly a year of weather and wear" (218). As the narrator daily watches "Crazy Abe" from his window, he describes him overtly as "in the pretty sketch which my window framed . . . a bit of local color," and as the last survivor of his grandfather's slaves—a man to be regarded "pictorially as a forlorn and expressive tail-piece to the last chapter of the old *régime*." This literary allusion is continued by the narrator's comment that, when Abe was no longer there, "the book would be closed," and that it was this which invested him with "a sort of pathos apart from his personality" (224). Thus, as with Uncle Mingo, the idealized black figure redolent with pathos and recorded as a local color sketch is a reminder to the white narrator/reader of antebellum loyalties and pleasures, and especially of a paradigmatically faithful slave whose passing must be mourned and recorded for posterity.

In a later novel, Stuart again re-creates this kind of poignant sketch of dying blacks clinging to the past. In *The River's Children*, an old couple lives between two levees in Carrollton suburb. Figures of southern legend, they typify the "faithfulness of the slave people during the crucial period when the masters had gone to battle, leaving their wives and babies in the

32. Ruth McEnery Stuart, "Crazy Abe," in *A Golden Wedding and Other Tales*, 218.

care of those whose single chance of freedom depended on the defeat of the absent." The old woman, Hannah, now surrogate mother to her dead mistress' daughter, nostalgically recalls antebellum plantation days when slaves and masters lived "for the possible preservation of a bit of local color—gone out in the changed light of a new dispensation."[33] This "local color" (as self-consciously constructed as its literary counterpart) includes a huge house-party on the plantation, at which New Orleans guests act as tourist consumers of the region's "local color"—the "amazing mammy-tales of voudoo-land and the ghost country" (74), fortune-telling (presumably by black women), and revival meetings and black church services. Hannah and her husband are now reluctant to go on living, even when their old master returns from the war to collect them and his daughter. They die peacefully, their cabin flooded by the Mississippi River, and after death they are immortalized through a sketch that their master makes of the cabin to hang on his daughter's wall.

But commemoration is not simply the province of whites. A black narrator is also made to re-create the glorious antebellum past, as in the story "Caesar." Caesar is an old man, ex-slave of a now impoverished, declassed white plantation owner, working as salaried overseer for the new owner. The story relates the white Colonel Taylor's determination to flee to New Orleans alone, escaping " 'like a runaway nigger' " to avoid admitting his extreme penury to Caesar.[34] But the loyal old man follows the colonel, rescues him on the steamboat from unscrupulous gamblers, and finds him a home in New Orleans, where the white man dies in peace and is buried in dignity because of Caesar's earnings from singing plantation songs and performing black dances in saloons.

Stuart makes Caesar a mock-heroic figure, but he is especially significant as emphasizing white Louisiana's view of Reconstruction in relation to black/white social and legal relations. To begin with, Caesar identifies himself completely with the colonel and is horrified that the latter should try to separate their fortunes by leaving him behind. On the boat, when "the finances of the firm were very low," he uses his own money to settle the colonel's bills and is referred to as "the silent partner in the firm" (206). However, this sense of economic equality and identification of the two men in one "firm" holds true only for Caesar; the colonel never knows the black man has paid his bills, nor could he guess his own funeral was to be subsidized by Caesar's work. But Caesar is selflessly loyal and silently

33. Ruth McEnery Stuart, *The River's Children, or An Idyl of the Mississippi* (New York, 1904), 49, 55.

34. Ruth McEnery Stuart, "Caesar," in *Carlotta's Intended and Other Tales* (New York, 1894), 193.

supportive to the end, taking his ex-master's part in every way. In a long monologue at the beginning of the story (ironically just before his master tries to give him the slip), Caesar denounces his own race: "a nigger slave-owner. Dem was *de* meanes'! . . . Dey warn't nothin' but a cross twix' a vampire an'—an' a wil'-cat—dat what dey was!" Referring to one such, "Kinky Jean Baptiste," Caesar proclaims that he is now "a-settin' up in a jedge's cheer, a-dolin' out jestice lak he knowed it when he seed it! He don't know no mo' 'bout jestice 'n—'n I does 'bout grammar—not a bit. He twis' it ter spress 'is own intruss, des' same as I does speech" (185–86).

These words anticipate Jerry's denunciation of his race in Grace King's *The Pleasant Ways of St. Médard*. And like Jerry, Caesar is made to speak on behalf of literate whites against the illiteracy and ignorance of his own race, in a speech designed to make the white reader smile with benevolent sympathy. In fact, the speech both denounces the black race as irresponsible and untrustworthy and also condones white Redeemer claims that blacks were unqualified and incapable of taking public office or benefiting from education. Caesar goes on to laugh at his master's attempts to teach him to read the Bible, which was beyond his comprehension. He explains this as the reason for his sitting "still-moufed" in the evening in Colonel Taylor's library: " 'I des' looks roun' dem walls an' views de still knowledge an' keep silence' " (186). Thus, however unintentionally, Stuart constructs Caesar—and by implication all freedmen—as inherently unsuited to literacy and education, real social status, and power. What Caesar goes on to demonstrate is the infinite adaptability, wiliness, and resourcefulness associated by whites with the black—qualities that of course do not derive from, and are anathema to, formal education. His loyalty to the colonel leads to his transformation into the mother of a dependent child (Caesar speaks "baby-talk" to the sick man, whose eyes water "even as a babe with tear-brimmed eyes crows aloud as his mother approaches the cradle" [216]). Thus both men are feminized through powerlessness and mutual dependence, with Caesar as soothing mammy to his white childish charge.

But most important, Caesar's popularity as singer and dancer, "drawing upon an inexhaustible fund of plantation-lore" (212), is what saves him and the colonel from poverty and humiliation. He becomes a local celebrity; makes white men weep and recall antebellum and wartime days; and comes to see himself as provider of an invaluable service to the white community. After Colonel Taylor's death, furthermore, he feels proud of his role as chronicler of the family's fortunes: following the colonel's burial on his old plantation, Caesar walks from the grave "with head erect, in full consciousness of the dignity that had descended to him as 'de las' one o' de

Dunbar-Taylor a'stokercy lef' ter tell de tale'" (225). This time the white protagonist is the dying figure, the black the interpreter. But of course Caesar's version has to be identical with the colonel's; the communality of interests and regrets is rendered poignantly in order to emphasize the inseparability of blacks and whites in the South, and to ensure a stable order based on an anachronistic fealty. And the feminization of both men that occurs in this story reinforces powerfully the orthodox gender definitions that are in play in many of these early stories foregrounding race. Feminine qualities are associated frequently with weakness, loss of power, even of life; kindly, sickly, childlike black men and declassed, feeble white southern gentlemen are denigrated by association with femininity. It is that kind of southern femininity which Grace King parodies in the figure of the little convent girl, and which Stuart also derides in some later work. But in the earlier fiction Stuart accepts traditional gender stereotypes, and by appearing to idealize some of her male characters (mostly black) damns them with faint praise.

Although so far the examples I have cited have been of male narrators and/or male black characters (rather more common than female in Stuart's work), there is an important exception which, as I suggested earlier, comes close to being Stuart's autocritique. In "'Blink,'" Stuart chooses a theme similar to that of many of her contemporary women writers. A young motherless woman, Evelyn Bruce, whose father's plantation has been sold as a result of wartime debts, has determined to make her living in New Orleans. Her father, after many careworn years, has given up: "The crisis of effort for him was past. He might follow, but he would lead no more."[35] The initiative is in the hands of women—Evelyn herself and her "withered old" black mammy, who (like Uncle Mingo) is horrified at the prospect of her mistress working for a living. The work Evelyn hopes to get is *writing*; she has always "scribbled" but now (like Ruth McEnery Stuart herself) sees publication as a way to save the family's fortunes. And significantly, although unlike Evelyn's father, Mammy can adapt and operate as "a most efficient deputy," it is she rather than Evelyn who is horrified at this obvious downward class mobility of her white owners/employers: "[T]his move to the city was violating all the traditions of mammy's life," and she can hardly bear to think of them arriving in New Orleans "'empty-handed, same es po' white trash'" (163, 165).

Like Uncle Mingo, Mammy sees her lack of formal education as something that leaves her vulnerable and makes her judgments questionable. And through dialect, like Mingo, she speaks of her own illiteracy and naïveté to deliberately comic effect: "'you know I ain't got educatiom, an'

35. Ruth McEnery Stuart, "'Blink,'" in *A Golden Wedding and Other Tales*, 160.

I ain't claim knowledge; b–b–b–but ain't you better study on it good 'fo' we goes ter dis heah new country? Dee tells me de city's a owdacious place' " (163). The comic effects of her self-proclaimed ignorance are further emphasized in her relating superstitious tales of candles like " 'sperityal steam,' " which Evelyn assures her are gas lights, and her ignorance of the vocabulary her mistress uses to describe the items for sale on the plantation (Mammy repeats "appurtenances" as "impertinences"). But humble though she is about her education, Mammy's identification with her white mistress' racial and social status is complete, as she shows "special contempt" for the Indian squaws in the market, dismissed by her because " 'dee ain't look jinnywine ter me. Dee ain't nuther white folks nur niggers' " (170).

And it is to Mammy that Evelyn, in her isolation and in the face of her father's helpless impotence, turns for literary advice. Of course Mammy cannot *read* her fictional local color stories, but Evelyn reads them to her and receives her most valuable criticisms. It is Mammy, not an editor, who rejects one of her manuscripts, who identifies the fault in her writing. When she tells her mistress, " 'I tell yer, honey, a–a–a pusson'd know you had educatiom, de way you c'n fetch in de dicksh'nary words,' " Evelyn realizes that she has failed as a popular writer—since "the *best* writing was *simple*" (172). She reflects on how "clever" the black woman is, and how "wholesome the unconscious satire of her criticism"; because of Mammy's subordinate relationship to literary language it *has* to be unconscious. So, by Mammy's promptings, she comes to realize that she can make literary capital out of their own experiences since selling the plantation.

Like Mingo's white narrator/employer, Evelyn constructs Mammy as a subject of fiction, her chicken "Blink" producing necessary comic relief. So thoroughly does she idealize the black woman in the story that when it is read to Mammy, she does not at first recognize herself. When it dawns on her that she is " 'dat noble ole black 'oman' " with " 'all dat book granjer what you done laid on me,' " Mammy is both flattered and appalled, and tells Blink to walk straight and step high " ' 'caze yer gwine in a book, honey, 'long wid de asstokercy' " (174–75). Uneasy as she may be at first, finally she assents happily to the distortion of her own experience, and Stuart makes Mammy connive in her own misrepresentation as paradigmatic loyal darky. Furthermore, Mammy takes in laundry while Evelyn's writing career is failing, ensuring the appropriate economic conditions for literary production of fiction in which she herself is mythified. And instead of adversely criticizing Evelyn for the distortion, she actively encourages a parodic reflection of herself in the stories: "I been a-thinkin' 'bout it, an' *de finer that ole 'oman 'ac', an' de mo' granjer yer lay on 'er, de better yer gwine meck de book.* . . . She de one wha' got ter *stan' by de battlemints an' hol' de fort"* (180–81). She urges Evelyn to include in her story details of reciprocal love, intimacy, and loyalty between white and black women of the household.

Mammy constantly refers to her own illiteracy and lack of "educatiom"; like "speculatioms," the mispronunciation represented in the story by a misspelling is intended to draw a reader's sentimental sympathy for black illiteracy and lack of formal learning. But as with Mingo, Mammy's innate good sense (she is a *natural* editor), generosity, and comic qualities—enhanced by her uncannily sensitive pet Blink—all serve to reinforce her natural subordination and servitude. The emphasis on language and learning is ideologically transparent; Mammy connives in her own literary exploitation, which subsequently she will not be able to read, in every sense of the word. But unlike Mingo, she is a survivor; in gender terms the nurturing, housekeeping, and maternal/sororal qualities of Mammy appear to have a role in the New South in a way that Mingo's backward-looking devotion does not.

In some ways, then, Stuart's fiction suggests that any hope of viable, lasting relations between the races in the postbellum South must lie with women, and/or feminized or childlike men, who recognize the need to maintain the "family" ties of slavery and surrogate kinship relations. The most ideologically transparent example of this is the novella *George Washington Jones,* in which a black boy seeks out a white family, convinced that is the only place he really belongs. This story, almost comical to a modern reader in its cloying racist sentimentality, was received enthusiastically by contemporary critics as "a pretty and pleasing little story," and "rare in its combination of pathos and humor." It tells the story of an orphan who wishes to follow in his slave grandfather's footsteps and find himself a white employer. Although since his relatives' death he has been cared for by a poor black family, he aspires to the special relationship with whites that his grandfather (chosen as a house slave) had enjoyed: "All his people had lived with 'folks,' and when an old-time darkey says 'folks,' he means quality white folks, 'none o' yo' po' white trash.'" On Christmas Day, dressed up so that he "reconstructed a very presentable 'little nigger'" (28), he walks up Prytania Street, where wealthy white families live, searching for "some great, fair lady of high degree" (25) to whom he will be a Christmas gift, as his grandfather was to *his* white mistress. Eventually he is adopted by a loving black woman, Sarah, whose own son is dead, and who finds him work in a white lady's home. This lady sees George handling a photograph of his grandfather with his mistress, and recognizes the lady as her own mother. Realizing that George is the grandson of her mother's faithful slave, she tearfully assures him, " '[Y]ou are back among your folks' " (123), and takes him to see a portrait of her mother with the slave beside her. The boy cries emotionally to his grandfather in the portrait, " 'Does you reco'nize me, gran'pa? Heah yo' boy! An' I'M ALL RIGHT! I DONE FOUN' DE FOLKS!' " (130). He then insists that Sarah be brought to live with him and his "folks," despite her objections that she values her own freedom.[36]

Thus Stuart reinforces most blatantly the mythic identification of black and white, both races nostalgic for antebellum social relations of intimacy and trust between the races—however unequal. The portrait before which the white woman and black boy stand is the romantic commemoration of such relations, and reflects significantly on Stuart's own unironic ideological position. The portrait depicts "a beautiful girl, in . . . evening dress. . . . She seemed to be strolling from a great old house through an avenue of trees, her faithful dog at her left, while a resplendent black serving boy in Continental dress at the other side bore her book in his arms—all pride and attention." The chapter in which George glimpses this portrait (before being taken to it by his mistress) is entitled "George Sees a Vision." The portrait, identical with the more realistic photograph George carries with him, is indeed a vision of black-white relations that only ever existed in fictional/iconographic representations. This—to a modern reader, grotesque—depiction of ideal relations fulfills Freud's conditions of secondary revision, in Renée Balibar's terms, "by showing how a fiction betrays (exhibits and parodies) the conflicts which activate it." Pet dog and pet boy are given equal representational weight and value in the loving attention and servility they offer the beautiful girl, whose presence is all they desire. Since the portrait only confirms George's belief that he *belongs* to wealthy white folks, it is used with the photograph to confirm the story's romantic purpose, the idealization of emotional ties between the races seen in deliberately ahistorical and apolitical terms. The conclusion of the story vindicates George's search for and discovery of a beautiful mistress to wait upon, locating his quest in the realm of the imaginary that is then privileged above real race and social relations: "But it must be remembered that the actual conditions of life count for very little to those

36. Ruth McEnery Stuart, *George Washington Jones: A Christmas Gift That Went A-Begging* (Philadelphia, 1903), 20; New York *Churchman,* April 7, 1904, Philadelphia *Lutheran Observer,* December 26, 1903, both in RMSC. This view is by no means generally discredited; in a recent biographical sketch written for the Ruth McEnery Stuart Clan, the story is described as "the finest portrait of a little Negro boy in all literature." Mrs. Henry P. Gamble, Jr., quoted in *Ruth McEnery Stuart Clan: A Brief History on the Occasion of Its Sixtieth Anniversary* (New Orleans, 1975), 3.

whose castles are in Spain, where they live in affluence, undisturbed by life's vicissitudes."[37]

By contrast, there is no question of the New Orleans Italian community being recuperated into white kinship and family structures. However, like Stuart's city and plantation blacks, they are treated as irrevocably subordinate, because threatening to the creole and Anglo-Saxon bourgeois hegemony. As with the black characters, dialect and incorrect English identify the Italians as quaint and comic and thus eminently suitable subjects of Local Color fiction. For instance, in "Camelia Riccardo," Stuart uses a dialect somewhat similar to that of George W. Cable's satirized creoles, to make the sexual rivalry over Camelia risible:

> ['Manuel says] "Ridges don' mague some*body* 'appy, Camelia!" . . . . ['Know sometheen, 'Manu*el*? Thad-a man wa's goin'-a ged marry weeth-a me, 's god-a mague plenny money, yas!"

Camelia is portrayed as financially hardheaded, and 'Manuel as winning her love only when he prospers as a stall-holder. Although the story plays lightheartedly on the themes of sexual jealousy and minor deception, it also tends to reinforce the notion of Italians as financially grasping and self-seeking (in a way Stuart's blacks *never* are).[38]

The Story of Babette, however, gives a more critical version of the Italian community.[39] A wealthy French creole family loses its daughter Babette to a poor Italian and gypsy family who kidnap her intending to demand a ransom. The family lives in a Gulf resort near Mobile and makes a sparse living by fishing and trading in other resorts and New Orleans. Nicholas Nicholas, putative head of the family, is drunken and dissolute and thus leaves provision for his children to his wily grandmother; nonetheless, the life of the Italian/gypsy family is seen by the author as fundamentally natural and good. Stuart's Italians are in tune with a benevolent natural environment (albeit pretty rough and dirty). She compares sophisticated New Orleans creoles and poor, unsophisticated Gulf-resort dwellers in much the way Chopin was to do later in *The Awakening.* Stuart's Italians live off the sea and on fruits and nuts in season; and their children (including the adopted Babette) eschew toys because of the many games and sports possible amid the natural landscape of the beach. But unlike Chopin's wholesome Acadians, Stuart's Arcadian Italians have a sinister

37. Stuart, *George Washington Jones,* 107, 146–47; Balibar, "George Sand's 'La Mare au Diable,' " 37.

38. Ruth McEnery Stuart, "Camelia Riccardo," in *A Golden Wedding and Other Tales,* 275–76.

39. Ruth McEnery Stuart, *The Story of Babette, a Little Creole Girl* (New York, 1894).

streak that reflects the distrust of Stuart's class for the "dagos" of her native city. Nicholas is an irresponsible drunkard, and the grandmother— wheeler-dealer and fortune-teller that she is—is distinctly witchlike. Her gypsy origins, allied with the Italians into whom she married, together create an ominous a-social aura around these people, and the heartbreak that Babette's kidnapping brings to the creole family reinforces definitions of the Italians as inherently evil.

The novella *Carlotta's Intended* has a more somber tone than most of Stuart's work, with an uncharacteristically tragic ending. It records the love of a crippled Irish cobbler, Pat Rooney, for a beautiful Italian girl, Carlotta, whom he hopes to marry. Carlotta's parents expect her to marry an old wealthy Italian, Socola, who is important in the Mafia. On the day of the wedding, Carlotta runs away and so Socola—proud Mafia representative that he is—simply marries her cousin to save face, warning the family and guests that anyone who reveals the truth of the wedding will be avenged by *"the knives of a hundred of Mafia's sons."* Pat Rooney, delighted that Carlotta has escaped Socola's grasp, inadvertently tells the truth to a group of Italians he hears laughing at Carlotta's reputed sexual forwardness, and realizes he is automatically condemned to death. Stuart's rather heavy-handed caricature of the Mafia emphasizes the patriarchal elements in their pride and their remorseless sense of honor. Socola, having fathered a son, feels "father to all the world" with an "intensely masculine heart," and he sees Pat Rooney's truth-telling as an offense "against this embodiment of sacredness—this woman—this infant."[40] Perhaps Stuart feared Mafia reprisals herself, since she does not allow Pat to perish by a Mafia hand. Instead, in a scene redolent with romantic pathos, she makes him overhear Carlotta avowing love to another young Italian—and, heartbroken, slip by mistake into the Mississippi, just in time to escape his two Sicilian assassins.

It is hard to see why Kate Chopin was so enthusiastic about this story, calling it "true to nature" and sounding a "wholesome, human note."[41] It seems to me a fairly uninteresting melodramatic novel using stock character types and situations. Its significance for this study lies in Stuart's particular use of the much-publicized hostility between establishment New Orleanians and the Italians and Mafia in the 1880s and 1890s. The writer's fictional critique of the Italians appears to derive from her feminism, and her antipathy to that intense male pride which was clearly at the heart of Mafia laws and punishments. There is an interesting comparison between *The Story of Babette* and *Carlotta's Intended* that points to such a

40. In Ruth McEnery Stuart, *Carlotta's Intended and Other Tales,* 44–79.
41. Per Seyersted (ed.), *A Kate Chopin Miscellany* (Natchitoches, La., 1979), 128.

reading. In both stories, the helpless exploited young girls are at the mercy of the Italian community itself, with its male-dominated lack of concern for the girls' individual rights and wishes. In both works, Stuart provides her female protagonist with a good helper figure who adores her and helps save her from a terrible fate—death, in Babette's case; a dreadful marriage, in Carlotta's. And in each case that helper is a non-Italian, also disabled—the Irish Pat Rooney was crippled in a political shooting, Noute is a deaf mute. The clear identification of both men with the girls' suffering and victimization makes an interesting comment on the possibilities of gender transference and identification (both men, crucially de-sexed themselves, deal with their young mistresses in *feminine* ways). And Stuart clearly has little sympathy with what she sees as the male-oriented, misogynist Italian social and family life that the men and female protagonists attempt to counter.

It is already clear that issues of gender are treated unproblematically in some of Stuart's early work. She makes clear her predilection for those qualities and characters associated with traditional stereotypes of feminine values, with her treatment of the meek and gentle blacks, and her clear loathing of patriarchal Mafia men. But unlike the strong, independent Italians, her weak, feminized blacks—often in the power of narrators—are demonstrably powerless themselves and in need of the support of their white confidant(e)s. Unlike the white Italians, blacks are almost never seen as having a vital, autonomous community life that is unmediated by white approval or control. And because of Stuart's paradoxical emphasis on the centrality for *all* races of the family, inevitably she privileges role models and gender positions that are most suitable to ordered familial relations, but which conflict with orthodox sex roles. This explains partly why many of her black male characters are given traditional feminine characteristics of gentleness, humility, and dependence. But there are considerable differences between her fictional treatment of gender in relation to blacks and whites, and it is significant that she excludes gender problems *only* from stories that deal exclusively with blacks. The black fiction operates largely in terms of a literary discourse, which self-consciously objectifies and thus seems to distance the writer and reader from real lived relations and uncomfortable historical realities. In the fiction that addresses itself specifically to questions of gender, Stuart's own experiences and ideas as a feminist woman, mother, and writer-in-exile all give an emotional immediacy to her work and avoid the excessive reflexiveness and cerebral detachment of the stories about New Orleans and Arkansas ethnic groups. Unfortunately, she never wrote a profound, complex feminist work. Her feminist themes are fractured throughout various stories, although she indicates original ways of examining problems of gender in a handful of key works. But Stuart's tone—lighthearted, comic, falling constantly into sentimentality and bathos—prevents her ideas from achieving anything but superficial, fragmented effects.

Nonetheless, it is worth examining selected stories in an attempt to understand the kinds of fictional critique that Stuart achieved around issues relating to gender. I will begin by exploring the ways in which a single theme—widowhood—is examined differently in relation to black and white women's sexuality. I will then discuss three stories that explore women's changing relationships to harsh economic reality and the changing demands of the New South. I will conclude by examining two works that seem to me the most interesting in terms of alternative visions of gender roles and possibilities: *Napoleon Jackson*, which displaces contemporary feminist questions about domestic labor into a comic story of postbellum black family life; and *The Cocoon*, which satirizes Dr. Weir Mitchell's "rest cure" for women but raises questions about sexual autonomy, women's freedom, and—again—madness and sanity. In my discussion, I shall emphasize the unevenness of tone, uncertainty of direction, and inappropriateness of closure that demonstrate the problems for a writer making fiction out of questions of gender that were close to the bone for a southern woman writing in the feminist 1890s.

The theme of widowhood is treated comically, both in relation to black and white women. In three stories about widows calculating to remarry in order to give their children and themselves economic security, Stuart takes an uneasily humorous tone. In the first published, "The Widder Johnsing," the black widow has seen three husbands die in five years, and the story appears to bear out vulgar white fears about black women's promiscuity. She is a caricature of female sexual dependence, beginning after the funeral (at which she fainted into a man's arms) "a worldly, rioting, rollicking war upon the men." Stuart suggests only at the end of the story the financial exigencies that led to such voracious determination to secure another husband. This notion of the merry black widow is repeated in "Moriah's Mourning" when another calculating woman describes how— within the first year of widowhood—she captures a new husband: "Any wide-awake widder 'oman dat kin get a widder man whar he can't he'p but see her move round at her work for two days hand-runnin', an' can't mesmerize him so's he'll ax her to marry him—"[42] Here, dialect is used to

42. Ruth McEnery Stuart, "The Widder Johnsing," in *A Golden Wedding and Other Tales*, 104; Ruth McEnery Stuart, "Moriah's Mourning," in *Moriah's Mourning, and Other Half-Hour Sketches* (New York, 1898), 10.

undermine blacks' autonomy, and to emphasize what is seen as humorous behavior, albeit catering to white fears about black female sexual calculation and voraciousness.

By contrast, the story "Weeds" about a *white* widow lays great emphasis on the subtle delicacy of her equally calculating plan to remarry, by constructing her as more passive and discreet than her black sisters. Indeed, the remarriage takes place because of newly widowed Elijah Tomkins' increasing sense of loneliness and emotional need, and his fascination for the widow he recurrently meets in the graveyard. The story leaves the widow's motives highly ambiguous for, though she *appears* to win Elijah's heart in a carefully calculated way, she makes no overt moves—and displays none of the comic manipulation of the black widows. Moreover, the story has an afterword that emphasizes the loyalty of the couple to their dead spouses and the fact that no courting actually took place in the graveyard, despite local gossip. However unconsciously on Stuart's part, these stories reveal a very different attitude toward black and white female sexuality; contrasted with white women, *black* women's economic and sexual needs are made a matter for only humor and satire, with just an edge of pathos to hint at individual dignity and tragic possibilities.

The postbellum economic needs of white women of Stuart's own class form the basis for a story that can best be compared with the work of some nonsouthern women writers she knew in New York. "The Woman's Exchange of Simpkinsville" is set in a small Arkansas town with a strong sense of community, despite the scarcity of men and devastations of war. Like Dunnet Landing in Sarah Orne Jewett's *The Country of the Pointed Firs* (1896) and the small forgotten communities in Mary Wilkins Freeman's work, Stuart's "Simpkinsville" is a town run largely by white women who reminisce about the past, about their youthful sexual opportunities, and the bourgeois financial security that the Civil War so rudely disrupted. The Simpkins twin sisters (originally from one of the "best" families in town, a fact underlined by their name) have lost their family's wealth over the years since the war, and since the death of their brother Sonny, who was a passionate naturalist. The story describes how they come to terms with "the informal guest called Poverty, with her startling command of 'Work!' "[43] As with Freeman's and Jewett's stories of women whose age forbids hopes of marriage, the story records their organization of a "Woman's Exchange" modeled on similar ones already running in cities and reported in women's magazines. The two women energetically run the Exchange, finding a new lease on life as they bring together goods, rearrange their house, and abandon traditional practices in order to earn a

43. In Stuart, *A Golden Wedding*, 313.

living (by dressing more cheerfully, and clearing out their brother's old room to accommodate paying guests).

This enthusiastic venture into commerce, unfamiliar as it is to women of their class and race, is shown to revitalize both the two women and the whole Simpkinsville community itself (" 'Simpkinsville ain't been so stirred up sence the fire' " (323). The goods for sale are described humorously (the cakes have names like "Confederate layer" and "General Lee"), but there is a sense of new life, bustle, and creativity: the town's "poetess" sends a cake for sale that she refuses to price since " 'that cake is jest the same to her as a p'try-verse' " (320). This mock-heroic tone anticipates Sarah Jewett's Bowden family reunion, in which the food is made as a tribute to the family itself and the magnificent gingerbread "house" (made by an "artist") is seen as a work of art to be devoured "as if it were a pledge and token of loyalty."[44]

Such commercial activity, perhaps because home-based and involving other women, is not regarded as demeaning to the sisters' social status, since they are "screened from the odium of professional bread-making by the prestige of the 'Exchange.' " However, when the sisters are the first in the town to take overnight lodgers for a fee, their social inferiors recognize that a shift is taking place in customary ways: "It seemed odd that [Simpkinsville's] leading family . . . should have been first to put a price on the bread broken with a stranger." The Simpkins twins also recognize "their changed social relations through the ever-present atmosphere of trade," but these changed relations are positive and life-affirming: "a new, youth-restoring life to be always professedly and really busy with work that left no time for repinings." Even when they are saved from the need to earn money by selling their dead brother's collection of stuffed birds and ornithological notebooks to the Smithsonian Institution, they use it as "lubrication" to give the Exchange "smooth and happy working."[45]

Stuart's lighthearted comic story suggests various feminist themes consistent with her own and her contemporaries' ideas about women's work, changed social roles, and relations after the war. The dead brother, idolized as he was, is put into appropriate perspective throughout the story, in terms of gender roles among the white bourgeoisie. Like other male characters in postbellum women's writing, Sonny "never grasped the changed situation after the war" (312). He is a somewhat emasculated figure, an absentminded naturalist without a clue about economic or political matters, who pursues his study of birds and dies appropriately after falling from a tree in which he was seeking a bird. The fact that the sisters

44. Sarah Orne Jewett, *The Country of the Pointed Firs* (London, 1927), 151.
45. Stuart, "The Woman's Exchange," 327, 331–32, 355.

cannot simply live in the clouds, or the past, leads them to espouse a mode of production rather than of consumption. They put to use the enshrined rooms of the house, demonstrating a youthful energy for work that gives them a real connection with the town from which (because of their class position) they had hitherto held themselves aloof. Stuart is giving cautious welcome to the New South, especially inasmuch as women can be freed from the role of corpse-watchers. And the story demonstrates how energy and life are enhanced when women lead useful rather than ornamental lives. The very title can be seen as an ironic comment on the radical shift of women's productive role from the domestic to the public sphere in postbellum years, the "exchange" of orthodox gender roles being such a marked feature of that period. Critics have argued that Local Color stories of this kind simply record with nostalgia the lives of old or aging women as testimony to the moribund nature of small-town life in the 1880s and 1890s.[46] But like Jewett's *Pointed Firs,* Stuart's "Woman's Exchange" exemplifies the vigor of such communities, which derives from their women's ability to adapt and change with new economic and social circumstances.

But in a later story Stuart takes a more somber perspective on Simpkinsville, questioning gender definitions within the community by featuring a female emotional breakdown. It seems that Stuart based her story "The Unlived Life of Little Mary Ellen" on an actual event, though it is also possible that she knew Kate Chopin's story "La Belle Zoraïde," published in 1894.[47] Chopin's story, set before the war, raises the question of mulatto women's favored treatment as house slaves and derives considerable irony from its framing within a bedtime narrative told by a black slave to her mistress. Zoraïde, pregnant with a field slave's child, sees her lover sold away from the plantation and her baby taken from her, pronounced dead. Her attachment to a bundle of rags that she treats like a child and her subsequent rejection of her real daughter are the manifestation of her deranged mind, which never recovers throughout her long sad life. Stuart avoids the mulatto theme and distances her female protagonist even more than Chopin within the narrative structuring. The story of Mary Ellen, jilted on her wedding day and so distraught that she claimed a talking doll for her baby, is constructed as a doctor's case study called "A Psychological

---

46. See, for instance, Wood, "The Literature of Impoverishment."

47. In Ruth McEnery Stuart, *In Simpkinsville: Character Tales* (New York, 1897). In the RMSC, there is a cutting entitled "Insane Mother Clung to Doll" (New York *World,* November 29, 1896), which records the death of a woman after trying to save from a traffic accident her doll which she treated like a baby. Seyersted (ed.), *The Complete Works of Kate Chopin,* 303–308.

Impossibility" and due for publication as an "authorized account" in a medical journal after its subject's death. The two town doctors discuss the case, with one urging the removal of the doll, the other (narrator of the story) emphasizing the innocence of such an attachment and the relative happiness of Mary Ellen compared with that of some families "where everything is regular and straight accordin' to our way o' lookin' at things." The desirability of this state of affairs is also questioned at a women's prayer-meeting where some women argue that the "hallucination" or "spell" should be broken, and one bitterly condemns "the man thet put words into a doll's breast, to be hugged out by a poor, bereft, weak-minded woman."[48]

Indeed, the focus of the story—original and disturbing as it is—is not Mary Ellen herself, but the very question of her imaginary relationship with the doll (itself bearing an uncanny relationship to a real child). Increasingly, the story reveals how unsettling the community finds Mary Ellen's behavior to its collective morality and indeed unconscious. This is apparent in the way the doctors disagree over the validity of allowing the lie to continue; the fact that the women of the church feel the need collectively to explore their attitudes to it at a meeting; and that when a decision is taken to give the doll a proper "funeral," after its despoilation by a dog in the rain, the townspeople do not know whether to laugh or cry. Perhaps not surprisingly, it is the "saddest funeral gathering in all the annals of Simpkinsville" (128).

In the only paragraph of unequivocal authorial comment, Stuart raises her central issue about Mary Ellen's case: "If the toy-baby gave her the greater pleasure, may it not have been because she dimly perceived in it a meeting-point between the real and the imaginary? Here was a threshold of the great wonder-world that primitive peoples and children love so well" (119). This is precisely what is undermining to the community, whose version of sanity and reality is circumscribed by familiar, established ideas and practices. The symbolic disruption of "normal" familial relations and attachments between women and children disorients everyone and produces new sets of relations and emotions. There is general relief when Mary Ellen dies during the mock funeral service, and an acknowledgment that what they had prayed for had been granted. The minister refers to the bedraggled doll as "this poor little symbol of our common sorrow" (130), and the author wrings a good deal of pathos from the service. Again Stuart uses a mock-heroic tone but this time to unusual effect; the story records a community coming briefly to terms with its own communal imagination and its relationship with little-understood areas of

48. Stuart, "The Unlived Life," 111, 113, 115.

human suffering and madness. Chopin focuses entirely on the pathos of Zoraïde herself, and in Jewett's *The Country of the Pointed Firs* and Charlotte Perkins Gilman's *The Yellow Wallpaper* (as well as much subsequent women's writing) madness is a solitary journey that excludes and renders irrelevant the wider community. But Stuart's concern here is a *general* one, and as with all her work there is an interest in the ways gender stereotyping functions within and against small communities, and how the individual woman adapts to or breaks with definitions of femininity and "normal" female behavior. Mary Ellen's fate is defined pessimistically; death is the only possible solution, and a mock funeral presages the real one.

This motif of the mock funeral followed by a real one was taken up again two years later in Stuart's story "Queen O'Sheba's Triumph," which also offers its protagonist a pessimistic relationship to her community, and a sudden death.[49] But Sheba is black, and this story lacks the pathos accorded to white Mary Ellen. Sheba's distance from her community derives not from madness but perversity, and her death is seen as an inevitable result of pride and ambition. The story describes the fate of a woman who has, against her friends' advice, left her native southern plantation home (Broom Corn Bottom) for New York City. Once there, she faces economic and physical collapse, while writing to her friends and family in such terms that they believe her to be prospering. When they plan a trip to New York to visit her, she cannot face them in her tenement, working as she does as a menial cook. Having already spent all her spare cash on funeral insurance to save herself from a pauper's burial, Sheba arranges a mock funeral service that the Broom Corn Bottom contingent attends. Her "full final triumph" is the loving homage her friends pay her, believing she has died wealthy and successful. Ironically, after her mock funeral, Sheba decides to confess to her people that she is alive and now wishes to return to Broom Corn Bottom. But this decision comes too late—since, at the height of a thunderstorm, she collapses melodramatically and finally into the arms of the funeral insurance agent. Conveniently in time for the burial, he substitutes her body for the wax replica over which her relatives have wept.

The story can be read both as a clear warning to southern blacks of the trials of northern life that face exiles, and also as a wry comment on upward social and geographical mobility of all kinds, including Stuart's own. By focusing on a woman attempting unsuccessfully to make a living alone in New York City, the story raises problems of race and gender that were pertinent both to women of Stuart's own class and race, and also to many disfranchised, impoverished blacks tempted to leave the South for

49. In Ruth McEnery Stuart, *Holly and Pizen, and Other Stories* (New York, 1899).

wider opportunities in northern cities. By emphasizing the economic difficulties and emotional isolation of such a move, as well as its dangers for
women from predatory figures like the insurance agent, "Queen
O'Sheba" sounds a conservative warning to both black and white women
who felt stirred by new freedom and possibilities in the 1880s and 1890s.
One white reviewer also read it as a satirical play on pretentious black
behavior: "Any one who knows the unctuous delight which the negro,
like the Celt, takes in a funeral, will appreciate the ease with which a poor
mulatto dishwasher in a Harlem boarding house suffers herself to be persuaded by the agent of the Afro-American Funeral Insurance Company to
mortgage her slender income . . . that she may be buried with all the
pomp and panoply of woe."[50] Just as Stuart was elsewhere seen as a
celebrator of the benign, childlike, and humorous qualities of the southern
black, so here she is praised for satirizing the gullibility and vanity of black
women. Sheba's aspirations seem increasingly distasteful, and the story's
dénouement, far from seeming tragic, looks merely perverse and men-
dacious. Although potentially a powerful feminist theme, the story has an
antifeminist tone: indeed it succeeds in betraying its author's thinly disguised horror at Sheba's flamboyance, sentimentality, and gullibility.

One of Stuart's later stories indicates the surer feminist touch she was
achieving in her stories about blacks, and sentimental and racist though it
is, it illustrates Stuart's interest in foregrounding within her fiction the
complex interrelationships of race and gender. The contemporary critical
reception of *Napoleon Jackson* praised the story's touching qualities. It was
called "one of the most humorously pathetic sketches that has appeared for
a long time"; "an idyllic romance of plantation life . . . full of rich humor,
subtle poetry, and suggestion of pathos"; and praised for demonstrating a
"tender undertone of sympathetic feeling . . . [and] exquisite, subtle insight into the human heart." Yet as I read it, the story has a strikingly
uneven tone; it betrays most interestingly the author's personal conflicts
and ambivalences, and those of her race and class at the turn of the century.
On the question of gender in relation to the black community, the story is
an original attempt to raise issues that only a woman familiar with, and
concerned by, the Woman Question could have aired so fully in fiction.[51]

Napoleon Jackson is "a man of color, of leisure, of family, and of parts"
(5) who sits all day long, dressed in considerable finery, in a rocking chair

50. New York *Current Literature,* n.d. (probably 1899), in RMSC. There is no evidence in
the story to suggest Sheba is a mulatto. She is referred to throughout as "colored" and must
be taken to be black.

51. Ruth McEnery Stuart, *Napoleon Jackson: The Gentleman of the Plush Rocker* (New
York, 1902); Springfield (Mass.) *Republican,* December 6, 1902, Washington (D.C.) *Times,*
November 9, 1902, New York *Christian Advocate,* November 6, 1902, all in RMSC.

bought for him with soap coupons by his hardworking wife Rose Ann. Atypical as *he* is among idle black husbands (by his clothes, rocker, and uncomplaining wife), Rose Ann is constructed as a typical black wife and mother: as a laundress, "jes a plain grass-bleachin', sun-dryin', clair-starchin', muscle-polishin' washerwoman" (3–4), typical—in Stuart's words—of many a "dusky 'madonna of the tubs' " (41), who supported her family often without a husband. Rose Ann is frowned upon by the black and white communities for condoning Napoleon's idleness on the grounds that his mother had worked so hard all her life that " 'she marked her chile for rest' " (15). She claims that she married for love and derives pleasure from Napoleon's familial affection and attractiveness in the rocker.

The tone of the story changes dramatically when a night visitor (typical of the notorious "whitecappers") comes to the house and warns Napoleon to engage in productive labor for his family or there will be trouble. Since Napoleon ignores this warning, he is brought to a simulated trial at night, organized by the young local attorney whose family had owned Rose Ann's ancestors as slaves (her own mother had suckled him). Condemned by the white "judge" and "jurors," Napoleon is then given a spirited defense by his wife and mother-in-law, on the grounds that he is a loving family man. Rose Ann goes further to compare Napoleon's "idle-ness"/child-care with that of " 'gen'leman wha' lived on dey wives' for-tunes' " and comments wryly, " 'nobody 'rested 'em or called 'em 'va-grams'—*but of co'se, dey was white*' " (123). The trial ends in disarray, and Napoleon's family walks home singing triumphantly.

Napoleon is thus presented ambivalently. Though everything in the book moves toward sentimental closure, nonetheless an uneasy tension pervades the story in terms of race and gender relations, a tension not defused completely by the failed trial. The story functions in a variety of ways and veers uneasily between reassuring and warning white readers about the nature of black family life. In one way, it must have confirmed white suspicions that black families were held together by hardworking, responsible women while their men posed a threat in the postbellum South because of their tendency to be idle, unproductive, thus vagrant and a threat to social order. But through the colorful, deeply domesticated fig-ure of Napoleon it also demonstrates the strong family bonds of blacks and the affection that white readers wished to believe black men had for their children so as to ensure black quiescence and self-control. When Napoleon assures his white judges that for him child-care " 'ain't work. . . . Dat's my pleasure' " (129), his dangerous and potentially subversive example is converted into one of tame domestication. Indeed, throughout the story

Napoleon is constructed as a comic figure who makes no distinction between his labor and pleasure. He tells the census-taker that " 'I's a family man, sir' " (43), and he denies that delivering the clothes Rose Ann has washed is work, since it is " 'on'y *'stributin'* of labor' " (31). Gathering herbs for medicines, looking after the children, and providing love and entertainment for Rose Ann are tasks he enjoys, and are discounted as labor by himself and indeed his judges—but not by his wife who values them and considers them fair exchange for her hard work. The story reassures the white reader fearful of black restiveness and revolt that the family unit is as crucial to freedmen and women as to whites, and therefore should be supported.

Napoleon's insistence on defining himself as a consumer, denying his own role in his family's and community's mode of production, is reinforced by Stuart through the story's comic elements, which underline the title's suggestion of Napoleon as an aesthetic rather than productive figure. The whole family is presented at the beginning in aesthetic terms: "The picture of the family group of Rose Ann, washerwoman, as gathered almost any day at her cabin door, was a pictorial expression of the great story of her life—its romance, its tragedy, and . . . its comedy" (3). This is, of course, conventional enough, but it is taken further when Rose Ann defends her hard life against Napoleon's idleness. She tells a friend that " 'a' able-bodied man *in sight* is a heap o' consolation [for hard work]' " (17, my emphasis), and she tells her mother that she chose the color red for his plush rocker so that it would set off his black skin, and together with the framing white evening-glory flowers make a handsome sight. Leading the family's afternoon dance, Napoleon is likened to "black royalty" (67). Rose Ann's spirited comparison of her idle husband with idle white "gen'lemen" can be read as an assertion of the right of black men to be both consumers and family men, and also the subjects of art, especially of sentimental fiction (even if the vogue for such "local color" portraits was passing). Indeed, the story could be taken by a modern reader as a satire on the whole Local Color movement and its distortion of black reality through fictional representation by white authors.

But more significantly, Napoleon can be read as a droll parody of white conspicuous consumption, that function which Thorstein Veblen ascribed to women.[52] Stuart's involvement with the woman suffrage movement and women's clubs sensitized her to the absurdity of the southern ideology of womanhood. A wage-earner and breadwinner for much of her life, she must have felt keenly the meaningless ascription of strict gender roles in

52. Thorstein Veblen, *The Theory of the Leisure Class: An Economic Study in the Evolution of Institutions* (New York, 1899).

southern white society, which clung to notions of female inferiority and unproductive, leisured consumption. By focusing on a *black* family—known to white readers as characteristically headed by a woman worker—the story makes humorous comment on the rigidification of roles and tasks. And it asks through Napoleon what the nature of productive labor really is, when domestic work is defined and accepted by most men and women as nonwork. Stuart's statements in interviews and her fiction about women demonstrate clearly that she saw this dismissal of housework and child-care as dangerous, especially as in her own life she always acknowledged her sister's role as housekeeper and surrogate wife. Napoleon acquires dignity not only through the loyal support of his wife and mother-in-law, but through his positive celebration of domestic skills and family duties—tasks his white judges devalue themselves and leave to their servants and wives.

But of course Napoleon is a comic figure precisely *because* he lacks traditional masculine qualities, allying himself instead with the domestic world and work of women. Napoleon's potential threat to whites (suggested at first by the whitecapping) is ultimately defused because he does not behave like a conventional man, and the women defend his right to be gentle, domesticated, and unproductive. He no doubt reminded contemporary readers of Uncle Tom, who shared many of these qualities. And it is significant that in recent years blacks have objected to Stowe's antebellum black hero on the grounds that he was exactly the kind of powerless, feminized darky whom whites preferred to the aggressively masculine, autonomous black exemplified by Nat Turner. James Baldwin spoke for others when he described Uncle Tom as "robbed of his humanity and divested of his sex."[53] Like Tom, Napoleon scorns active resistance in favor of humble endurance. Associated with women and validating the tame, united family unit, he confirms for white readers the harmlessness and political irrelevance of his race.

It is thus only in works about *white women* that Stuart can confront feminist issues without undue equivocation; as with *Napoleon Jackson,* her black stories return inevitably to racial stereotypes and use the transgression of gender roles to confirm black subordination. I have already referred to Stuart's avowed wish, in the last years of her life, to write an overtly feminist novel about a southern girl in New York, following the examples of Mary Johnston and Ellen Glasgow. *The Cocoon,* her last published novel, is the nearest Stuart ever comes to tackling the difficult contemporary problems of women of her own race and class.[54] But despite focusing

53. James Baldwin, "Everybody's Protest Novel," in *Notes of a Native Son* (London, 1965), 12–13.
54. Ruth McEnery Stuart, *The Cocoon: A Rest-Cure Comedy* (New York, 1915).

on a promising theme and achieving some satiric effects, it lapses quickly into Stuart's characteristic comic sentimental narrative mode. The novel features an unwillingly childless wife who has been sent by her husband to a sanitarium to take the "rest-cure" of a godlike Doctor Jacques. The cure bears obvious resemblances to that of Dr. Weir Mitchell; although to my knowledge Stuart never took the cure, her son was treated for his broken back by Dr. Mitchell, and Mitchell's fame and notoriety were by then considerable (and were probably a matter of some interest to Stuart, since both she and her sister had suffered forms of mental breakdown after Stirling's death).

Weir Mitchell's cure for women's nervous diseases, developed in the 1870s and 1880s as an alternative to then-fashionable cauterization treatments, consisted of "a combination of entire rest and of excessive feeding, made possible by passive exercise obtained through steady use of massage and electricity." The cure was dependent on the physician's "commanding personality and charismatic will"; women were encouraged to worship the physician who "could become almost god-like." By the time Charlotte Perkins Gilman went to him for treatment in the late 1880s, his vanity "had become colossal. It was fed by torrents of adulation, incessant and exaggerated, every day, almost every hour." Gilman undertook the cure shortly after her daughter's birth. In her autobiography she described the rest cure and Mitchell's instructions thereafter: "I was put to bed and kept there. I was fed, bathed, rubbed, and responded with the vigorous body of twenty-six. [After sending her home because he could find nothing wrong with her, he told her] 'Live as domestic a life as possible. Have your child with you all the time. . . . Lie down an hour after each meal. Have but two hours' intellectual life a day. And never touch pen, brush or pencil as long as you live.' "[55]

It was in following these strict instructions that Gilman came near to an utter nervous breakdown, which culminated in her rejection of all his advice and abandonment of her husband and daughter to become a writer and public speaker. In her short story that records this experience, *The Yellow Wallpaper* (1892), Gilman provides a powerful critique of Mitchell's theory and methods. In a gothic tale, much influenced by Poe, a disturbed first-person narrator describes her increasingly distressed state of mind as a result of confinement in a strange colonial mansion in the country by a

55. S. Weir Mitchell, quoted in Ann Douglas Wood, " 'The Fashionable Diseases': Women's Complaints and Their Treatment in Nineteenth-Century America," in Mary S. Hartman and Lois Banner (eds.), *Clio's Consciousness Raised: New Perspectives on the History of Women* (New York, 1974), 5, 9; Mitchell's biographer, quoted in Barbara Ehrenreich and Deirdre English, *For Her Own Good: 150 Years of the Experts' Advice to Women* (London, 1979), 91; from *The Living of Charlotte Perkins Gilman* (1935), quoted in Gail Parker (ed.), *The Oven Birds: American Women on Womanhood, 1820–1920* (New York, 1972), 374–75.

husband, John, who is carrying out Mitchell's methods. The wallpaper of the title becomes a metaphor for her confused state of mind, then for her derangement—and that of countless other women whose postnatal depression is misdiagnosed and wrongly treated. The story's conclusion, with the husband/jailor unconscious before his deranged wife, offers nothing but despair and chaos. This story, read in the early twentieth century as a gothic fantasy, is now understood as a powerful feminist indictment of the Victorian medical profession and its patronizing prescriptions for women's depressive illnesses.[56]

Ruth McEnery Stuart's story begins promisingly enough, and appears to be making conscious reference to *The Yellow Wallpaper*. The protagonist's husband is also called John, and like Gilman's confined heroine she writes a secret diary and takes a confidential, slightly subversive tone, calling into question the nature of her treatment. The "cocoon" of the title refers to the single cots on the sanitarium roof into which patients are tucked for hours at a time for "rest-in-the-open." The opening of the novel suggests that a radical critique of Weir Mitchell's methods is planned:

> *My dear Jack:*
> I am a cocoon; or must I say *in* a cocoon? Is the cocoon the shell or the shell *and the worm*? Dictionaries are downstairs and "hours for consultation" limited. . . . Anyway, I'm it—the poor worm going into oblivion to get its wings.

Like Gilman's wallpaper, Stuart's cocoon is the place women escape to for recuperation, solitude, and often childlike regression. Dr. Jacques is satirized as the godlike creature Mitchell assumed: "He just walks around, smiling in his white halo, and seems to impersonate the love of God, all unconsciously, of course."[57]

Aware that the doctor is keeping a special eye on her either because she is "an interesting patient or an element of danger" (7), the protagonist tells both her husband and—more confidentially—her diary the ways in which she rebels daily against the strict regime, and is sardonically critical of her treatments. Like Gilman's narrator, she breaks the rules by writing and reading; she uses her diary as friend and place of refuge, seeing it like Gilman's as "book of my Heart, chum, pal, confidant—and before we get through, perhaps my confederate, even my accomplice" (73). Significantly, she values the "sacred bosom" of her diary because "there may be those who will come after me—daughters, not sons, for this—to whom I shall be only too glad to commend your utmost confidences . . . hoping

56. See, for instance, Elaine R. Hedges, "Afterword," in Charlotte Perkins Gilman, *The Yellow Wallpaper* (Old Westbury, Conn., 1973), 37–63.
57. Stuart, *The Cocoon*, 41, 1, 6.

in this trivial record of miserable tears and narrowly-averted disaster, possibly to guard them against similar pit-falls in life" (142–43).

Stuart thus signals to her women readers that this is a cautionary tale for them, though the hinted possibility of the protagonist's overt rebellion and outspoken criticism of her degrading and absurd treatments is never translated into meaningful action. The narrator, like her author, becomes more sardonic and skeptical, but also more humorous and light-hearted as the story proceeds. She comments on the absurdity of the sanitarium's treatments for women such as "sand-sopping," "thermo-electric cabinets," "hot dip and cold spray," the "flesh-reducing horse," and indeed "cocoonery" itself. Her main complaint, however, is not the nature of the ludicrous and humiliating treatments, but rather the fact that everyone takes them with utter seriousness rather than with humor: "This is a deadly place" (24). Indeed, she sees herself as the clown of the whole sanitarium, with everyone else playing parts and adopting roles: calling her fellow inmates "the dramatis personae in the great tragedy of 'Life and Death,'" she writes of her fear to stir "lest I jostle my cap and ring my bells. Of course mine must be a comedy part with my playful nose and yellow hair" (12). The humor she derives from the place predominates over her awareness of the sanitarium as a prison for women. It is almost incidental that she speaks of "serv[ing] this sentence" (30), and of the patients at one point: "I nearly wrote inmates, although prisoners would be even better, for it's quite the thing for one to ask another what he's 'in for'" (17).

In brief references like this, the novel makes oblique if flippant and superficial allusion to problems around definitions of femininity that led women to seek medical care, specifically the rest cure. Although the reasons for her confinement are never clarified, the protagonist's childlessness is seen as problematic—and after leaving the sanitarium she immediately conceives. While undergoing the cure, she pretends to be unmarried—a deception that, to her mixed pleasure and dismay, seems to leave her prey to sexual attentions from male patients and infantilizes her in the eyes of other patients: married women patients whisper about childbirth in her presence, assuming sexual ignorance and naïveté. She mischievously enjoys the freedom of this childlike status, and in another way too she relishes the freedom afforded by the rest cure:

> Servants! Bills! Mistakes in bills! The telephone! Wrong wash sent home! Right wash not sent out! Telephone! Soft icecream! Subsided soufflé! Wrong entrée sent in from caterers, doubling home course. . . . Callers and telephone adjuster and C.O.D. parcel "to be tried on" all arrive at same moment with Angelic Husband who wonders why wife didn't arrange to have them call separately. Tears! Coaxing! Temporary control—then hysteria—Angelic Hus-

band assumes all blame and calls himself a brute! Reconciliation and gr-r-r-r-eat
happiness followed by "nerve disturbance"—and then this place! (63)

As I have argued, a consciousness of the burden of domestic production is
demonstrated in a few of Stuart's stories and is made a central issue in
Napoleon Jackson: Stuart may well have felt with other feminists that the
problems of running a home were as likely as anything else to drive
women of all classes into nervous collapse. Furthermore, she may have
known that intense domesticity was precisely what almost destroyed her
contemporary Charlotte Perkins Gilman. But this is an isolated reference
to the whole issue, and Stuart gives little weight and emphasis to it, as well
as to the protagonist's insecurity and excessive fawning upon her husband
in letters, and the near-breakdown she experiences when suspecting his
infidelity.

While suggesting weighty problems associated with gender, as well as
with the states of marriage and motherhood, Stuart characteristically
evades the political logic of the subject. The story develops into an absurd
romantic comedy of misunderstanding, in which the husband is used as a
go-between in order to secure marriage between one of the sanitarium
inmates and her lover. The unraveling of this narrative is tedious and
unwieldy, and the novel's conclusion is predictably sentimental, with husband and wife reunited, she braiding pink ribbons over the bassinet ready
for her new baby. As in earlier works, Stuart airs feminist issues but is
either unwilling or unable to create sustained serious fiction around them.
Many of the problems facing middle-class white women at the beginning
of the twentieth century are contained here: the trials of married life; the
desire for escape from marital and childbearing responsibilities; the need
of women for self-expression; the importance of independent work for
women; the problems of facing sexual infidelity. But Stuart defuses all
these themes through a comic story that finally laughs away the conflicts
and questions which needed to be explored, and sadly fails to take further
in fiction the concerns about women's psychology that Gilman had begun
to define in *The Yellow Wallpaper.*

There is one example in Stuart's work that does not defuse feminist
themes but deals directly with woman suffrage and women's rights. It is a
short chapter, "The Women," in the novel *Sonny's Father,* in which a
seventy-five-year-old white grandfather narrates a rambling monologue to
his doctor, describing the changing nature of his town Simpkinsville as it
copes with the new century's influences and pressures.[58] Sonny's illiterate
father is the voice of the past and traditional ways, while Sonny (school

58. Ruth McEnery Stuart, *Sonny's Father* (New York, 1910).

director and famous naturalist author) and his wife represent educated, progressive ideas and methods. One of these is their enthusiasm for "perfessional lady speakers" (59) who come to address the town's women on feminist issues; Sonny's father records his bemusement as his daughter-in-law and her friends begin to ride bicycles, agitate for woman suffrage, and sport "Social Purity" badges.

The story is an isolated incident in the book, and its effects are not referred to later, but it is an interesting example of Stuart's comic mode being put to effective ends. To mediate feminist ideas through a quizzical old man speaking in dialect works well, especially as he is shown to move from a skeptical and mocking to a respectful, tolerant position. The story raises many of the objections that were made to woman suffrage in the 1880s and 1890s, and comically defuses them through the old man's reflections. For instance:

> I was werried, some, lessen in all this tumult they might git mannish, an' I'd be the last one to like that; but they tell me thet they's thess ez many or*gander*-lawns an' furbelows sold in the States where they vote ez they ever was, an' no mo' small-sized pants. (88)

> . . . they ain't no 'casion to fret about our women. They ain't banded ag'in' the men no mo' 'n the men has been banded ag'in' them all these years in their Odd Feller an' Freemasonry an' all sech. (95)

There is a pointed use of irony when the narrator talks of the women's rising up "in insurrection," and in response to the doctor's questioning of the term he says, "I don't know why not use that word. They talk about emancipation. Looks like they must 'a' felt in bondage to use a slave-term like that" (73). This reference to slavery suggests to the reader (or reminds her of) the analogies that suffragists had made since 1848 between their own situation and that of blacks, and by distancing the notion through an old man's reflections, inserts it cleverly into the fictional agenda. So, despite the somewhat patronizing comedy that derives from the old man's imperfect use of standard English (identical to that used in relation to Stuart's blacks), nonetheless his increasing openness to change and his liberal attitude to feminist issues give him a dignity that is not merely sentimental. Stuart demonstrates here an ability to introduce unfamiliar (and still, to many readers, risible) ideas within a comic narrative that makes a persuasive argument for women's rights with gentle, undogmatic humor. Her failure to sustain such an argument in a full-length fictional work such as *The Cocoon* points to her limitations and/or lack of courage as a writer. But in "The Women" her qualities of economy and subtle use of humor indicate the strengths that she might have developed as a feminist writer.

Of the three main writers in this study, Ruth McEnery Stuart was most immediately and consistently successful, and had she returned to New Orleans would undoubtedly have acquired the same status as Grace King, a major southern woman of letters in her home city. At the height of the vogue for Local Color, she catered well to a northern demand for regional materials, especially comic and sentimental fiction about southern blacks and other nonmetropolitan figures and types. I suggest that her very success, and her permanent move to New York where editors and critics were near at hand, probably ensured that she continued to produce conventional material and consistently played safe in order to make a good living. As with George W. Cable, her assimilation into northern letters was too easy and comfortable for her own good, and although she had none of his political and social radicalism in relation to questions of race, I believe her writing about women and feminist issues suffered as a result.

As writers, Grace King and Kate Chopin benefited from the freedom of their marginality and produced work at odds with prevailing ideologies— largely from innocence and lack of sophistication. But Ruth Stuart learned quickly how to appease and please her paymasters, and threw her energies and talents into acting the part of southern hostess, writer, and public reader in New York (though significantly she broke down under the strain). Of the three writers, Stuart is the one who most emphasizes and privileges sectional harmony and unity, reconciliation between the races, and nostalgia for a mythic antebellum past. In this way she is more typical of her contemporary Louisiana women writers than King or Chopin, who dared to focus on difficult issues like miscegenation, race, and gender conflicts. Unlike them, too, she used dialect extensively, stressing the differences between the races and the particularity/peculiarity of subordinate ethnic groups. Her discomfiture at being defined as a dialect writer may have stemmed from an uneasy sense that this very difference between races was precisely what led to social conflict and disruption, and indeed to interracial strife. She knew these were the very factors that had led to the bitter struggles of Reconstruction and after, and to the Hennessey riot in New Orleans (from all of which she may have been escaping by moving north). The decision to move away permanently from the region that furnished material and experience for her fiction appears to have weakened Stuart's critical perspective, as it did for Cable and to a certain extent the Chopin of the short stories. Hamlin Garland recognized the dangers of permanent exile for certain kinds of writers and so returned to the Midwest, while Grace King (wisely for her) stayed put; Stuart was content to make a comfortable living and career out of a fashionable minor literary vogue.

Stuart's career demonstrates well the constraints and limitations of the northern world of letters, which drew heavily on southern materials in the postbellum period. Like other Louisianians, she was encouraged to produce work that reinforced a sense of national well-being through conciliation, and this meant repeatedly constructing the paradigmatic black as a nostalgic conservative figure of loyalty to the Old South and also peaceful conformity to the New. In a decade of serious racial tension and considerable feminist activism, Stuart satisfied a demand for lighthearted regional material the ideological project of which was to ensure that conflicts could be shrugged off as temporary frictions and the very real differences of interest of races and sexes soothed with laughter and the healing power of human love. The chorus of praise and approval that greeted each new story and novel from Stuart bears testimony to the importance of anodyne regionalist literary materials in the literary construction—indeed creation—of a unified corporate America.

But whereas Stuart's role in the North bears many similarities to that of a conservative, conciliatory male figure like Thomas Nelson Page, she departs from him and others because of her more reformist adherence to feminist ideas. In "Queen O'Sheba" and *Napoleon Jackson,* Stuart was unusual in displacing concerns central to white women of her class onto black characters. These characters are both constructed as harmless and subordinate, but are also used by the author to challenge gender assumptions by implicit analogy with the similarly disfranchised and politically powerless female sex, black and white. The uneasy tone of "Queen O'Sheba" and the sentimental triumph of the figure of Napoleon Jackson must alert a modern reader to the political flaws in this analogy much employed by contemporary women suffragists. In the late fiction, a considerable degree of self-censorship operated to exclude strong feminist arguments of the kind Stuart made in articles and interviews, in favor of a bland light-hearted tone and sentimental closures—those very elements that make the *black* fiction distort and simplify lived experience. Stuart illustrates well the problems for a postbellum exiled southern white woman adopting liberal political ideas in one sphere while clinging to the learned responses of her upbringing in another. Although throughout the 1890s, at the height of concern about the Woman Question, Stuart was much concerned with the social conditions and subjectivity of her own sex, she never managed radically to challenge vulnerable white male supremacy. The incompatibility of her two main political positions—orthodox southern white racism and northeastern feminism—virtually neutralized her radical insights and cancelled out the more progressive elements in her fictional writing about gender and women.

III

Kate Chopin

Of the three writers discussed in this book, Kate Chopin (1850–1904) is likely to be the most familiar to modern readers. Her novel *The Awakening*, which led to a scandal on its publication in 1899, was reprinted for the first time in 1969, significantly by a European scholar, Per Seyersted. It quickly became a classic within the Women's Liberation Movement, admired by American and British feminists who recognized in it their own revolt against socially prescribed roles and especially definitions of female sexual behavior. The novel has since become a considerable critical and commercial success in the U.S.A., where its new position in university freshman-level English classes has given it minor canonical status, and in Britain, where it is generally included in women's studies syllabi. The enthusiasm for *The Awakening* has been followed by interest in Chopin's entire work, though it is generally agreed that she wrote nothing to compare with this extraordinary novel.

Kate Chopin was less prolific than Grace King or Ruth McEnery Stuart; she began to publish later, and finished before the others. Altogether she published approximately one hundred short stories, including two collections, *Bayou Folk* (1894) and *A Night in Acadie* (1897); a handful of poems and essays for magazines; several translations of Maupassant stories; a piece of music; and two novels, *At Fault* (1890) and *The Awakening*. The second novel was so heavily condemned by critics and friends that Chopin apparently lost the will to continue writing for a hostile reading public and subsequently wrote only a few stories and poems, including some not offered to editors. She achieved minor critical success as a Local Color writer, a reputation that was virtually obliterated with the scandal of *The Awakening* and her death shortly afterwards, of a brain hemorrhage in 1904. Of the three writers, Chopin made the most conscious references to

European writing and the most original intervention in late nineteenth-century American letters. Her significance, as I would define it for this study, lies in her particular use of Local Color techniques, and of regional and historical themes and allusions, that challenged European male and English and American female fictional definitions of femininity and female sexuality. She made an important contribution to debates about gender of relevance to the South of the 1890s.

Although she quickly established herself in the eyes of the northern reading public as a "Louisiana writer," Kate Chopin had a briefer and more tenuous biographical connection than Grace King or Ruth Stuart with the state that provided her with fictional materials. She began to write only after permanently leaving the state, and she made few return trips. Unlike the other two, she was never celebrated in Louisiana as a native writer, and King and Stuart make no reference to Chopin in their private papers and correspondence, though Chopin and Stuart met. Yet despite, or because of, Chopin's marginality to Louisiana's literary and social life, the state had a strong imaginative attraction for her; and while she resented being labeled a "Local Colorist," she returned to New Orleans and especially the Cane River community for literary subjects. She lived in Louisiana throughout her marriage, for approximately thirteen years, and because she had been born into a southern creole family similar in some ways to her husband's, found little trouble in adjusting either to New Orleans city life or the plantation community of Cloutierville and its district. Her fiction makes little direct reference to political questions (especially about race), and her papers afford virtually no evidence as to her explicit views on key southern problems of the war, Reconstruction, and questions of regional and racial identity. This has therefore led most critics to avoid historical and political readings of the texts, focusing instead on Chopin's formal strengths of narrative structure, characterization, dialogue, and so on. In recent years there has been a spate of feminist interpretations, especially of *The Awakening,* but these have given general rather than historically specific interpretations and have failed to recognize the different ways Chopin's feminism is mediated through her implicit positions on race and regionalism.

Chopin's biography has been written twice, first by Daniel Rankin in 1932, including interviews and information from living friends of the writer (but making no reference to the scandalous *The Awakening*), secondly by Per Seyersted who—encouraged by Edmund Wilson—"rediscovered" Chopin in the 1960s and collected her works. Seyersted's pioneering persistence produced a body of work that remains the most valuable contribution to Chopin scholarship. However, though excellent, his biography leaves many questions unanswered, and only some of them are clarified by his later collection of diaries, correspondence, and other materials, *A Kate Chopin Miscellany*. Recent scholarship by feminist critics has offered different perspectives on the writer, and a new biography is being prepared, but there still remain open questions about Chopin's personal relationships, her attitudes to her own and others' writing, and to problems of gender and race. In the absence of a large body of letters and documents comparable with the Grace King Papers, for the purposes of this study several biographical details have had to be conjectured or deduced from the fiction and nonfiction. Constructing Chopin's biography from extant publications has the major drawback that there is little documentation about the precise nature of her parents' and husband's class and economic positions. Both Rankin and Seyersted concentrate on Chopin's genealogy and personal history, skating over the writer's social and financial circumstances at different periods of her life, including her relationship with black Louisianians. What is clear from all sources is that she suffered several severe shocks from family deaths and economic reversals of fortune during her life, and that she learned early on from the women in her family to develop independence and an emotional resilience to crises and shocks. These stood her in good stead as an increasingly iconoclastic writer.[1]

She was born Katherine O'Flaherty in 1850, in St. Louis, Missouri, daughter of a creole mother from a wealthy bourgeois background and an Irish immigrant father who was a successful businessman and entrepreneur. Thomas O'Flaherty ran two stores and a commission house, and was one of the founders of the Pacific Railroad. When Kate was almost five, he rode the inaugural train of the St. Louis–Jefferson City track and was killed as it crashed through a bridge. Katherine O'Flaherty was to follow the pattern of her female relatives in experiencing the deaths of male relatives at crucial points in her life. By the time she was thirty-five she had lost her father (as a child), her beloved half-brother (at puberty), and her husband (when a mother of six). The family's economic position after Thomas O'Flaherty's death is not clear from Rankin's and Seyersted's biographies. It seems Kate was afforded the standard education and recreational opportunities of other girls of her class and race, and was expected to

1. Daniel S. Rankin, *Kate Chopin and Her Creole Stories* (Philadelphia, 1932); Per Seyersted, *Kate Chopin: A Critical Biography* (Baton Rouge, 1969); Seyersted (ed.), *The Complete Works of Kate Chopin* (subsequent references to the *Complete Works* will use the abbreviated form *CW*); Seyersted (ed.), *A Kate Chopin Miscellany* (subsequent references to this title will use the abbreviated form *KCM*). See *The Kate Chopin Newsletter* (later called *Regionalism and the Female Imagination*), 1975–1979. A new biography of Chopin by Emily Toth will soon be published by Atheneum.

take part in a busy social life. The trauma of male family deaths was clearly not followed by financial hardships; the women of the family must have had resources, and they demonstrated that managing without men was not only possible but also quite acceptable.

The importance of women relatives and friends in Kate Chopin's development cannot be overstated. She was brought up, after her father's death, in a household dominated by a great-grandmother, grandmother, and mother, none of whom remarried after early widowhood. She spent her adolescence at a convent school. Thus she came to trust and respect women for their independence, intelligence, and courage. As recent critics have demonstrated (in contrast to the "aristocratic" image Rankin and Seyersted ascribed to the family), she came from a family of early French settlers, many of them free-thinkers and rebels against legal, sexual, and racial conventions. There had been divorce, adultery, and some miscegenation in her mother's side of the family (there is little information about her father's family).[2] Kate O'Flaherty's great-grandmother, generally acknowledged to have been a raconteuse and a strong influence on the young girl, had legally separated parents, and herself married in 1797 when three months pregnant. She enjoyed telling her great-granddaughter tales of the early city's founder Pierre Laclède's adultery with his lieutenant's mother, Madame Chouteau. Stories such as this are said to have inspired Kate with the knowledge of unorthodox, daring women, providing subjects for her fiction. The many examples of her own immediate family and her ancestors can thus be seen as offering role models and possible subjects for her later work.

The influence of the women of the family is rightly seen by her biographers as positive and liberating. However, in many ways the strong Catholic piety and religious fervor of her female relatives must have stifled Chopin, especially as she grew older and also became a strong independent widow with apparently no intention of remarrying. This is apparent in her many references to convents and to the constraints of the Catholic faith on Louisiana creoles and on particular kinds of women. It is also suggested by her apparent abandonment of any serious Catholic practices immediately after her mother's death in 1884, and by her diary note ten years later that spoke of "the past ten years of my growth—my real growth."[3] This diary entry notes that, were her mother and husband to return to earth, she

2. See Mary Helen Wilson, "Kate Chopin's Family: Fallacies and Facts," *Kate Chopin Newsletter,* II (1976–77), 25–29, and Elizabeth Shown Mills, "Colorful Characters from Kate's Past," *Kate Chopin Newsletter,* II (1976–77), 7–12.

3. Kate Chopin, "Impressions," May 22, 1894, in Seyersted (ed.), *A Kate Chopin Miscellany,* 92.

would willingly give up everything she had become since their deaths, so the sense of freedom is by no means unequivocal. But in terms of writing, female relatives' deaths appear to have been crucial: it was immediately after her grandmother's death in January, 1897, that Chopin began work on *The Awakening*. All those women whose Catholic propriety and conservatism might have inhibited Chopin's work were now dead, and she was free to experiment in ways she may have evaded earlier.

The constraints of the Catholic faith on women she loved were even more obvious in the case of her lifelong friend Kitty Garesché. They had met at convent school, and their friendship was encouraged by Kate's mother because Kitty was Catholic. As children, they played music and read together, and wandered St. Louis alert to its political and social changes. They were both more studious and literary than their contemporaries. In 1870 they were symbolically separated, and Daniel Rankin records Chopin's memory of this date: "[In 1860] I formed a friendship with Kitty Garesché; a friendship which, I will not say ended—but was interrupted by her entering the Sacred Heart Convent as a religious in 1870—the year that I was married." Beside her notes is pasted a portrait of Kitty. Rankin points out that this was "the one unbroken friendship" of Chopin's life; it is perhaps significant that Kitty was recalled on Chopin's honeymoon and after Oscar's death, when the widow visited her friend at her Michigan convent.[4] At all major life events and crises, Kate Chopin's thoughts turned to her women friends and relatives. Although she made fewer friends of women writers and activists than Grace King or Ruth Stuart, she relied heavily on women as confidantes, role models, and strong, unorthodox subjects of fiction.

The St. Louis in which the young Kate O'Flaherty grew up, and which she left in 1870 upon her marriage to Oscar Chopin, was a busy cosmopolitan city with a tight creole community that gave its bourgeois and mercantile community a southern Gallic atmosphere. A city established in the eighteenth century by French and Spanish settlers, it was rapidly growing as the "Gateway to the West" to which traders, settlers, and groups of new immigrants (including Thomas O'Flaherty's family) came from the mid-nineteenth century. But in spirit and political sympathies, St. Louis remained a *southern* city, very similar in many ways to the New Orleans to which the newlywed Kate Chopin moved. Since the Missouri Compromise of 1820, the whole state had been a focus of debates around slavery and abolitionist activity. Slave auctions took place on the steps of the St. Louis courthouse, which in 1857 saw the *Dred Scott* v. *Sandford* case. The U.S. Supreme Court ruled that Dred Scott, a slave who had resided in a

4. Rankin, *Kate Chopin*, 42; *KCM*, 85.

free state and territory, was nonetheless still a slave. This generated heated national debate and is often cited as a contributory factor to secession and the Civil War. In 1860 the citizens of St. Louis elected a secessionist governor, but Missouri remained in the Union mainly because of northern economic ties, and St. Louis became a strong center of Union support and activity thoughout the war.

Katherine O'Flaherty's family were in a minority as Confederate supporters; she herself tore down the Union flag that was placed on the family's porch, and her brother died while serving in the Confederate army. Though she left the city for thirteen years after her marriage, St. Louis became her home again in 1883. By then, the French/Spanish creole influence and atmosphere were disappearing from a city that was becoming a major manufacturing center and by 1900 was the nation's fourth largest city. Ironically, St. Louis had passed various progressive measures relating to women—the licensing of prostitution (later repealed), and admission to Washington University and the state university. But blacks enjoyed few progressive measures, and renowned as the city was for its innovative educational methods, during Reconstruction it insisted on segregated schools and colleges. In 1917 the city saw major racial violence.

The conservative and racist positions of Kate O'Flaherty's immediate family were entirely consistent with those of her Louisiana creole husband and thus her adopted state. The attraction of Louisiana almost certainly derived from its function as an imaginary "Other" that did not require Kate Chopin to accept a version of the South different from that of her family and class. Indeed, her childhood excitement at the St. Louis slave auctions, her family's anti-Union passions, and the death of her beloved half-brother during the war had left her with as emotional a support of the Confederate cause as many Louisiana natives, and with a bitter suspicion of emancipation that must have accorded well with her husband's overt racism.

Oscar Chopin met Kate in 1869, when he was working temporarily in St. Louis. The son of a wealthy Louisiana Cane River planter, he worked as a cotton factor in New Orleans, and it was there that the couple settled after a European honeymoon. They had six children, and like other wealthy creole families spent each summer on Grand Isle, then a fashionable resort, which was destroyed by a hurricane in 1893 and provided the setting for some of Chopin's fiction. When Oscar's business collapsed in 1879, they moved to northwest Louisiana to the Chopin family plantation. Oscar's father Dr. Victor Chopin had married a wealthy creole from Cloutierville and had gone into exile in France during the Civil War, prospering well. He bought his vast Red River plantation after the death of its owner Robert McAlpin; according to legend, this was the site of the plantation in *Uncle Tom's Cabin,* with McAlpin himself the model for the cruel Simon Legree. Chopin alludes to McAlpin, reputedly vicious to his slaves, in two works—*At Fault* (1890) and the short story "The Return of Alcibiade" (1892). But McAlpin was also confused in popular memory with his successor Victor Chopin, who before the war (according to Daniel Rankin) was "outrageously cruel to his slaves."[5] Dr. Chopin also mistreated his own wife (providing Kate Chopin with a model for Edna's father in *The Awakening*). Since overseers refused to work for Chopin, he tried to force the young Oscar to work in this capacity, but the boy ran away. Thus by the time the young Chopin family moved to Cloutierville in 1879, they were associated with, and had to live down, the legendary reputations of Chopin/McAlpin, as well as local resentment at the family's wartime exile.

Apart from the Chopin family's distasteful history and reputation, the new arrivals were by no means settling in a troublefree paradise. Phanor Breazeale, married to Oscar's sister, left an account of the activities of the White League in the Natchitoches area in the 1870s; although thousands of men were involved in these leagues across the state, this was one of the most active branches.[6] Breazeale describes the racial tensions that arose from Democratic accusations of Republican ballot-rigging, the fears of black insurrection, and the violence surrounding the 1878 election. He writes of hopes for an end to "the rule of the carpet bagger and scalawag and the negro in this parish and in North Louisiana" (162). After the election, he describes the "many objectionable negroes who had to be killed . . . by a company of patriotic democrats" (163) and boasts of how "thoroughly organized" the whites were. With relish, he describes their armed march on a group of blacks to disperse and terrify them, and relates the achievement by two white jurors of a not-guilty verdict in a white conspiracy trial by a poker game in which the black jurors "of course . . . lost." These comments are significant for an analysis of Kate Chopin's somewhat Arcadian view of black-white relations in her parish, since Breazeale was a major source of information for her and must surely have recounted these swashbuckling tales to his sister-in-law.

Cane River was an extremely heterogeneous area in terms of racial mix. Apart from its wealthy white creole planters who owned most of the fertile land, there was a large community of poor white French Acadians whom the British had driven from Acadia in 1755, and an even more

5. Rankin, *Kate Chopin,* 121.
6. Phanor Breazeale, "Statement on Reconstruction Natchitoches," n.d., quoted in *KCM,* 157–66.

significant number of *gens de couleur libre*—mulattoes who had owned land and slaves since the early nineteenth century, supported the Confederacy, but been thoroughly displaced and disfranchised since the war. Kate Chopin was fascinated by these different groups and got to know them in the four years she lived there. After Oscar Chopin's sudden death of swamp fever, Kate took over the running of the family's plantation and village store, and came to know more intimately the working people she was to describe in later years in her fiction. Seyersted speaks of her local popularity as a "magnificent, gracious, and efficient châtelaine," and quotes her daughter's description of the writer's "Lady Bountiful" role in the neighborhood. But the language used here should alert readers to suspect Seyersted's assertion that Chopin was unequivocally welcome. She could hardly have been oblivious to the many class and race tensions in the area, or to the considerable shifts in economic and social power and influence (especially away from the mulatto community in favor of the wealthy creoles). It would be surprising if all Kate Chopin's charms managed to live down the reputation of Oscar Chopin's father, the considerable status and power of the Chopin clan (most of whom had married into other wealthy neighborhood families), and Oscar's own well-known White League activities.[7]

In 1884, Kate Chopin returned permanently to live with her mother in St. Louis; tragically, her mother died suddenly a year later. At this period, Kate was experiencing considerable economic difficulties—Oscar had been a rather unsuccessful businessman both in New Orleans and in Cloutierville. After his death, Oscar's widow found many debts and had to sell most of the property. Seyersted notes that she supported her family on the profits from two small plantations she retained, as well as from some real estate her mother left her.[8] It was shortly after the traumatic deaths of these two people closest to her that Kate Chopin began to write. She never remarried, and as single parent of a large family probably saw publication as a way of supplementing her meager income. Social and economic independence was something she understood and valued highly, and the importance of which was underlined by her experiences of family deaths. Furthermore, the new role of women in her home city must have emphasized this. Women of her class were taking an active, energetic part in transforming St. Louis' political, economic, and social life. Like Grace King, Chopin was involved in the life of a city at a time of its ascendancy, and at a time when women were taking a meaningful part in public affairs.

7. Gary B. Mills, *The Forgotten People: Cane River's Creoles of Color* (Baton Rouge, 1977); Seyersted, *Kate Chopin,* 45.

8. Seyersted, *Kate Chopin,* 205–206 n.6.

This must have helped develop both her confidence and her increasingly individual and unorthodox voice. The deep divisions in and often irreconcilable barriers to independent action for Chopin's women characters were not Chopin's own. She had become, even by the time of her first publications, a stronger and more autonomous being than any of the women she portrayed in her fiction; unlike many of them, she was not alone.

Like Grace King, Kate Chopin was in a cosmopolitan city at a time of considerable intellectual activity. Most critics emphasize her isolation from other writers and especially from the mainstream of American literary culture in northeastern cities; however, as Per Seyersted points out, the St. Louis to which she returned in 1883 was a lively cultural center. It was the home of the Philosophical Society, founded in 1866, the St. Louis Movement, and its Hegelian *Journal of Speculative Philosophy,* for which William James and John Dewey wrote. Following these initiatives, in the 1880s younger intellectuals interested in post-Darwinian scientific and naturalist texts—writers, editors, and critics such as William Schuyler, Alexander DeMenil and Sue V. Moore, W. M. Reedy, and Chopin's friend Dr. Frederick Kolbenheyer—kept the city's cultural life alive. Kate Chopin herself was described by one of her journalist friends as having come "closer to maintaining a salon than any woman that has ever lived in St. Louis," and like Grace King in New Orleans she was renowned for the welcome she gave to residents and visitors to the city on her "Thursdays." In 1898 the St. Louis *Star-Times* named her as one of the four leaders of the city's "working literary colony."[9] Also like King, she was briefly involved in a women's club that was set up by forty St. Louis women (including T. S. Eliot's mother) for the welfare and education of women. Seyersted does not list feminist topics among the subjects they discussed at their biweekly meetings (though he records that Chopin contributed a paper herself on one occasion), but he notes that they campaigned on behalf of poor and unemployed women. Although Chopin found the women's campaigning zeal and intellectual earnestness distasteful, she must have been encouraged to value her own writing by the very existence and seriousness of such a group.

Charlotte Eliot, the main force behind the club, probably provided the kind of example to Kate Chopin that Julia Ward and Maud Howe did for Grace King. Charlotte Champe Stearns was an intellectual New Englander who married Henry Ware Eliot, the first of an intellectually distinguished establishment New England Unitarian family to go into business. This marriage produced seven children, the last of whom was the poet Thomas Stearns Eliot, whose writing was early encouraged by his

9. *Ibid.,* 63.

mother—herself a prolific poet who achieved a minor literary reputation. But most of her energies went into her reform activities in the areas of education and legal safeguards for young people; she helped establish the Missouri juvenile court system. Her establishment of the Wednesday Club and her strong sense of reformist zeal were far more in tune with New England reform societies and women's clubs than with southern women's organizations. Not surprisingly, therefore, they were anathema to the creole Kate Chopin, whose upbringing and education within a Catholic French, then Louisiana-French family had instilled in her a horror of women's participation in social reform and public life. There seem to have been few women in Chopin's literary group, and the preciosity she noted among the women of the Wednesday Club probably served to encourage the ironic, detached view she expressed in her fiction and nonfiction writing towards women's rights questions.

Apart from intellectual women who stimulated and sharpened Chopin's ideas, there were other figures who influenced her writing, taking the place that northern editors occupied in the lives of many of her contemporaries. Besides the writers and editors who were part of her salon life, a great friend of Chopin's was a local doctor who had been her obstetrician even when she lived in Louisiana. Her biographers emphasize the importance of Dr. Frederick Kolbenheyer both throughout Chopin's married life (when she made frequent trips to St. Louis) and after her husband's death. She named one of her sons after him, and when she resumed living in St. Louis he became (in Rankin's cautious words) "a cordially accepted intimate friend, almost an ardent admirer of Kate Chopin."[10] During his constant visits to her home he read her the letters she had written him from Cloutierville and Grand Isle, and urged her to write for publication.

Dr. Kolbenheyer was a major figure in St. Louis' intellectual life. As a radical republican agnostic, he had been forced to leave his native Austria. He settled in St. Louis in 1870, where he engaged in medical practice and became interested in progressive philosophy. He undoubtedly encouraged Chopin's philosophical skepticism and rejection of the Catholic faith after her mother's death. He also encouraged her to read the works of Darwin, Huxley, and Spencer, and contemporary European and American writers such as Zola, Whitman, and Swinburne. Although there is insufficient evidence to prove that the two were lovers, they clearly had a close and profound friendship that gave Chopin the support and confidence to begin to write. As with Charles Dudley Warner for Grace King and Ruth McEnery Stuart, and Longfellow for Sherwood Bonner, Kolbenheyer demonstrates the importance to a southern woman writer of a male mentor who

10. Rankin, *Kate Chopin*, 89.

could reassure her that her status as woman and sexual being would not be threatened by writing seriously for payment. But he was a more critical mentor than Warner or Longfellow; radical and unconventional himself, Kolbenheyer was qualified to make Chopin see Genteel Tradition values and strictures in perspective, and to encourage her to defy them.

After some early rejections and a few stories and sketches published in St. Louis journals, Chopin achieved recognition from national editors and then placed her work regularly with major eastern magazines. She achieved critical success in the 1890s through her Local Color fiction, a success that was obliterated by the scandal of *The Awakening* (ironically, the only work for which she is celebrated today). The national construction of Louisiana as mythic and romantic site had been well established by the time she came to national attention; Chopin was thus shrewd to follow Kolbenheyer's advice to write fiction that drew on her knowledge of the state. From the beginning of her literary career, she was identified unequivocally as a *southern* writer and—though her essays reveal her impatience at being identified as part of the Local Color "school"—she continued to exploit (and romanticize) Louisiana settings and characters. The whimsical *Bayou Folk* was her own choice of title for the first collection of stories. Both her published novels are set firmly in Louisiana and refer to specific historical events and local legends as well as topographical detail to enhance atmosphere and create an appropriate medium for her themes. Chopin clearly wished to be regarded as a national writer, and her best stories and *The Awakening* escape the narrow provincialism associated with some Local Color fiction. Nonetheless, the regional emphasis and descriptive strengths are unmistakable and must be confronted critically rather than brushed aside in favor of the author's "universal" qualities. In discussing her fiction, I will examine the nature of Chopin's special relationship with her adopted state. Apparently more ethereal and remote than Grace King's, and certainly evoked more in terms of myth, symbol, and ambience, Chopin's fictional Louisiana embodied many of the political and social complexities and ambivalences of her own class, race, and gender positions.

Perhaps because she never became the protégée of a northern editor committed to protecting his provincial "genteel" reader, and because she could rely on the advice of her cosmopolitan intellectual friends in St. Louis, Chopin did not completely succumb to the values and censorship of Genteel Tradition letters. Gradually, she moved away from initial deferences toward northeastern editors to an indifference to and defiance of critical values she came to despise. As with other contemporary writers, there were conflicts between her ambition to be recognized in the North and her desire to write in the way she chose. And like others in the 1880s and 1890s, she came under the influence of powerful editors such as Richard Watson Gilder, who rejected some of her stories and insisted on changes in others. He objected particularly to her heroines, as her correspondence with him suggests: of a revised version of "A No-Account Creole," she wrote, "I hope I have succeeded in making the girl's character clearer. I have tried to convey the impression of sweetness and strength, keen sense of right, and physical charm beside." It is clear that she had to take notice of editors' criticisms if she wanted to become commercially successful, and so she capitulated to some genteel pressures. It is known that she destroyed at least one story and one novel the subject matter of which editors condemned, and she selected stories for her third collection (which was never published) by excluding those with strong, independent female protagonists. And she was grateful for and responded positively to editors' critical comments. In 1894, at the peak of her national success, she had good reason to feel pleased with the literary establishment that was publishing and commissioning her work. Responding to Hamlin Garland's condemnation of the East as a literary center (in *Crumbling Idols*), she claimed, "There can no good come of abusing Boston and New York. On the contrary, as 'literary centers' they have rendered incalculable service to the reading world by bringing to light whatever there has been produced of force and originality in the West and South since the war."[11]

Later in her career, when conflicts with northeastern editors became more frequent as her subject matter became more dangerous, Chopin came to sympathize with Garland's position. She learned early what the limitations of genteel editors were and paid for private publication of her first novel *At Fault,* realizing that its theme (divorce) and treatment were too strong for any national publishing house. She was also happy to send her work to unorthodox journals with a small circulation, like *Yellow Book* and the *Chap-Book,* and willingly accepted *The Awakening*'s publication by the avant-garde Herbert S. Stone. In an essay written in 1897, she related an anecdote that revealed her cynicism about the relationships involved in publishing fiction. She sent a story to a "prominent New York editor" who returned it saying that the public was "getting very tired of that sort of thing." She then sent it to a prominent Boston editor who welcomed it as

11. She went to Boston only once, on the advice of friends. As Rankin says, "the atmosphere was supposed to be literary. She went, and after three days fled home to St. Louis." Rankin, *Kate Chopin,* 31; Kate Chopin to Richard Watson Gilder, July 12, 1891, quoted in *KCM,* 106. She wrote a second novel rather than another collection of stories; and she adopted briefly a pseudonym, "La Tour." Kate Chopin, St. Louis *Life,* October 6, 1894, in *CW,* 694.

certain to delight his readers. She also relates how she did the same thing in reverse—with the Boston editor refusing a story that the New York editor called "clever and excellent." Her final comment is, "I wonder if the editor, the writer, and the public are ever at one."[12]

It is interesting to note her extreme disgust at the attention focused on Thomas Hardy's *Jude the Obscure* after it had been critically condemned for its "immorality." Chopin herself disliked the book, calling it "detestably bad . . . unpardonably dull; and immoral, chiefly because it is not true," and claimed that for young people seeking forbidden texts in libraries, "books which are withheld from their perusal are usually not worth reading."[13] Chopin's uncharacteristically irritable and unironic response to the case of *Jude* suggests her sensitivity over the issue of writing about sexuality and the Woman Question. While angry that what she considered a poor work had become a *succès de scandale,* she must have been alerted to the dangers of creating a female protagonist who defied orthodox codes of female sexual behavior. Her comments are particularly ironic to a modern reader who is aware that only two years after she wrote this, Chopin's own novel *The Awakening* would be banned from the St. Louis circulating library. Her response to Hardy's censure also reveals a deep ambivalence to contemporary morality and to her desire for literary success on her own terms rather than those of the Genteel Tradition.

Per Seyersted argues that Chopin was never a critic of the social values of the Gilded Age, but I believe the truth is more complex. *The Awakening,* far from being a startling achievement at the conclusion of an orthodox career, was the culmination of many of Chopin's less ambitious attempts to push at the limits of hegemonic northeastern publication traditions and demands. It is sometimes suggested that Chopin was naïve or simply foolish to create the kinds of heroines she did and to treat the sort of themes she repeated. But I suspect that she learned early how far it was possible to go and that her impatience with northeastern American puritanism, opposed as it was to her own favored European frankness and literary iconoclasm, led her to challenge it repeatedly in its most vulnerable area— namely, female sexuality. And her challenge to the northern puritan literary version of female adultery, which defined it as a sin to be expiated (as in *The Scarlet Letter*), gave her a certain mischievous pleasure. This is clear in her sardonic "apology" for *The Awakening,* published in response to the deluge of hostile criticism following the book's publication: "Having a group of people at my disposal, I thought it might be entertaining (to myself) to throw them together and see what would happen. I never

12. Kate Chopin, St. Louis *Criterion,* March 27, 1897, in *CW,* 717–18.
13. Kate Chopin, St. Louis *Criterion,* March 13, 1897, in *CW,* 714, 715.

dreamed of Mrs. Pontellier making such a mess of things and working out her own damnation as she did. If I had had the slightest intimation of such a thing I would have excluded her from the company."[14]

A friend of Chopin's, Anna Moss, acknowledged the difficulty that the reading public must have had with the writer's refusal to preach. She deplored "the cant, the pretence, the smotherings of the human heart that disfigure that . . . great and grand factor in our civilization—puritanism." As Chopin was to discover to her cost, St. Louis newspaper editors were happy to publish Maupassant and other European writers, but found Edna Pontellier too hot to handle; this heroine was, after all, an *American woman*. As the author's friend W. M. Reedy, editor of the St. Louis *Mirror,* wrote of the American Purity Alliance's demand for a single standard relating to free love, "the woman who is polyandric commits a sin against Nature . . . the man who is polygamic does not." As late as 1940, an American critic condemned *The Awakening* for being too "continental."[15]

Even more than Grace King or Ruth McEnery Stuart, Kate Chopin had considerable ambivalence toward the Woman Question, women's rights activities, and women's clubs. She dissociated herself in essays and interviews more thoroughly than they from feminist struggles and other women writers. But her family and recent male critics have taken these public statements and read her work too literally. Her son Felix said categorically that she "was not interested in the woman's suffrage movement," and Per Seyersted agreed with this. He saw only *The Awakening* as embodying "a fundamental female protest," while in general he regarded her as "a woman author who could write on the two sexes with a large degree of detachment and objectivity." Feminist critics have revised this view by offering different readings of her work, discovering a certain amount of feminist irony in her essays and stories. And as Anne Goodwyn Jones says, Chopin understood the public definition and expectations of a female artist and "was fully conscious of the implicit contradictions between lady and artist and made the best of them, largely through irony." Furthermore, Chopin went to considerable lengths to dissociate herself from the special category of "lady writer." Since much of her fiction was centrally concerned with sexuality and the problems of gender definition, it is not surprising that she found the sexual and critical double standards of her time particularly irksome. Furthermore, because (unlike King and Stuart)

14. Kate Chopin, *Book News,* XVII (1899), 612, quoted in *KCM,* 137.

15. Anna L. Moss to Kate Chopin, June 25, 1899, quoted in *KCM,* 138; W. M. Reedy, St. Louis *Mirror,* June 11, 1896, p. 7; A. H. Quinn, *History of the American Novel,* quoted in *KCM,* 176.

she had been raised a Catholic and, having abandoned her faith, was at the center of a liberal intellectual group, she was especially aware of the contradictory expectations made of her as a woman writer writing mainly about women.[16]

Kate Chopin went against the contemporary image of a committed woman writer in St. Louis. The journalist Sue Moore described her somewhat ambiguously as "the exact opposite of the typical blue stocking. She has no literary affectations; has no 'fads' or 'serious purpose' in life." Chopin herself apparently enjoyed fostering this image, perhaps recognizing the freedom it gave her to experiment in her work without being identified immediately with the much-maligned excesses of feminist campaigns. In an essay that describes the kinds of question journalists posed to her about writing, she suggests that she writes anything that comes into her head, sitting casually in a chair, when there is no task more appealing. Saying that for material she is "completely at the mercy of unconscious selection," she thus reinforces a romantic notion of the artist that obfuscates gender considerations. But she expresses impatience, too, at those "questions which some newspaper editors will put to a defenseless woman under the guise of flattery," and in answering such questions claims "the victim cannot take herself too seriously." Ironic though this is meant to be, the words *defenseless* and *victim* perhaps suggest a deeper sense of grievance at the power and prejudice of male critics.[17]

Chopin's many contacts with feminist ideas meant that she must have been aware of the impossibility of taking the detached view of the sexes that Seyersted and others have claimed for her. Like Grace King, at a formative stage in her life she had met a northern suffragist who considerably impressed her: while on her honeymoon journey, she met and described in her diary Victoria Claflin (later Woodhull), who urged her to use her brains and not sink into the "useless degrading life of most married ladies."[18] Apart from her many independently minded women relatives and friends, her literary club associates in St. Louis undoubtedly discussed women's rights and suffrage in a decade in which some of the liveliest controversies and campaigns were taking place in the South as well as the Northeast. Although she denounced *"précieuse"* women, Chopin admired independent, active women. She was fairly typical of many women (es-

16. Felix Chopin, "Statement on Kate Chopin," January 19, 1949, quoted in *KCM*, 167; Seyersted, *Kate Chopin*, 169; Jones, *Tomorrow Is Another Day*, 146.

17. Sue V. Moore, St. Louis *Life*, June 9, 1894, p. 12, quoted in *KCM*, 114; Kate Chopin, "On Certain Brisk, Bright Days," St. Louis *Post-Dispatch*, November 26, 1899, in *CW*, 721–23.

18. Kate Chopin, "Common Place Book, 1867–1870," June 13, 1870, quoted in *KCM*, 69.

pecially those outside northeastern intellectual circles) who tacitly believed in women's rights but for family and/or career reasons distanced themselves from those public campaigning elements of the 1890s women's movement. But her work indicates an intense personal interest in and engagement with women's issues. Two of her earliest stories ("Wiser than a God" and "A Point at Issue") deal directly with women's rights questions, and much of the fiction is concerned with the impact on individual women—of different classes and races—of feminist ideas about free love, girls' education, courtship patterns, marriage relationships, and celibacy.

Earlier I discussed briefly the importance of Chopin's relationship to Catholicism—a crucial element in her upbringing and in the lives of women relatives and friends, but a faith that she abandoned soon after her husband's and mother's deaths. Catholicism provided a good deal of material and motifs for Chopin's critique of women's lives, especially since the fiction repeatedly demonstrates the repressive and/or dangerous nature of that faith for women's sexuality and thus full human potential. And at crucial points in her writings the specter of her friend Kitty recurs as a reminder and warning of other possibilities of female passional life. On honeymoon, then as a widow, and finally as a writer disgraced for her fictional representation of female sexual feelings, Chopin wrote fondly of her friend—though in her 1894 diary she expressed a clear repugnance to Kitty's life choice. She implicitly recognized a sensual parallel between her own and Kitty's experiences by referring to the nun's "lover who lavishes all his previous gifts upon [her] in the darkness," and her own "lovers who were not divine." But she records her response to a traveling companion who asked if she yearned for the nun's "vocation and happy life": seeing a child with a dog, she says, "I would rather be that dog."[19]

Like other nineteenth-century women writers from Madame de Staël and George Sand to Charlotte Brontë and Grace King, Chopin saw the convent both as a site of emotional intensity and also as a kind of death—certainly a retreat from adult female sexual life. She uses the convent theme overtly or suggestively in much of her work, and also in two of her most unorthodox short stories, "Lilacs" and "Two Portraits"—the latter of which was so unpalatable to 1890s editors that it was never published in her lifetime and was even rejected by the avant-garde magazines *Yellow Book* and the *Chap-Book*. These two stories, written within a year of each other, are interesting examples of Chopin's fictional use of the dialectical relationship between the convent and society, the nun and the wanton,

19. Kate Chopin, "Common Place Book, 1867–1870," August 24, 1870, quoted in *KCM*, 85; "Impressions," May 22, 1894, quoted in *KCM*, 92; (poem) "To the Friend of My Youth: To Kitty" (probably) August 24, 1900, in *CW*, 735.

sublimated and sated sexual desire. And in each story, with its echoes of de Staël's *Corinne* and Sand's *Lélia*, Chopin emphasizes the differences and suggests the similarities between the women: for both, the central problem is the nature of desire and the impossibility of fulfillment.[20]

In the more autobiographical "Lilacs," the widow Adrienne (like Corinne) annually visits a convent for spiritual rest and refreshment. Unlike Corinne, she is dissolute and selfish, and each year she arrives bearing lilac blossoms, to share the room and temporarily monopolize the company of Sister Agathe. One year she is barred entry, her lilacs cast out of the convent while Agathe weeps within. The story thus underlines the irreconcilable differences between the two opposing social constructions of femininity and female erotic feeling, while allowing the images of the weeping nun and scattered lilac blossoms to suggest a more diffuse and uncontainable notion of desire.[21]

In "Two Portraits," this theme becomes more explicit and thus more challenging (and so unpublishable): in this story, wanton and nun are the possible fates of the *same* woman. Each "portrait" begins with an identical paragraph emphasizing Alberta's sensuality: ripe for a rich future, she has "mysterious eyes and love looked out of them." Both Albertas have been constructed through adult female influences at vulnerable ages. The "wanton" is alternately indulged and abused by a surrogate mother who allows her to be sexually handled by men and finally leaves her to be taken into prostitution; while the "nun" is taken in hand by "a very holy woman" who teaches her "that the soul must be made perfect and the flesh subdued," and thus impels her toward the convent. The wanton Alberta learns the arts of love and of using men through beauty and wiles, but is capricious and insatiable; at the same time men must beware of her since she "has added much wine to her wantonness [so] she is apt to be vixenish; and she carries a knife." On the other hand, the nun has found such "oblivious ecstacy" and "holy passion" in God that she sees visions that make her "swoon in rapture" so often that "it is being talked about a little in whispers."[22] More explicitly than elsewhere, this story links eros and thanatos, desire and its containment.

This dialectical pattern recurs in Chopin's fiction, often around ques-

20. Kate Chopin, "Lilacs," written May 14–16, 1894, published in New Orleans *Times-Democrat*, December 20, 1896; "Two Portraits," written August 4, 1895, published in Rankin, *Kate Chopin*, 240–44.

21. Kate Chopin uses lilac in the way Whitman does, to suggest sexual desire and eroticism.

22. Kate Chopin, "Two Portraits," in *CW*, 462–66. This heretical passage is strongly reminiscent of Gustave Flaubert's description of Emma Bovary's sensual delight in her last rites—significantly one of the passages that were condemned at the book's trial.

tions of Catholic marriage and the threats posed to its sanctity by adultery and divorce. In several short stories and both the novels, there are struggles between "the living spirit" of desire and "the dead letter" of the Catholic laws governing personal conduct. In Chopin's first novel, *At Fault*, the emptily pious observances of a young Catholic girl are articulated to a black woman servant (like Grace King's Marcélite) whose skepticism exposes the sexual hypocrisy that underlies many of the Church's ritual practices. When the girl Lucilla solemnly tells Belindy that she is counting thousands of "acts" in order to win twenty-five years' indulgence, the black woman says she had assumed Lucilla was "studyin' 'bout dat beau you lef' yonda to Sent Lous," and she scorns the girl's claim that she wishes to enter a convent. Since the girl gives no convincing replies to Belindy's penetrating questions, the servant dismisses her observances easily and comments that Lucilla's mother is "all dress up fittin' to kill. Don' 'pear like she studyin' 'bout ax." There is of course considerable irony in this, since a modern reader is uncomfortably aware that Belindy is a familiar literary type of sensual, phlegmatic black woman—but she shares with Marcélite a wry perceptiveness about the way sanctified sublimated desire is used by the Catholic Church as a means of social control over sexually vulnerable white young women.[23] In *The Awakening,* which challenges sexual taboos most radically, these conflicts again center round Catholic sexual codes: the indissolubility of marriage is used by the creole community as both a constraint on sexual freedom (especially for women) and also as license for ritual sexual games. These must be played according to unspoken rules, the breaking of which inevitably signals ostracism and (in the case of Edna) ultimately death.

Although Chopin's works and personal writings point to a considerable critical engagement in questions of gender and the position of women, they indicate no such involvement in the problems of race and southern blacks. When one considers the various elements of Chopin's biography, it is perhaps not surprising that she shared with Grace King and Ruth McEnery Stuart a thoroughly orthodox southern line on race. The factors contributing to this have already been discussed: her southern half-creole and pro-Confederate family background; the presence of slaves in her home throughout childhood; her marriage to a planter's son who was a White League activist; and her making a permanent home in that very southern city St. Louis. Chopin's critics are inevitably uncomfortable with her racism and have evaded its full implications. For instance, her biographer Per Seyersted is surprised that Chopin rarely treats directly the subjects of

23. Kate Chopin, *At Fault,* in *CW,* 872, 841–42.

slavery, miscegenation, black integration, and education—and then only in a few early stories. He suggests (without offering evidence) that Chopin "disapproved of slavery" but argues that she was "not interested in society and issues, but in the individual and character, and whatever views she held on Southern problems she usually hid behind a serene objectivity."[24] The use of the word *hid* is significant; I think Seyersted comes closer to the truth when he says later that Chopin's attitudes on the subject "were well hidden." I would argue that Chopin's racism is a central element in her writing, and cannot be ignored or simply excused. As with King and Stuart, her inability or refusal to confront it created critical problems and severely limited her achievement.

There is clear evidence of Chopin's southern orthodox views on race. In 1894, when her collection *Bayou Folk* was published containing several stock portraits of (mainly comic) black figures, William Schuyler (a close friend of the author in St. Louis) wrote: "Her father's house was full of negro servants, and the soft creole French and patois and the quaint darkey dialect were more familiar to the growing child than any other form of speech. She also knew the faithful love of her negro 'mammy,' and saw the devotion of which the well-treated slaves were capable during the hard times of the war, when the men of the family were either dead or fighting in the ranks of the 'lost cause.'" Like Grace King, Kate Chopin clearly expressed herself to close and sympathetic friends in terms of an affectionate nostalgia for the intimate black/white relations of childhood. Three years later, she wrote an essay in praise of Ruth McEnery Stuart, whose "whole-souled darkies" she admired. Revealing her admiration for the fiction of Page and Harris, she claims Stuart surpassed them "in the portrayal of that child-like exuberance which is so pronounced a feature of negro character, and which has furnished so much that is deliciously humorous and pathetic to our recent literature." For Chopin, as for Page and Stuart, literary black characters were best suited to provide peripheral amusement and pathos—the very elements of that Local Color from which Chopin always claimed she was eager to dissociate herself.[25]

When one examines the work for complex treatments of race, what emerges is a sentimental and anodyne view of Louisiana blacks and mulattoes, one that confirms their simplicity, fidelity to and love for whites, and constructs them as cheery figures acting out a pastoral subplot to the comic or tragic dramas of white communities. Like Stuart, Chopin provided stereotypical black characters and black dialect to satisfy that nationalist

24. Seyersted, *Kate Chopin*, 93, 96.
25. William Schuyler, *The Writer*, VII (1894), quoted in *KCM*, 115–16; Kate Chopin, St. Louis *Criterion*, February 27, 1897, quoted in *CW*, 711.

project of northern editors which she soon realized would provide a regular income. This meant that her short stories and sketches, set mainly in
Louisiana's Cane River area, had to ignore the historical realities of extreme poverty and racial violence, its anachronistic plantation economy,
and the tensions between poor whites and freedmen/women, and land-
owning whites and free mulattoes. And she used the dialect of her subordinate black figures as Page and Stuart had done, to patronize and amuse.
But from the beginning, her work featured black characters and motifs
around the themes of slavery and emancipation: her first piece of writing
used that very term—"Emancipation: A Life Fable"—about an animal
escaping nervously but joyfully from its cage. Anne Goodwyn Jones suggests that throughout the fiction, Chopin used blacks "as an objective
correlative for her feelings about oppression," and in terms of *female* oppression this seems to be the case, especially in the later works. As with
other southern women writers, black suffering, slavery, and oppression
are all linguistically and thematically appropriated for white women. The
complexity of blacks' own lived experience is sacrificed.[26]

Part of the reason for this may well have been Chopin's strong identification with European, rather than American, realist writing. Her fiction is
a response to European writings that focused on gender, rather than to
those works by Stowe, Cable, and Twain that foregrounded issues of race
in relation to American history. Unlike Grace King, she did not identify
herself as a southern cheerleader. Though using southern themes and
characters, her texts work in opposition to, or dialogue with, European
writers who shared her concern with questions of sexuality, bourgeois
marriage, and woman's role—primarily in relation to women of Chopin's
own race and class.

Kate Chopin was not alone in her enthusiasm for European models. Other
late nineteenth-century American women writers had rejected their
female forebears' sentimental Christian and/or didactic fiction in favor of
(predominantly male) European realism. Sarah Jewett made the ascetic,
amoral Flaubert her mentor, while Willa Cather respected realists such as
Tolstoy and Ibsen, as well as Flaubert whom she defended in 1896 against
charges of "uncleanness" and "immoral" subject matter.[27] Such models
were important for these realist women writers since they needed to dissociate themselves from that highly successful but critically devalued

26. Kate Chopin, "Emancipation" (n.d. but, according to Seyersted, late 1869 or early
1870), in *CW*, 37–38; Jones, *Tomorrow Is Another Day*, 151.

27. Quoted in Sharon O'Brien, "Sentiment, Local Color and the New Woman Writer:
Kate Chopin and Willa Cather," *Kate Chopin Newsletter*, II (1976–77), 20.

school of women's writing which preceded them. In the case of both the young Willa Cather and Kate Chopin, this led to a careful distancing of themselves from other American women writers, and in Cather's case from women's writing altogether, including Chopin's.

Cather declared that "the great masters of letters are men" or women who are "anything but women," which included "the great Georges, George Eliot and George Sand . . . Miss Bronte . . . and . . . Jane Austen." This reflects both that common deference by American writers to European models, and also a respect that women of Cather's generation clearly felt for those professional English women writers who had gained serious critical acclaim from a male literary establishment. Her stern rejection of women's writing and female subjects led her to pour contempt on women during her 1890s journalism period, and she condemned the "innate temperamental bias" that led a writer like Kate Chopin to deal with the "trite and sordid" theme of adulterous love.[28] Thus, Cather's own fear of sexuality, distrust of love between men and women, and revulsion against cultural definitions of femininity—compatible as all these were with Flaubert—led her to reject and condemn a work by a woman who created an American realist novel out of the subject matter of a woman's sexual life. Chopin used European male realists and both European and American women writers as inspiration for and confirmation of her own project as a writer who privileged the natural and sensual in fiction.

There is ample testimony from friends and relations that Kate Chopin regarded Guy de Maupassant as one of the greatest writers and influences upon her work. The St. Louis editor and publisher Alexander DeMenil said that Chopin regarded Maupassant's "artistic methods" as "superior to those of any other French author of late days," and Sue V. Moore, William Schuyler, and Chopin's son Felix also bear this out. Schuyler explains her fascination with the French school of Molière, Daudet, and Maupassant in terms of a reaction against Zola and Ibsen, both of whom she found took life too clumsily and seriously. The French critic Cyrille Arnavon said that (to a French reader) *The Awakening* suggested Maupassant or Boylesve, and of Chopin's story "Désirée's Baby" he says, "As is often the case in Maupassant, the tragic irony of fate makes us feel a kind of pity tinged with bitterness."[29]

Kate Chopin herself acknowledged her debt to Maupassant in the first draft of an article she submitted to *Atlantic Monthly* in 1896. She records how she accidentally discovered Maupassant's stories some "eight years

28. O'Brien, "Sentiment, Local Color and the New Woman Writer," 21, 22, 20.
29. Alexander DeMenil, in *KCM,* 157; Seyersted, *Kate Chopin,* 51; *KCM,* 119, 166; William Schuyler, in *KCM,* 119; Cyrille Arnavon, "Introduction to Kate Chopin, *Edna*" (Paris, 1953), quoted in *KCM,* 169, 174.

ago" (thus indicating how he influenced her early in her career) and that they were a revelation to one who had been "in the woods . . . groping around; looking for something big, satisfying, convincing." She accounts for their appeal to her thus: "Here was life, not fiction; for where were the plots, the old fashioned mechanism and stage trapping that in a vague, unthinking way I had fancied were essential to the art of story making. Here was a man who had escaped from tradition and authority, who had entered into himself and looked out upon life through his own being and with his own eyes; and who, in a direct and simple way, told us what he saw." She continues by saying how pleased she is to hear Maupassant has gone out of fashion, and expresses a proprietorial enthusiasm for him: "I even like to think that he appeals to me alone. . . . Someway I like to cherish the delusion that he has spoken to no one else so directly, so intimately as he does to me." The tone of the whole passage is excited, secretive, and possessive. The author is mentor and confidant to Chopin— he shows the way and, like an indulgent father or lover, gives her permission to be herself, to express the simple truth as she sees it, however shocking or unorthodox.[30]

Thus Maupassant had a special role in Chopin's life and work, and was an important reference point to be interrogated and challenged in her fiction. Seyersted has well documented the ways in which her subject matter, themes, tone, and patterns of imagery are drawn from her master; my interest in the Frenchman's influence lies more in the ways Chopin built on and departed from his narrative structure, characterization, and emphasis to develop an individual voice. What she valued in Maupassant was his ability to disregard the authority of tradition and to trust to the individual's perceptions. It seems clear that he taught her to have confidence in her inclination to do that, and in some ways to go further than he did—certainly to invite more censure. Although Seyersted is probably correct in asserting that "what Kate Chopin wanted was nothing less than to describe post-Darwinian man with the openness of the modern French writers," nonetheless she faced different problems from her mentors because of an attempt to create a post-Darwinian *woman,* especially in *The Awakening.* Edna Pontellier was bolder than anything Chopin's (male) French masters could have conceived, and more original than any of the female characters created by her American male contemporaries—naturalist Norris, veritist Garland, and realist Crane.[31]

I will discuss later the two works by Maupassant that bear directly on

30. Kate Chopin, "Confidences," in *CW,* 700–701.

31. Seyersted, *Kate Chopin,* 125–30, 90. Pamela Gaudé briefly addresses this in her discussion of two Maupassant stories and one story by Chopin in "Kate Chopin's 'The Storm': A Study of Maupassant's Influence," *Kate Chopin Newsletter,* I (1975), 1–6.

Chopin's novel *The Awakening*. But one can come close to understanding Maupassant's general importance to the writer through examining those of his stories she chose to translate.[32] It may be assumed that these eight were stories for which she felt a special affinity or wished to rewrite in her own terms. Certainly they all touch on themes and problems in Chopin's work, and their titles anticipate some of *her* abstract and cryptic titles (unusual among short story writers of the period). Moreover, close reading of Maupassant's originals throws a significant light on Chopin's selection. If this group of stories is examined together, and if it is borne in mind that they were translated over a period of two years midway through Chopin's career, at a time of considerable literary productivity, it becomes apparent that through the discipline and challenge of translation Chopin was rethinking her mentor in terms of her own work. Although the greater daring and experimentation of her work in the late 1890s may be attributed to other literary models and to the liberal journals of a "decadent" period, nonetheless these stories contain elements that she was to emulate: the choice of an isolated world-weary and misanthropic hero who revels in his own sensuality; who trusts in nature and distrusts human relationships, especially love; who experiences a sense of liberation through solitary walks and confidences in his writing (be it journal, letter, or scribble); and who is strongly drawn to death as a solution to the repetitive meaninglessness of life's pleasures.

With one exception ("Le Père Amable"), all the stories concern the reflections and/or obsessions of a male protagonist, usually expressed in his writings "discovered" by the narrator. The stories are similar in tone. All are strongly reminiscent of Poe, and a couple quote French symbolists influenced by Poe—Baudelaire and Rimbaud. The stories are informed by the agonies of isolation and a horror of the specters that haunt the imagination; they are bitter about women and love, and are suffused by a general misanthropy and more specific misogyny. The only positive descriptions are the sensations of the flesh, experienced alone in the natural world, especially by the sea. This freedom by the sea is echoed in Chopin's *The Awakening*, and Maupassant's "La Nuit" describes a faith in the natural world that undoubtedly spoke to Chopin:

> There is nothing that inspires the spirit to soar and the imagination to wander as being alone on the water, beneath the sky, on a warm night. . . . Intelligence, that unseeing, toiling Stranger, can know nothing, understand nothing, dis-

32. Seyersted lists the following eight, with dates of composition, in his bibliography, *CW:* "A Divorce Case," July 11, 1894; "Mad," September 4, 1894; "It?" February 4, 1895; "Solitude," March 5, 1895; "Night," March 8, 1895; "Suicide," December 18, 1895; "For Sale," October 26, 1896; "Father Amable," April 21, 1898.

cover nothing except through the senses. It is they alone that nurture it, and form the link between it and universal Nature.

Discussing the tentative way in which mid-nineteenth-century women writers and feminists began to "construct the idea of a libidinized female imagination and, through it, women's right to reason and desire," Cora Kaplan argues that they had to seek authority from *male* radical romantic manifestos. For Chopin, the poetry of Whitman and the romantic elements in Maupassant legitimized and suggested models for her own development.[33]

Chopin's response to Maupassant's stories is suggested in her firm identification of an isolated, disillusioned type with a female rather than male protagonist and in her intimation that, because of her reproductive role, a woman's relation to the natural world is more responsive and responsible than a man's, thus more joyous but potentially more tragic. She cannot evade nature through a cynical decadence nor through blame of *women* for failing to live up to the ideal. And since any experiments with sexual freedom have weightier resonance for Chopin's heroines than for Maupassant's weary men, the solutions of solitary meandering, adultery, and death take on very different meanings for both. In the Grace King chapter, I cited P. M. Stoneman's argument that it was socially and politically impossible to conceive of a woman as romantic solitary figure, unless she was irrevocably doomed.[34] It must have seemed provocative when Chopin chose to call her second novel *A Solitary Soul,* and kept this as the book's subtitle, bowing eventually to her publisher's preference for *The Awakening* (ironically a translation of Maupassant's story title, "Réveil"). Thus she indicated her intention to feminize Maupassant's solitary male figures, revising the sneering, detached bachelor or reluctantly married man. And by refusing to make men the central target of her women characters' despair, she could focus more directly on the institutions and social frameworks in which they were trapped. Producing Edna Pontellier, a female equivalent of the angst-ridden heroes of French fiction and poetry—a type she knew to be inadmissible in American women's fiction—Chopin interrogated her predecessors' misogyny and demonstrated the limitations of fashionable naturalism and decadence for women.

33. Guy de Maupassant, "La Nuit," *Oeuvres Complètes* (Paris, 1926), 15 and 23, translation by Mary Shepherd; Cora Kaplan, "Wild Nights: Pleasure/Sexuality/Feminism," in *Formations of Pleasure* (London, 1983), 27.

34. P. M. Stoneman, "The Brontës and Death: Alternatives to Revolution," in Barker *et al.* (eds.), *1848: The Sociology of Literature,* 79–96.

Kate Chopin's ability to reread and counter Maupassant depended to a certain extent on her response to other women writers she knew and admired. In order to develop as a writer, she relied on reading women's writing in her schooldays and throughout adult life. Kitty Garesché records the girls' childhood reading, which included popular male authors like Scott, Dickens, the Grimms, and Enlightenment and Romantic poets, but also many fashionable works by women such as Susan Warner's *The Wide Wide World* and *Queechy,* and Dinah Mulock's *John Halifax, Gentleman.* There are references in Chopin's diary to Madame de Staël's *Delphine* and *Corinne,* and she named her only daughter after George Sand's Lélia. Since from an early age she read novels and poetry in French, she undoubtedly read many works by French women as well as men, and it seems that in both life and art she appeared more European than American. A St. Louis journalist compared her "Thursdays" to the salons of French women such as Ninon d'Enclos and Eugénie de Staël, while another called her "the Lagerlof, the Audoux, the Olive Schreiner of America."[35]

She was apparently impatient with much fashionable sentimental writing by English women. William Schuyler wrote that "she calls them a lot of clever women gone wrong, and thinks that a well-directed course of scientific study might help to make clearer their vision; might, anyhow, bring them a little closer to Nature," though he adds that she respected Mrs. Humphrey Ward's "achievements" while deploring her reformist tendencies. Chopin had confided to her diary a couple of months earlier her view of "the hysterical morbid and false pictures of life" of certain English women. Earlier, in her diary of 1867–1870, Chopin quoted two pages of Dinah Mulock's *The Woman's Kingdom,* which argues that until women recognize their power and duties within the home, *"it is idle for them to chatter about their rights."* Chopin underlined these words, the last word twice. Although Per Seyersted reads this as a sign of agreement, I would suggest it indicates the author's early sense of irony and skeptical view of woman's role. It is perhaps significant that the only book from Kate Chopin's collection that has survived is by an aristocratic English woman, a witty satire on the subject of marriage and women's rights, Elizabeth von Arnim's *Elizabeth and Her German Garden*; I will discuss this later in relation to *The Awakening.*[36]

35. St. Louis *Republic,* September 11, 1910, in *KCM,* 152–53; Orrick Johns, St. Louis *Mirror,* July 20, 1911, in *KCM,* 155.

36. William Schuyler, "Kate Chopin," *The Writer,* VII (1894), 117, quoted in *KCM,* 119; Kate Chopin, "Impressions," May 12, 1894, in *KCM,* 91; Kate Chopin, "Common Place Book, 1867–1870," in *KCM,* 62.

It is possible to deduce a certain amount about Chopin's own project as a writer from her comments on the American women writers she admired. In 1894, after reading a manuscript quadroon story by a neighbor and noting in her diary its lack of originality, she recommended as models the two women with whom Chopin herself has frequently been compared: "I know of no one better than Miss Jewett to study for technique and nicety of construction. I don't mention Mary E. Wilkins for she is a great genius and genius is not to be studied." After commenting on the press notices of *Bayou Folk,* which she felt to be disappointingly unperceptive, she noted by analogy that Mary Wilkins' *Pembroke,* which she had found "the most profound, the most powerful piece of fiction of its kind that has ever come from the American press," had received critical notices full of "senseless abuse of the disagreeable characters which figure in the book. No feeling for the spirit of the work, the subtle genius which created it." The censure of *Pembroke* is something she may well have recalled when her own novel was condemned five years later. Such apparently unjust critical treatment must have endorsed Chopin's decision to exercise overt censorship of her own material and increased her sense of the importance of maintaining a healthy skepticism about the critical establishment's judgments.[37]

Finally, it is important to note Chopin's great admiration of Ruth McEnery Stuart, the only nationally known woman writer she mentions having met. Stuart is also the only writer (known to critics at present) to whom Chopin inscribed a copy of her *Bayou Folk* and about whom she published an article, so it is reasonable to assume a special attraction. Chopin's inscription is lyrical, almost passionate: "I heard the voice of a woman: it was like warm music; and her presence was like the sun's glow through a red pane . . . the voice of the woman lingered in my ears like a melting song, and her presence, like the warm red glow of the sun still infolded [*sic*] me." In the same month, the *Criterion* published her eulogistic article on Stuart in which she praised *Carlotta's Intended* for being "true to nature" and for sharing with her other work a "wholesome, human note." She describes Stuart's humor as "rich and plentiful, with nothing finical or feminine about it"—something in which "few of our women writers have equalled her." Effusively she comments on Stuart's "no sharp edges [to her soul]" and "no unsheathed prejudices." In short, Stuart struck Chopin as "a delightful womanly woman." She identified strongly with Stuart's fictional interpretation of the Louisiana black and her strict refusal to use fiction for overt political or social comment. For Chopin, Stuart's "womanliness" was related to her ability to represent

37. Kate Chopin, "Impressions," May 12, 1894, and June 7, 1894, in *KCM,* 90, 96.

rural life and people as uncomplicated, spontaneous, and happy—qualities associated in Chopin's mind with the "natural" from which she felt English women held themselves apart. Chopin's sympathy and admiration for Stuart in part derived from a similar romantic, idealized view of Louisiana and its people, which both writers were constructing at a physical and social distance. In her first novel, *At Fault,* Chopin appears to emulate Stuart in presenting both French Acadians and blacks in the Cane River area in terms of picturesque ideal fictional subjects. She also makes extensive and rather forced use of both dialects—possibly in an attempt to provide that "fidelity" and "humor" she found in Stuart's work.[38]

It is interesting that the two writers about whom she enthused most maintained a kind of detachment from their material, Maupassant with a tone of ironic distance and cynicism, Stuart in terms of a physical and emotional distance from the region and people featured in her fiction. Chopin valued spontaneity in life as well as art, and for her, Maupassant and Stuart were writers who trusted their own subjective responses and concurred with Chopin's view that great art should seem to be apolitical and uncontrived. In essays and interviews, Chopin had carefully defined herself as a paradigmatically romantic writer, who made no notes and was "completely at the mercy of unconscious selection." As her work developed, it seems that this description of her method of literary production (however untrue or exaggerated) indicates an intention to achieve that "unmediated and eroticised relation to art and life" that Cora Kaplan argued was necessary for some women to write out their feminism and sexuality together.[39]

THE FICTION

By choosing for herself the role of romantic writer, Chopin consistently repudiated any definition of writing that located and delimited literary production, and that identified her with the Local Color movement. In two essays published in 1894 (the year of her greatest success as a writer of Louisiana stories), she argued against the provincialism of the Western Association of Writers, and of the writer Hamlin Garland. She claimed that the world to which art should address itself was not northern Indiana (where most of the association members lived) but "human existence in its subtle, complex, true meaning, stripped of the veil with which ethical and

38. Kate Chopin, Inscription in *Bayou Folk,* February 3, 1897, quoted in *KCM,* 128; Kate Chopin, St. Louis *Criterion,* February 27, 1897, quoted in *CW,* 711–13.
39. Kate Chopin, St. Louis *Post-Dispatch,* November 26, 1899, quoted in *CW,* 722; Kaplan, "Wild Nights," 27.

conventional standards have draped it"; and she emphasized this further by disagreeing with Garland: "social problems, social environments, local color and the rest of it are not *of themselves* motives to insure the survival of a writer who employs them." Her own ambition to "survive" clearly made her anxious not to be dismissed along with the James Whitcomb Riley type of American regionalist writer—especially since she saw her mentors to be major European realists of a different stature.[40]

But despite her distaste for Local Color, Chopin used regional material repeatedly in her work, and I would suggest that her original contribution to southern women's letters results from a combination of specific regional motifs with feminist themes and preoccupations. Her ironic and resonant use of historical, topographical, and mythical Louisiana materials, worked through responses to European romantic and realist fictional writing, functions to interrogate both the southern ideology of womanhood and contradictory constructions of southern femininity in the 1890s.

Since Chopin's writing focused persistently on issues of gender and sexual definition, and the fiction increasingly exploded taboos around female sexuality and desire, it is perhaps not surprising that she turned to unfamiliar and exotic locations and subjects for fiction. The rural Cane River community of northwest Louisiana, the cosmopolitan city of New Orleans, and the fictional Italian and French settings of her European models all operate as symbolic sites of that elemental sensuality and erotic bliss that were unattainable for a woman writer living in the St. Louis of the 1890s. The Cane River area, which as I have argued Chopin knew to be in the process of social, racial, and economic shifts and transformations, is constructed in the fiction as a homogeneous organic region of close relationships between families, generations, races, classes, and sexes. A serial reading of the stories emphasizes unity at the expense of divisive complexity: characters recur and are used as minor figures in one story then protagonists in another; place names, social activities such as Acadian balls, even natural elements such as the weather (especially storms), all serve to create a strong atmosphere of harmonious rural tradition. This is adaptable to new and unpredictable economic, social, topographical, and climatic influences. The area is constructed nostalgically and ironically as a place of fixed social relations and ideologies; within that mythic space, characters are allowed limited autonomy and the possibilities of change or minor revolt. Altered social relations are hinted at through the existence of freed blacks, volatile sexual relations, and changing women's roles. But these

40. Kate Chopin, "The Western Association of Writers," *Critic*, July 7, 1894, in *CW*, 691; "'Crumbling Idols.' By Hamlin Garland," St. Louis *Life*, October 6, 1894, in *CW*, 693 (Chopin's italics).

remain peripheral and rarely destroy or impinge on the pastoral lightheart-edness and optimism that compound the region as a haven of well-being and plenty.

Typical of her tone are two stories about potential social friction in this tight community: the sketch "A Little Free-Mulatto," which records the social isolation and personal misery of Aurélia, a mixed-race girl, and the story "The Storm," which describes the adulterous relationship between two near neighbors. In the first, the problem is solved through Aurélia's father moving the family away from a plantation of whites and blacks to live within the free mulatto community on "L'Isle des Mulâtres"—thus ensuring that all her social contacts will now be with other mulattoes; while "The Storm" suggests that as a result of their illicit passion, the adulterous couple will now be more generous and loving toward their respective spouses and children. The community's racial and sexual codes, although ridden with flaws and contradictions, in most cases allow for compromise solutions. The only tragic fictional closures occur in the few examples where those codes are ruptured—in the case of miscegenation or a rejection of bourgeois marriage, both of which could irrevocably disrupt unified social relations. Unusual in Chopin's work (and significantly, they are two of her most powerful works) are "Désirée's Baby," about a dis-graced wife's suicide after bearing a black baby (which, as her husband discovers too late, comes from his own mixed blood), and *The Awakening*, in which the female protagonist swims to her death unable to live freely outside an orthodox family structure.[41]

However, her first published novel, *At Fault* (1890), does indicate Chopin's early capacity to experiment with regional material and conven-tional Local Color techniques. The novel's title gestures toward general moral concerns, and its central narrative problem concerns the ethical debate between a Louisiana Catholic creole widow and a St. Louis (defined here very firmly as northern) Unitarian divorcé, who love and wish to marry. In many ways the novel is typical of postbellum fiction, though it does interrogate that fiction through its subplot and its contrived happy ending.

Like most Louisiana women's fiction of the period, *At Fault* is a ro-mance with gothic motifs, a conspiracy subplot, and a melodramatic reso-lution. Its black and French Acadian characters are superstitious and sim-pleminded, speakers of a largely quaint and comic dialect. Northerners are seen as crass and grasping, while the plantation is on the whole harmo-nious, fiercely community-spirited, and unmaterialistic. Again like many

41. Kate Chopin, "A Little Free-Mulatto," *CW*, 202–203; "The Storm," *CW*, 592–96.

others, the novel even makes a direct reference to *Uncle Tom's Cabin*. Unlike most Louisiana women writers, Chopin does not depart from the conventional theme of other postbellum fiction, that of reconciliation between North and South symbolized by the marriage of a northern man and southern woman. The novel is clumsily organized, reading more like a series of the sketches in which Chopin specialized than a full-length novel. Thérèse Lafirme, like Kate Chopin the widow of a French creole plantation owner, has inherited a huge Cane River plantation that she manages single-handedly. The plantation once belonged to the notorious McFarlane who, as I discussed earlier, clearly echoes Robert McAlpin, both the model for Stowe's Simon Legree and confused in popular memory with Victor Chopin, Oscar's father. Like Kate Chopin for the few years she managed the Chopin plantation, Thérèse Lafirme is a shrewd and capable businesswoman, well liked, and admired for her moral rectitude. Madame Lafirme is loved by David Hosmer who, much against local wishes, has bought timber rights on her land and erected a sawmill. His sister Melicent, visiting from St. Louis and flirting with Thérèse's nephew, the hot-headed creole Grégoire, tells Thérèse of Hosmer's divorce. The widow assures him it is his Christian duty to remarry and save his alcoholic ex-wife Fanny; Hosmer returns to St. Louis and does so. Returning with his bride to Place-du-Bois, Hosmer is wretched with frustrated love for Thérèse and with his inability to prevent Fanny drinking. Going in search of alcohol and resting in a precariously placed cabin belonging to Thérèse's retired black servant, Fanny topples into the flooding river. Hosmer fails to save her and is injured. A year later, he and Thérèse are reunited and marry at Place-du-Bois. The ethical problem is solved both by Fanny's death and by Thérèse's acknowledgment that she was "at fault" in seeing only one truth, while Hosmer concludes that truth is relative, and the secret is to "learn to know the living spirit from the dead letter."[42] The novel contains two curious subplots that have little clear narrative function. Joçint, a surly half-black, half-Indian boy who loathes his work at the sawmill, burns it down and is shot dead by an angry Grégoire. Grégoire, rejected by Melicent, leaves the plantation on a drinking bout and is killed without motive in a bar.

In terms of regional concerns, the novel is revealing both in its overt themes and also its dissonant elements. It begins conventionally, like Ruth McEnery Stuart's fiction, presenting the Cane River community as a series of fascinating customs, characters, and dialects. The plantation with its "negro quarters . . . breaking with *picturesque* irregularity" (742, my

42. Kate Chopin, *At Fault* (1890), in *CW,* 872.

emphasis) is surveyed with "comfortable satisfaction" by its owner, Thérèse Lafirme, who looks from her back door at the classic "picture" of Negro servants, one slowly raking magnolia leaves, one asleep beneath a tree, one, "a piece of youthful ebony" (743), crossing to the poultry-yard. Throughout the novel, black servants and white creoles and Acadians are conceived as part of the Cane River community which, especially within the Place-du-Bois plantation, is one happy extended family. The blacks are simple, loyal, superstitious, and supportive to their white employer/ mistress; idealized antebellum social relations remain, and Joçint's dissatisfaction is the only indication of the racial tensions and conflicts that were a very real part of Cane River's daily life in the 1870s and '80s. Such autonomy as the blacks have is indicated by brief references to their potential untrustworthiness (because of that "savage instinct" that past generations have left "in dormant survival" [755]), and more pointedly through their sets of resistance to the northerners who visit Place-du-Bois and have little comprehension of their nature and ways. The St. Louis visitors' lack of ease with the blacks serves to underline the real understanding that Chopin (following other white southern writers) suggests white Louisianians have for "their" blacks, while the amusement or exasperation of the visitors speaks of the superior knowledge that the South claimed in its own defense of the racial status quo.

The fate of Marie Louise, Thérèse's old servant, is revealing in terms of Chopin's treatment of issues of race. Appearing halfway through a novel that has presented the plantation community in terms of respect and love between the races, Marie Louise is visited by Thérèse, who goes to her for the comfort she bestows so well. Her pet name ("*Grosse Tante*") speaks her familial status; she lights up and indeed cooks up at the sight of Thérèse, and there is "soft music" in her speech, which is "seemingly made for tenderness and endearment"; the only times she has hitherto left her riverside cabin were to "install herself" at her mistress' sickbed and to cook for special dinners (807). As in other postbellum fiction, she is presented in the most idealized terms, especially as a nurturer of white women. Herself scornful of "those lazy niggers" (808) employed by Thérèse, she massages her mistress' head with her "big soft hands," which almost transcend her subordinate racial identity—since they stroke "as gently as if [they] had been of the whitest and most delicate" (809). She is thus represented as akin to Thérèse, and akin to all white women, yet Chopin foregrounds her difference from, and exotic appeal to, white culture and sensibility. For instance, her dress and speech must be explained to the white noncreole reader: her purple garment is "known as a *volante* amongst Louisiana Creoles" (807), and her words of defiant refusal of Thérèse's offer to move her and/or her cabin are first quoted in black creole dialect, then translated into standard English.[43]

As with Grace King's black women characters, it is to white *women* that Marie Louise and her kind are unquestioningly loyal, a loyalty that is by no means always reciprocated. The drunken Fanny taking refuge in *Grosse Tante's* cabin finds an emotional and physical release with the black woman, who then colludes in a lie to her husband Hosmer. But while Fanny tries to escape the toppling cabin and Hosmer attempts a rescue, the only reference to the black woman is a simple sentence: "Of Marie Louise there was no sign" (867). And, as at the conclusion to Grace King's *Monsieur Motte,* the white woman whose closest and most loyal black servant and friend has disappeared makes no further reference to her existence. A year later, as Thérèse returns to Place-du-Bois after a long trip away, she recollects "that one terrible day of *Fanny's* death" (870, my emphasis). By the last chapter, all the blacks on Place-du-Bois have lapsed into silence and virtual invisibility, featured only as "a troublesome body of blacks" (870) who will now be controlled by the mistress' return, and as an anonymous crowd of spectators who are occupied in the "absorbing theme" of the marriage between Thérèse and David Hosmer, fittingly described as "a royal love" (873). Significantly, for the first time Thérèse shares that amused patronizing attitude to her servants that has hitherto characterized the St. Louis northerners (and by implication, northern readers). Marrying a northerner means that when David imitates the dialect Mandy normally uses to announce supper, Thérèse laughs with him at the girl's speech (at which she "retreat(s) from their laughter" [876]). By the novel's conclusion, the black characters have all retreated into quaint perspective, a background to frame the white marriage that restores social order and a racial harmony that depends on the speechlessness of the black community.

And what of the two murdered men—Joçint and Grégoire? Although in formal terms their deaths appear awkwardly integrated into the novel, in terms of the work's oblique references to the problematic nature of Local Color, both are highly significant. Joçint is of mixed blood (Negro and Indian), thus, as in much postbellum fiction, signaled as potentially disruptive. Indeed, the first reference to him describes his "open revolt" and "revolting youth," though these feelings are described as referring specifically to the "intrusive Industry" that brought the mill to Place-du-Bois, thus to that northern capitalism that had spoiled the peaceful woods (747).

43. "'*Non-non, Tite maîtresse, Marie Louise 'prè créver icite avé tous son butin, si faut'* (no, no, *Tite Maîtresse,* Marie Louise will die here with all her belongings if it must be)," *At Fault, CW,* 809.

The night he burns down the mill, Joçint is breaking codes both of the black and white communities—the black, since he not only ventures out on the one night, Halloween, when all Negroes stay home, furthermore to bite the white hand that feeds him; the white, in destroying valuable property. The boy's wounded body is dragged from the fire by his frail old father Morico, who then dies beside him. Joçint has betrayed his own father, but worse, the Place-du-Bois "family" of which he was a reluctant, revolting member. His unarmed shooting is described as "not altogether laudable . . . [yet] in a measure justified by the heinousness of his offence, and beyond dispute, a benefit to the community." The Negroes are "of one opinion" that he got what he deserved; Grégoire is seen as having meted out the Lord's justice, and "the occurrence pointed a moral which they were not likely to forget" (824). Thus insurrection is appropriately punished, and Grégoire's murder of an unarmed arsonist is accepted by the community without further question. It is only Melicent, with a St. Louis fastidiousness that she later comes to question, who cannot forgive Grégoire—though it is her cruel rejection that is seen to lead to his meaningless death. However, within the novel's moral context, Grégoire's own murder—essential as his deed was to restore social and racial order—can be read as just retribution. Shortly before he is shot, he has caused trouble in a local bar, urging blacks and whites to drink together (a normally taboo practice). His attempted rupture of racial codes is recognized by the Place-du-Bois blacks as likely to lead to further trouble, and thus his death is presaged and in a sense condoned. Nevertheless, compared with Joçint, the white Grégoire's challenge to racial and thus social order is seen as less threatening and forgiven more easily by the whole community. Unlike the unmourned Joçint and Morico, Grégoire is grieved over by all: masses are said, reminiscences exchanged, and letters written to relatives, while the black reaction is epitomized by the distraught Aunt Belindy.

At Fault, Chopin's only full-length extant novel about the Cane River community, gives an insight into her conflicting attitudes both to regional fiction and to the community in which, like Thérèse Lafirme, she had had a powerful socio-economic base. In many ways, the novel is highly ambitious, though far less flawlessly constructed than the later novel *The Awakening.* It draws on and alludes to contemporary issues of the Louisiana Chopin had left only a half-dozen years earlier, mediated through a somewhat autobiographical perspective on race and gender. In Local Color fiction, Thérèse Lafirme is an unconventional figure who represents contradictory meanings of the South and southern experience. Her moral self-righteousness is seen as both necessary (in order to protect her symbolically from northern industrial capitalist domination) and also excessively rigid, since it denies her the personal happiness to which as a white property-owning Catholic woman she is entitled. Thérèse represents those qualities that Chopin and others admired in the southern lady, and especially in the Louisiana French creole. Her sensuality and warmth distinguish her from other American women: indeed, she is the epitome of the Louisiana belle, "so wholesome, so fair and strong; so un-American" (801). As I will discuss later in relation to Adèle Ratignolle, Chopin focused on this romantic figure, seeing her as both socially restricted but emotionally potentially liberated and liberating. In *At Fault,* Thérèse's desires are fulfilled by external forces through conventional melodramatic narrative devices; unlike Edna Pontellier in the later novel, she is unable to speak for herself and act autonomously. But the seeds of Edna are there, and (as Per Seyersted points out) the amoral treatment of divorce suggests a daring and profoundly unconventional approach to sexual and social relations that *The Awakening* takes much further.[44]

What is significant in terms of the Local Color movement is the way this novel solves a white woman's dilemma and rewards love in a triumphal reconciliation of North and South, agnostic industrial and Catholic rural traditions. But this resolution can only be achieved through the elimination of those elements that threaten to disturb and destroy the hierarchical socio-economic structure of Place-du-Bois. The emphasis on its familial and community relationships mythifies the plantation as a haven of almost complete harmony—similar to those sites familiar to readers of the ante- and postbellum novel. Joçint's death is pronounced to be a moral lesson for blacks; Tante Louise's drowning goes unremarked. The white lovers marry, restore order, and ensure symbolic national peace and mutual understanding; consistent with her impatient rejection of parochial literature, Chopin refuses a restrictedly regional resolution.

As with the closure of *Monsieur Motte,* the interdependence of white and black prevails, so long as white interests are accepted as paramount and blacks embrace their own subordinate position. The novel's narrative organization compels a political reading consistent with Phanor Breazeale's version of the Natchitoches area's racial history and Oscar Chopin's White League affiliation. Nevertheless, in the unsatisfactorily integrated and too easily dismissed black insurrection and the three blacks' deaths, *At Fault* manages to suggest a different reading of that history—one that can in no way be integrated into a conventional southern romance.

At Fault appears to make conscious and unconscious reference to other Local Color writing and to the plantation and postbellum southern novel.

44. Seyersted, *Kate Chopin,* 93.

If one examines the nature of Chopin's regionalism, it is important to discuss the ways she mediated that romantic and exotic Other, the imaginary site of Louisiana, by comparison with other contemporary writers. Several Louisiana writers had already demonstrated their fascination with the various waters that are such a prominent feature in the topographical, historical, and legendary character of that state, especially the Mississippi River and the bayous of north and southwest Louisiana. *At Fault*'s climactic scene takes place in the Cane River, which features throughout the novel. The Gulf of Mexico is, however, the richest source for Gulf State writers, combining as it did so many romantic and dramatic elements of southern history: piracy, devastating hurricanes, the plantation and slave economy that was abruptly ended by the Civil War, and the vacation spots of wealthy creoles.

The Gulf waters were particularly associated with the legendary figure of Jean Lafitte, leader of a band of Louisiana privateer-pirates who preyed on mainly Spanish ships between 1810 and 1814, selling plunder in New Orleans and dividing up spoils on Grand Isle. Although there had been a death warrant on Lafitte's head, he became a temporary national hero during the Battle of New Orleans, when he helped repulse the British through superior knowledge of the network of Louisiana waterways. Alice Dunbar-Nelson records one of Lafitte's less savory dealings: he and his brother Pierre supplemented their piracy income by smuggling slaves into the territory through Barataria Bay; Governor Claiborne of Louisiana spared their lives because of this economically useful activity. Lafitte was a popular folk-hero, his activities an important part of the mythification of the Gulf.[45]

The small islands in the Gulf were subject to destruction or annihilation from the frequent storms and hurricanes. Writers were drawn to the tragic drama of l'Île Dernière, which was destroyed before the Civil War, and the peninsular Chênière Caminada and the small barrier island Grand Isle, which were both devastated in the hurricane of 1893. Before the hurricane, Caminada had been heavily settled by fishermen who lived in virtual isolation from other parts of the state. A beautiful island of live oak trees (as its name suggests), lush vegetation, and gardens before the hurricane, it lost most of its families, buildings, and vegetation to the storm: "The very ground . . . was torn and rent as though some gigantic ploughshare had passed capriciously over it, and the scene was one of heart-rending pa-

45. There is a large body of writing about Lafitte. Grace King discusses him in her Louisiana histories, and Lyle Saxon wrote his biography, *Lafitte the Pirate* (1930). The information about Lafitte on Grand Isle is from the Houma *Courier*, March 6, 1970; Dunbar-Nelson, "People of Color in Louisiana, Part II," 53.

thos . . . [for days after the storm] half-crazed survivors were picked up floating clinging to debris, burned black by the sun, their clothing in shreds, some naked."[46] Not until the 1930s did a seafood fishing and packing community begin to grow there again. The hurricane was a natural disaster that made national news; Kate Chopin read of it in the St. Louis press and made it the subject of a story and part of a novel.

But the islands of the Gulf were not only sites of pirateering, ravaging storms, and associated legends. Both Grand Isle and Chênière Caminada had been drained and cultivated by Spanish sugar-planters from the early nineteenth century; Grand Isle had also been covered by cotton plantations. Although fishing and orange-growing were more profitable on Caminada, Grand Isle was relatively productive in sugar and cotton, and the planters supplemented their income by building hotels for summer vacationers escaping New Orleans' heat and yellow fever outbreaks. Lafcadio Hearn describes in his novel *Chita* this shift in the island's economy: "Since the war the ocean reclaimed its own;—the cane-fields have degenerated into sandy plains, over which tramways wind to the smooth beach;—the plantation-residences have been converted into rustic hotels, and the negro-quarters remodelled into villages of cozy cottages for the reception of guests." Neither Hearn nor Kate Chopin spells out Grand Isle's past in political terms, but both suggest it: Hearn by referring to the ocean's "reclaiming its own" and his heavily naturalistic view of the malevolence of nature toward man's attempts to own the land; Chopin in *The Awakening* by making implicit links between the island's planter slave-owning history and the patriarchal, proprietorial creole community that enjoys its summer pleasures.[47]

Hearn and Chopin are the two writers who best captured the atmosphere of the Gulf in their novels. Anticipating them both, however, George W. Cable had learned a great deal about the history of southern Louisiana from his own reading and from his friend, the writer Sidonie de la Houssaye; he in turn passed on many stories to Hearn, a newcomer to the state. Indeed, Hearn aroused Cable's anger when he used in *Chita*—without acknowledgment—the story Cable had told him of l'Île Dernière's destruction. As Longfellow had already done for the bayou country in "Evangeline," so Hearn captured for many readers a sense of the magic

46. Mark Forrest, *Wasted by Wind and Water: A Historical and Pictorial Sketch of the Gulf Disaster,* quoted in Betsy Swanson, *Historic Jefferson Parish from Shore to Shore* (Gretna, La., 1975), 167.

47. Swanson, *Historic Jefferson Parish,* 160. Also, see Frederick Stielow, "Grand Isle, Louisiana, and the 'New' Leisure, 1866–1893," *Louisiana History,* XXIII (1982), 239–57; Lafcadio Hearn, *Chita: A Memory of Last Island* (New York, 1889), 11.

and horror of a Gulf that contained islands and people of considerable beauty and harmony, and also hosted hurricanes, storms, and floods of vast power. His description of Grand Isle anticipates Chopin's own in *The Awakening*: "with its imposing groves of oak, its golden wealth of orange-trees, its odorous lanes of oleander, its broad grazing-meadows yellow-starred with wild camomile, Grande [*sic*] Isle remains the prettiest island of the Gulf."[48]

Two other southern women writers had published stories about the Gulf before Kate Chopin: Hearn may have known Sherwood Bonner's account of the destruction of l'Île Dernière, "Two Storms" (1883); while Grace King's "At Chênière Caminada" appeared in *Harper's* seven months before Kate Chopin's story "Tonie" (later given the same title as King's) came out in the *Times-Democrat*. Bonner's story uses the setting of Last Island just before the final hurricane as a site of sensuality, seduction, and betrayal, with a final passionate reconciliation between daughter and hitherto neglectful widowed father—confirming rightful patriarchal relations. King's story is of more immediate relevance to this discussion of Kate Chopin, since like hers it was published within a year of the destructive hurricane that hit both Caminada and Grand Isle. King follows Bonner and Hearn in referring to the Gulf's romantic associations—especially its "sea-folk . . . discoverers, adventurers, merchant-men, filibusters, buccaneers, privateers, pirates" at the name of which "the imagination . . . takes flight." Somewhat uncharacteristically, King constructs the peninsula as a harmonious community and makes the night of the storm an ironic farewell feast for her female protagonist, who is due to become a nun. King uses the hurricane itself as ironic comment on convent education and the Catholic asceticism and hypocrisy that much of her fiction satirizes.[49]

Chopin's story, however, is more characteristic of her general regionalist style. It has a lighthearted, sensual tone, and focuses more intimately than Bonner or King on the quality of daily life and the people of the peninsula. The story relates how Antoine Bocaze, a young fisherman, is enraptured by a sophisticated New Orleans woman, Claire Duvigne, who comes from Grand Isle to play organ at his church. Chopin's setting is a midsummer day, the atmosphere sensual and languorous. Chopin makes no reference to the hurricane and concentrates instead on the temporary

48. Hearn, *Chita*, 11–12.

49. Sherwood Bonner, "Two Storms," *Harper's*, LXII (April, 1881), 728–48; Grace King, "At Chênière Caminada," *Harper's*, LXXXVIII (May, 1894), 871; Kate Chopin, "Tonie," New Orleans *Times-Democrat*, December 23, 1894, renamed "At Chênière Caminada" for *A Night in Acadie*.

madness and rejection of his community to which Tonie's pursuit of Claire leads him. He haunts her on Grand Isle and pursues her to New Orleans— a pursuit that is described as a natural extension of his sensual life attuned to the elements on Caminada: "He obeyed it [his love] without a struggle, as naturally as he would have obeyed the dictates of hunger and thirst. . . . From a cluster of orange trees a flock of doves ascended, and Tonie stopped to listen to the beating of their wings and follow their flight toward the water oaks whither he himself was moving."[50]

The playful coquetry of Claire, inspired both by the atmosphere of Grand Isle and her own self-dramatization, contrasts with the earnest purity of the young man's love. But it is the city woman who perishes, ironically of "a cold caught by standing in thin slippers, waiting for her carriage after the opera" (316), while Tonie feels liberated from her thrall. He returns to Caminada to his home and humble duties, cheerfully offer-ing to light the fire for his mother's bread in full assurance that Claire will know in the afterlife who loved her best. As with the Cane River stories, Chopin here confirms the Gulf islands as sites of conflict-free organic unity, and she celebrates the sense of community that she helped con-struct in a region already rich in romantic associations. She also uses Caminada—vulnerable to the elements—as a poignant reminder of the precariousness of all things, thus the ideal literary subject for nostalgic and lyrical pathos.

However, Chopin's evocation of Chênière Caminada in *The Awakening* is used for more subtle and complex effects. In order to set it in context, the novel needs to be briefly summarized. It is set on the pre-1893 Grand Isle, which was a vacation resort for wealthy creoles. Edna Pontellier begins to question her role as wife of a creole and, through other women and a young admirer Robert Lebrun, begins to act independently. Back in New Orleans, she rejects her role as society hostess and conscientious house-wife, and moves out of her husband's house. Installed in her own space, she paints, wanders the city, and takes a roué lover, Alcée Arobin. Robert returns and she tells him they can live and love together, regardless of her husband. He flees, frightened by her free spirit; she is chastened by her friend's agonizing childbirth; and so returns to Grand Isle where she swims to her death.

The novel contains several references to the legends associated with the Gulf, Grand Isle, and Caminada in particular. In chapter 13, Edna's trip to Chênière Caminada with Robert is associated with fairy tale, legend, and especially the illicit: Robert jokes with Edna about her "Gulf spirit" that

50. Chopin, "At Chênière Caminada," in *CW,* 312.

one day will lead her to the very island where pirate treasure is buried, and she replies with a sexually suggestive allegorical speech that makes him blush: "I'd give it all to you, the pirate gold and every bit of treasure we could dig up. I think you would know how to spend it. Pirate gold isn't a thing to be hoarded or utilized. It is something to squander and throw to the four winds, for the fun of seeing the golden specks fly."[51] The sharp-eyed Acadian girl Mariequita recognizes the two for what they do not yet know they are; she immediately asks Robert if Edna is his sweetheart. When they reach the peninsula, Edna is overcome with drowsiness and is taken to rest in Madame Antoine's simple cottage (also the home of Tonie—a reference perhaps to the earlier story) where, as in a fairy tale, she takes off her clothes, lets down her hair, and sleeps a deep, dreamless sleep that is seen as a transitional, transformational experience: " 'How many years have I slept? . . . The whole island seems changed,' " to which Robert replies, " 'You have slept precisely one hundred years. I was left here to guard your slumbers.' " She is revived and changed so that her eyes are bright and her face glows, and she eats with a healthy animal appetite, "tearing it [a brown loaf] with her strong, white teeth" (38). As in many of Shakespeare's comedies, the book is full of characters sleeping and wak-ing, with the suggestion of active dream-work that can clarify and heighten desire. Like Shakespeare, Chopin uses this transitional scene to compound a sense of magic, to confuse reality and illusion, self-awareness and self-delusion. A growing awareness of the erotic self and of romantic love is also central to the scene. The chapter ends with the distinctions between categories blurred again, and the magic of the Gulf and its prom-ises held out to Edna are enhanced by Madame Antoine's storytelling: as the sun sets, she relates to the couple legends of the Gulf and the Bar-atarians—presumably mainly pirate stories, so that "Edna could hear the whispering voices of dead men and the click of muffled gold" (39).

This conclusion to the episode on Caminada is important in that it presages Edna's own death in the Gulf as well as ironically reminding the contemporary reader of the "dead men" who were to join those before them, after the hurricane. The pirate stories also suggest strongly the breaking of taboos on ownership of property--a vital consideration for Robert as potential adulterer and Edna as possible source of metaphorical gold and buried treasure, and maybe a strong reason why he leaves for Mexico the next day. The glamorous yet illicit nature of the pirates' activity also provides an ironic example to the two undeclared lovers, who arrive

51. Kate Chopin, *The Awakening,* ed. Margaret Culley (New York, 1976), 35–36. All subsequent references to the novel (in parenthesis) will be to this authoritative text.

back at Grand Isle to face the fretful worries about their lateness from the adults and the vengeful naughtiness of Edna's younger son in her absence. The last words she exchanges with Robert before they part for the night (and before he makes his decision to go to Mexico in order to seek treasure as a pirate on perhaps less treacherous ground) are of a heightened intensity, carrying as they still do the poetic feeling of Caminada: " 'Do you know we have been together the whole livelong day, Robert—since early this morning?' 'All but the hundred years when you were sleeping. Goodnight' " (40).[52]

The Gulf and its atmosphere are central to Edna's liberation, a fact that many critics have noted. But I would suggest that the Gulf is central to the book not simply because of all the (mainly literary) romantic and emotional associations of the sea, but also because the Gulf is the repository and graveyard of legend and dreams, and the entirely logical site of Edna's willing death. As I have discussed, the Gulf is a place rich with association for Louisianians. Sailing from New Orleans south toward the Baratarian Islands is used by Bonner, Cable, Hearn, King, and Chopin to suggest a shift from the mundane and real into a sphere of heightened existence, poetic intensity, and legendary richness. Chopin, following Hearn in *Chita,* shows that the transition by boat from the mainland to Grand Isle, and in Edna's case from Grand Isle to Chênière Caminada, exalts the spirit through escape from the brutal realities of city and thus social life. In Hearn's *Chita,* the doctor who experiences such exhilaration after leaving behind yellow fever-infested New Orleans is bringing the deadly fever with him and will be swept away in the hurricane of l'Île Dernière; but in Edna's case the freedom of the legendary Gulf is something she can only experience outside the world that defines her. She is in tune with, and as free as the Gulf, with none of Hearn's doctor's contamination from the city.

And the Gulf is not only a place of romantic legend, as both Hearn and Chopin demonstrate. Strongly influenced by the naturalists as they were, they saw the Gulf as destroyer and site of perils; Hearn makes the omnivorous hurricane the central action of his novel, while Chopin sets much of her novel on an island that she knew had been virtually destroyed by the 1893 hurricane. For Chopin, the irony is implicit, but I believe it informs the entire work (and would not have been lost on contemporary readers). The Grand Isle of the novel is already economically moribund; its plantation/slave economy has been destroyed by emancipation and the Civil

---

52. Chopin perhaps anticipates this connection in the first chapter when referring to Robert's intention to go to Mexico "where fortune awaited him," *The Awakening,* 6.

War, and it is now merely a resort. As Chopin's readers knew, it was shortly to be devastated and so the seemingly endless rituals of the creoles' summer vacations are about to be abruptly concluded.

Chopin knew from her married life and economic misfortunes with Oscar (like Pontellier, he was involved in the cotton business that was shortly to crash) that the creoles were an anachronistic social group in New Orleans. Their economic and social lives were resistant to the many changes that came during Reconstruction, and their old sense of aristocratic superiority and privilege became increasingly vulnerable. Cyrille Arnavon is right to say that the author "has succeeded in evoking a whole world which, now that the Anglo-Saxon influence has become predominant, is definitely a thing of the past," but not when he says "there are still a few lingering traces of something exotic and picturesque in the local customs to which Kate Chopin is sensitive, though she has no political motive in describing them."[53] Since the author's intention should be discounted in favor of the effect of Local Color themes and regional allusions, *The Awakening* may be read as a critique of obsolescent creole social and (especially) patriarchal attitudes. Jean Lafitte hoped he could outwit his victims and pirate forever in peace; the Grand Isle planters believed they could own their land and slaves in perpetuity; the creoles believed they could live each summer in Arcadia, endlessly and harmlessly flirting. The story of Edna Pontellier demonstrates vividly and ironically what the reader knew already of the Gulf's inhabitants: Jean Lafitte, according to legend a free-spirited, independent mythic pirate, was engaged in slave trafficking and took the pragmatic self-protective course of making peace with and helping the United States during the 1812 war against the British in order to protect his "business" interests; the Grand Isle and Caminada planters lost their rich land and slaves after the war; and the creoles lost their summer vacation island in 1893, as well as much of their status and social and economic power after Redemption, which favored Anglo-Saxon entrepreneurial newcomers. Adèle warns Robert to leave Edna alone because " 'she is not like us. She might make the unfortunate blunder of taking you seriously' " (21). And it is this seriousness, this ability on Edna's part to expose the anachronisms around her, that reveals the hypocrisies and ideological disjunctions in the taken-for-granted creole philosophy.

Although in many ways Chopin's regionalist stories are conventional in their treatment of race, community, and minor social conflicts, some of them do suggest radical or anarchic possibilities for *women*, which make

53. Arnavon, "Introduction to Kate Chopin," in *KCM*, 179–80.

for startling and ambiguous endings. Myra Stark has discussed the different uses made by male and female writers of the "epiphany" conclusion to
the short story. Arguing that for male writers the epiphany tends to be one
of freedom, illumination, and ecstasy, she claims that for women it is a
moment of insight into the condition of women that overwhelms and
defeats the characters. Thus she describes women's short fiction as "notes
from underground, letters from the prison house," riddled with "shock,
rage, despair, defeat." Stark's theory, typical as it is of the most deterministic readings of women's texts, does not hold true for Chopin. Her stories
are impregnated with metaphors of epiphany—awakening, discovery, the
breaking of light, spontaneous laughter, and sensual awareness. Many of
her stories conclude with a woman's exultation or sense of her own power,
however momentary: Mildred Orme in "A Shameful Affair" with her
frank admission of sexual desire that leaves the man blushing; 'Tite Reine
in "In Sabine" who escapes with another man from her oppressive
drunken husband, on the husband's horse; Mrs. Baroda, in "A Respectable
Woman," with its final enigmatic hint of her future adultery; finally, the
triumphant Calixta of "The Storm," who gives full vent to her sensuality
with another woman's husband, then welcomes her own husband and son
home with new carefree gaiety. Far from conforming to a grimly pessimistic model of women's writing, Chopin's work develops an increasingly euphoric, anarchic force that achieves its most powerful expression in *The Awakening*. But because of the constraints of Genteel
Tradition editors, Chopin's ambivalence about feminism, and the influence of European realism on her work, the fiction is consistently ambivalent about gender definition, and especially about the possibilities
available to women to challenge patriarchal values. Her most defiant text is
anticipated by several earlier stories, which may be considered briefly as
first drafts of parts of the novel. "A No-Account Creole" (1894) and
"Athénaïse" (1896) are significantly more timid and ambivalent precursors of *The Awakening*.[54]

"A No-Account Creole" prefigures the novel in its focus on the poly-
morphous, uncontrollable nature of sexual desire and its relationship with
the exotic and distant, rather than the known and familiar. It describes the
sexual awakening of a conventional Catholic Cane River girl who is appropriated by a young man from New Orleans, Wallace Offdean, whose
firm's capital has appropriated the plantation on which she lives. Visiting
New Orleans at Mardi Gras (significantly an Other Place and a festival of

54. Myra Stark, "No Transformation, No Ecstacy: Short Stories by Women," *Regionalism and the Female Imagination*, IV (1978), 4–7; Kate Chopin, "A No-Account Creole," *CW*,
80–103; "Athénaïse," *CW*, 426–54.

sexual license), Euphrasie is aroused by Offdean and then offers her "no-account Creole" fiancé Placide her first passionate kiss. The story's social and political subtext lies in the fact that her local fiancé is far less glamorous to the ex-convent girl than the man who indirectly owns the plantation, who comes from the city, and who has considerable fortune as well as geographical and social mobility. The story suggests perverse elements in sexual feeling and also points to economic changes that structure such feeling: the rural area's postbellum devastation, in conjunction with a shift from a traditional planter's economy after the war and emancipation, had increased the economic importance and attractions of the cities. Also, absentee landlordism was growing and breaking up traditional hier-archical, fixed patterns of family and social life. Euphrasie's rejection of an old pattern—for women—of long courtship through childhood and ado-lescence, followed by a move from the father's to the husband's house, in favor of the new confusion and ambiguity of free sexual expression and choice, is a result of the exposure of apparently closed, secure social groups to outside influences.

Euphrasie is a motherless child whose surrogate mother, the parish's Lady Bountiful, has raised and educated her and, indirectly, made her into the appealing creature her city admirer desires. Like the many motherless heroines that feminist critics have noted in nineteenth-century women's fiction, Euphrasie needs the *right kind* of love. When Placide, overhearing her weeping for Offdean, withdraws from their engagement, she realizes she has been saved from the "sin" of being untrue to her desires. But she remains the passive pawn of the two men, and the story concludes with her sitting in a traditionally female posture—silent, her head "bowed upon her arm" (102), tacitly assenting to her lover who kisses her hand and cheek before leaving to give her time to consider his proposal.

"Athénaïse"—a later story—anticipates *The Awakening* even more di-rectly, since it confronts the problems of the institution of marriage itself. Its interest lies in Athénaïse's resistance and repugnance to the very state of being married, and in its analogies (more explicit here than elsewhere in Chopin's work) between marriage and slavery. It is also significant as an early working out of the problems confronted in the later novel in its acknowledgment and reluctant acceptance of a biological determinist defi-nition of woman that does not include her as desiring subject. The story describes Athénaïse's escape from her husband's house, first to her parents' home then to New Orleans—on each occasion helped by her brother. At the New Orleans boarding house where she spends a month alone, desul-torily looking for a teaching post, she befriends Gouvernail, an intellec-tual, rather effete bachelor who serves as a welcome relief from her patriarchal husband and brother.[55] Learning finally that she is pregnant, she rushes home to her husband, to whom she responds for the first time with genuine passion.

Athénaïse's husband Cazeau is one of Chopin's least attractive male characters. He is a model patriarch, a mixture of Victorian melodramatic villain and cruel slave-owner: he is "severe looking," with hair like "the breast of a crow," and a sweep of mustache a tuft of which he twists; his eyes are "narrow and overshadowed," and he wears a spur (even in the house) that "jangled at every step" (426–27). The analogies with a slave-owner are legion: thinking of fetching Athénaïse back from her parents, he concludes that "he would find means to keep her at home hereafter" (428), and later he plays with the idea of "compelling" her to stay (the word is used three times in one sentence [438]); Athénaïse's father speaks admiringly of his son-in-law's "steady hand to guide . . . [her] disposition . . . a master hand, a strong will that compels obedience" (434). The analogy is spelled out most starkly after Cazeau has collected Athénaïse from her parents' home; riding back, they pass a solitary live oak tree, and he recalls an incident in his boyhood:

> He was . . . seated before his father on horse-back. They were proceeding slowly, and Black Gabe was moving on before them at a little dog-trot. Black Gabe had run away, and had been discovered back in the Gotrain swamp. They had halted beneath this big oak to enable the negro to take breath; for Cazeau's father was a kind and considerate master, and every one had agreed at the time that Black Gabe was a fool, a great idiot indeed, for wanting to run away from him. (433)

Montéclin, her brother, is the only figure not to see Athénaïse as "a great idiot indeed" for wanting to run away, and he understands her "revolt", though only from his own selfish perspective. Montéclin's incestuous, possessive behavior toward Athénaïse only intensifies her passivity and locks her more firmly into patriarchal power structures.

Athénaïse, like Euphrasie, is unable to take any responsibility for her own life—except to hand it back to the men who wish to control it. When she becomes pregnant, she happily and unreservedly chooses to be wife and mother, and insists that her brother meet her at the station so as to deliver her back to Cazeau. She is literally an object of exchange throughout the story. Subject to various kinds of patriarchal institution and relationship, she goes from her father's house to the convent, whence she is taken by her brother; then to her husband's house, from which she is also

---

55. This is the same Gouvernail who unwittingly attracts a married woman in "A Respectable Woman," and who attends Edna's dinner party in *The Awakening*.

brought away by Montéclin, who finally returns her. At other crucial points she refuses to control her own destiny: denying her role as mistress of Cazeau's household she throws down the bunch of keys (with its echoes of Bluebeard's castle) for the black servants, saying " 'Je ne veux plus de ce train là, moi!' " (436); at the train station she hands her purse to Gouvernail, who is expected to buy her ticket, find her a seat, and get her and luggage safely aboard. She needs to be taken from the train to her husband. All her men take control; even the gentle Gouvernail (his name meaning "rudder/helm" with its overtones of "governor") assumes "such an air of proprietorship" (447) and thinks of a time when he will have "a right" to her (450).

Understandable as all these may be, they signify the bleakness of such a woman's life; the only autonomy she can show is to refuse, throw down, give over control—even in her positive assertion of motherhood she is abandoning herself to the claims and demands of a biological destiny of which she is ignorant (she did not realize she was pregnant). The epitome of vulnerable southern belle and ideal woman, Athénaïse is at the beck and call of her own impulses and others' power; returning to her shrewd businessman and good manager-husband, she avoids coming to terms with her nameless anguish. Like Euphrasie, she sees marriage as an inevitable result of passive expectancy—"it was customary for girls to marry when the right opportunity came" (430)—and can find few words adequately to explain to her parents why she has "a constitutional disinclination for marriage" (431). The relish that the latter feel at the prospect that her "master" will somehow lick her back into shape adds an insidious edge to Athénaïse's dissatisfaction, and explains why she turns so unquestioningly to her brother. The weight of the community's view that she has a good husband and nothing to complain about helps exacerbate her passivity. Like Euphrasie she is in a weak position to choose her own fate: her parents live on and manage property owned by a merchant in Alexandria, so she has no wealth to inherit. Furthermore, her attempts to obtain work in New Orleans come to nothing.

"Athénaïse" is the provincial, conventional version of the more cosmopolitan and daring novel. Athénaïse embraces the pleasures of social recuperation by returning willingly to a tyrannical husband and accepting motherhood in place of freedom. Edna Pontellier, given an apparently more liberal husband, is made to reject any compromise with her awakening self, which is defined as a process rather than a completed state. "Athénaïse" outlines the problems of self-definition for women, defined and spoken for as they are by men. In *The Awakening,* other women play a more significant role in Edna's understanding of this process, by actively or implicitly countering patriarchal pressures and oppression.

There has been considerable concentration on the figure of Edna Pontellier in *The Awakening*; studies have been written on her as romantic heroine, Whitmanesque solitary, and embodiment of an 1890s naturalistic determinism. Excellent articles have been devoted to the book's patterns of imagery, especially relating to Nature, the sea, waking and sleeping, and to metaphoric and emblematic sexuality. The qualities for which the book was censured and banned in 1899 are now praised and analyzed as the essence of its originality—notably its frankness about female sexuality, its daring amorality, and its very modern concern with the female individual's right to freedom and autonomy. Since *The Awakening* is the author's most ambitious and daring work, and the one that most defied contemporary critical taste and was most heavily censured, for my purposes it is the most interesting. I thus make no apology for discussing it at length, and for reviewing Chopin's entire *oeuvre* in the light of this novel. And because insufficient emphasis has been placed on the literary sources and influences on the book, I will devote a considerable amount of space to such consideration.

The important ingredient in Chopin's development from a compromising critique of to a more iconoclastic and overtly critical attack on patriarchal values is her reading of European writing by male realists and feminists. This attraction and reference to Europe is mediated in *The Awakening* to a highly sophisticated degree, which partly explains the bewildered and furious condemnation of the book by puritanical American critics—a response that took aback its thoroughly Europeanized author.

The hostile critical reception of *The Awakening* is a familiar story to scholars of eighteenth- and nineteenth-century women writers. Writers such as Mary Wollstonecraft, Madame de Staël, George Sand, and Charlotte Brontë had all published novels with strong, self-determining heroines who spoke their minds and were assumed to speak those of their authors. Like Maria, Corinne, Lélia, and Jane Eyre, Edna Pontellier was condemned for her independence, defiance of society's rules and values, and most particularly for her expression of and joy in sexual passion. Willa Cather's review of *The Awakening,* published in the same year the novel appeared and typical of its reception, referred to the "trite and sordid" theme, and accused Edna of sharing with Emma Bovary a demand for "more romance out of life than God put into it" and for making "the passion of love . . . stand for all the emotional pleasures of life and art." As Ellen Moers says, "if women writers do succeed with the expression or the dramatization of passion, if they do create an attractively erotic male character, their real-life experience at once becomes the only subject of critical discussion" (and in the two most extreme cases, de Staël was known as Corinne, Sand as Lélia, the latter even by her modern biographer André Maurois).[56]

Kate Chopin was no exception. What is interesting is the vehemence of the critical response, a response that indicates how much bolder was this treatment of illicit love by a woman writer than anything yet published in America. Though the "New Woman" and adulterous wife were by then commonplace features of European fiction and drama, America's women writers, almost all firmly in a puritan Protestant tradition, avoided direct reference to female sexuality except as an expression of deviance (see, for instance, a work Chopin admired greatly, Mary Wilkins Freeman's *Pembroke*, 1894). Kate Chopin herself, assumed to have been an unfaithful wife and negligent mother, suffered the fate of Mary Wollstonecraft rather than of George Sand; notoriety led not to fame but to cold silence, her novel dropped from libraries, polite company, and soon from print. Unlike Europeans, American genteel puritan critics had difficulty absorbing writing by women about sex. Chopin's creole links with French literature and culture, with European ways of thinking about sexual love, and especially with the long tradition of women's writing on love, marriage, and adultery, were to make a great difference both to the liberties she took in her writing and the ways she was received and misconstrued in her own country.

Edna Pontellier is by no means the "*femme de génie*" depicted by de Staël, George Sand, or the Elizabeth Barrett Browning of *Aurora Leigh*.[57] But she echoes many elements of their works and creates interesting variations on their central feminist themes. Motifs from *Corinne* and especially *Lélia* recur in the novel to such an extent that the book cannot make sense when read just in the light of late nineteenth-century European naturalism and realism, and of male authors only. The comparison that is frequently made between *The Awakening* and *Madame Bovary*, seductive as it is, seems to me to locate Chopin's novel in a male tradition which, as I argued in relation to Maupassant, she was writing her way out of throughout her career. In her

56. Quoted in Sharon O'Brien, "The Limits of Passion: Willa Cather's Review of *The Awakening*," *Women and Literature*, III (1975), 11, 13, 14; Moers, *Literary Women*, 144.

57. Chopin wrote a few stories that feature women writers as protagonists, though the characters are usually seen ironically: for example, "Wiser than a God," "Miss Witherwell's Mistake," and "Charlie."

final novel, I believe she succeeded by returning to questions and themes raised by earlier women writers. The novel is usually read as an apolitical work, and even when a recent critic tried to rectify this he still asserted that, in this "political romance," "for roughly the first half of the novel Chopin subordinates the political implications of Edna's predicament to the solitude and tentative self-exploration that begins to occupy her heroine during the summer idyl on Grand Isle."[58] My analysis of the novel is an attempt to argue through the highly political subtext, demonstrating how the work makes an original contribution to women's writing about the Protestant/Catholic divide, about nationality and regionalism, and about patriarchal institutions and the "New Woman" in the 1890s South. These are all questions Chopin's foremothers had wrestled with, and which American women writers were aware of. Chopin's novel is the first to use mainly English and French feminist themes in an American and especially a southern context.

Several texts by English and French nineteenth-century women writers foreground the social and political differences between European nations. Madame de Staël and Elizabeth Barrett Browning emphasize the contrast between cold, northern Protestant England and warm, southern Catholic Italy; Charlotte Brontë uses France (and French Belgium) as a symbolic site of revolution and moral and sexual laxity in contrast with the bracing self-control and common sense of England. Cora Kaplan writes of *Aurora Leigh*: "As in *Corinne,* and in so much Protestant writing about Italy, classical architecture, Catholicism and warm weather come to represent a blurred sensuality, missing in England, which opens the self to its permitted corollary, love."[59] For European women, and indeed for an American like Margaret Fuller, Italy—followed closely by France—stood for revolution in the widest sense, and both Grace King and Kate Chopin felt stimulated and liberated when visiting France. For Margaret Fuller and Elizabeth Barrett Browning, political revolution was exhilarating, while for Tory Protestant Charlotte Brontë it was terrifying; but for many European women writers, the farther south one moved, the more a woman could relax, feel free to be herself, and relish sensual pleasures. This geographical transition is also a metaphysical and emotional one—from the ascetic rigors of Puritanism to the lavish "indulgent" rituals of the Catholic faith, away from repression toward satisfaction of desire.

It is the complex dialectic between these contrasting attractions for women—documented as it was in such well-known texts as *Corinne* and

58. Lawrence Thornton, "*The Awakening:* A Political Romance," *American Literature,* LII (1980), 52–53.
59. Kaplan, "Introduction," in Browning, *Aurora Leigh,* 19.

Villette—that Chopin borrows from European women's writing and neatly transposes to Louisiana, by choosing a strictly reared, repressed Presbyterian heroine from Kentucky who marries into the relaxed New Orleans creole Catholic community that takes its vacations on a warm, sensuous island in the Gulf of Mexico. This clash of cultures, sited initially on Grand Isle and expressed mainly through the ripening friendship and understanding between Edna and creole "mother-woman" Adèle Ratignolle, is seen very much in de Staël's terms. Corinne tells Oswald of the difference between her Catholic and his Protestant faith and practice:

> Yours is stern and serious, ours is bright and tender. . . . in Italy Catholicism has taken a character of gentleness and indulgence, while in England . . . the greatest strictness both in principles and morals. Our religion . . . breathes life into art, inspires poets, makes a part of all the joys of our life; whilst yours . . . has taken a character of moral austerity from which it will never depart. Ours speaks in the name of love; yours in the name of duty.

Ellen Moers records that Harriet Beecher Stowe felt "an intense sympathy" with Corinne but wrote that in America "feelings vehement and absorbing like hers become still more deep, morbid, and impassioned by the constant forms of self-government which the rigid forms of our society demand." Stowe, a Puritan New Englander, shied away from *Corinne,* but Chopin—raised a Catholic, and with strong fascination for literary locations associated with the exotic and sensual—found in that text a set of contrasts which would be employed in her own work.[60]

When she returned to her hometown after her husband's death, Kate Chopin was known as the "Corinne of St. Louis," and Ellen Moers suggests that she patterned her salon life on that of de Staël and other versions of this *femme de génie,* Margaret Fuller in Boston and George Eliot at the Priory. She may also have heard from friends of the salon life established by the Howes in New Orleans, taken up by women such as Grace King. But Corinne is not the most obvious model for Edna in *The Awakening;* the exceptional, independent artist was inappropriate for an 1890s American woman writer steeped in European naturalism. De Staël's disciple George Sand adopted a tone in *Lélia* (1833) that was more attractive to Chopin. The "threnody of sexual despair and bitter skepticism which made the *maladie du siècle* a female as well as a male disease" was ripe for intertextual reading by a *fin de siècle* novelist who was appropriating overwhelmingly male-created and male-oriented European and American romantic and realist themes and forms for herself. As Patricia Thomson has demonstrated, *Lélia,* of all Sand's novels, had huge popular success and

60. Madame de Staël, *Corinne: or Italy* (London, 1911), 178; Moers, *Literary Women,* 205.

succès de scandale, and was widely known and referred to by the very Victorian novelists Chopin had known from childhood. Several of Chopin's stories, and especially *The Awakening,* amount to a dialogue with and response to *Lélia,* and indeed to Sand herself, who clearly attracted Chopin because of her "introduction of passion as a major theme in the novel."[61]

Lélia's crisis is very different from Edna Pontellier's; she has lived too richly and fully and now cannot love or feel sexual desire for the man she cares for, Sténio; instead, she feels maternal and protective toward him—but cannot prevent his suicide by drowning. Lélia can find no peace, neither that of orgasm nor of celibate retreat; instead, she goes to confide in her sister Pulchérie, a prostitute, who offers her a stark choice between the options of becoming a courtesan or a nun (a choice that Chopin explored in "Two Portraits"). Instead, Lélia plays a cruel trick on Sténio, offering to make love then substituting Pulchérie in her bed, later writing him to explain it was done to avoid his idolizing her. Sténio becomes throughly debauched but is saved temporarily by Trenmor, who takes him to a monastery where the young man sleeps deeply and awakens to see the world transformed in a new light. Then, after hearing Magnus' story of hopeless love for Lélia, Sténio—feeling betrayed and cheated—drowns himself.

The oblique uses Chopin makes of the novel in *The Awakening* are legion. There are obvious parallels: the older woman loving a young man who cannot cope with her complexity; the young man's sleep in the monastery only to wake to a new world, like Edna on Caminada; the suicide by drowning. But there are more significant parallels that are less obvious. Pulchérie's long description of her first sexual arousal in girlhood while lying peacefully in Lélia's arms suggests the sensual arousal that Adèle produces in Edna on the beach; Pulchérie's state of mind then suggests the lesson Adèle tries unsuccessfully to teach Edna: "for me nothing revealed itself through suffering. I didn't tire myself out as you did with useless questions. I found because I didn't seek."[62] Lélia is the first object of beauty Pulchérie recognizes, and this daring description of homoerotic, incestuous love is adapted more delicately by Chopin to suggest early in the novel the bisexual nonspecificity of love and desire. When Sténio loves her

61. Moers, *Literary Women,* 33; Patricia Thomson, *George Sand and the Victorians: Her Influence and Reputation in Nineteenth-Century England* (London, 1977). Thomson makes the point that for Victorian English writers (and this also applies to Americans)·"what each chose to concentrate on is as revealing of his personality as of her achievement" (1). She also notes that the first reviews—like those of *The Awakening*—called Lélia "a monster" and the book itself a "revolting romance" and "a regular topsyturvification of morality" (12, 19, 9).

62. George Sand, *Lélia,* trans. Maria Espinosa (Bloomington, Ind., 1978), 102.

sister as herself, Sand's cynical theme is reiterated, while in Chopin there is a difference of tone: she gives her heroine a joyous adulterous experience with a man who she well knows is not the beloved, and this liberates rather than destroys Edna.

By using Adèle as a first, and Arobin as the second and last erotic encounter for the heroine, Chopin has transformed Sand's weary cynicism into feminist defiance. And in terms of the theme of motherhood and mother-love, Chopin turns the tables on Sand's maternalistic heroine. While Lélia tells Stenio's corpse, "I would have liked to be your mother and be able to press you in my arms without awakening in you a man's sense," Edna rejects her primary role and feelings as those of a mother—to her children or her lover—and challenges the man who sees her as someone's wife and mother to enjoy her only as a woman.[63] In *The Awakening*, it is the child who flees Edna, daunted by a woman who refuses to be her husband's property. Lélia's sad, solitary retreat is translated by Chopin into the "solitary soul" who "dares and defies," and who, like Sténio (but not Lélia), has the dignity of death by her own hand.

The defiance of Edna Pontellier may well have been suggested by that sole surviving book in Chopin's library, a curious, sardonic text, *Elizabeth and Her German Garden*.[64] For the first half, the novel appears to be a light satire on marriage, with an absurdly misogynist patriarchal husband—called by the wife/narrator "the Man of Wrath"—from whom Elizabeth escapes to her beloved gardening. But the second half is dominated by a prolonged discussion of women's rights and duties, occasioned by the visit to the couple's home of an English woman writer. The tone alters as the writer Minora hears to her horror that in Germany women are "literally nobodies," classified in law with "children and idiots" (145–46)—the very status of women in the Louisiana of the Napoleonic Code. Elizabeth's husband rails unpleasantly against the vanity and gullibility of all women, to the considerable disgust of his own wife.

Significant parallels exist between *Elizabeth* and *The Awakening*, which are worth noting since it is possible Chopin used its subject or tone for her own final novel. The relationship of both with feminist ideas is strikingly similar—though the dénouement, with Elizabeth retreating farther into a strange obsession with her garden, has more links with Charlotte Perkins Gilman's gothic "The Yellow Wallpaper" than with Chopin's work. Both protagonists find their husbands' houses stifling and imprisoning, and reject domestic labor and indoor child-care for the liberating atmosphere of the natural world. Both women relish solitude (to the puzzlement of

63. *Ibid.*, 225.
64. Elizabeth von Arnim, *Elizabeth and Her German Garden* (New York, 1898).

others around them) and define themselves in relation to Nature and aesthetic pursuits rather than as wives and mothers. Each woman has an oppressive husband, and children are referred to in both novels as "a troop." In both, a woman artist appears to offer a critique of patriarchal relations and attitudes—Minora, with her masculine pseudonym, parallels the "unfeminine" Mademoiselle Reisz. Most important of all, *Elizabeth and Her German Garden*—like the later novel—stresses the right of women to be happy rather than their duty to accept suffering and tyranny. Though each rebellious wife is regarded as eccentric, both Elizabeth and Edna exult in that definition, which at least allows them freedom to be different.

I have emphasized the influence of European women's writing, since it seems clear that throughout her career Chopin used and reworked feminist themes associated with that exotic, remote site of the female libido, Europe. In many of her writings there are indications of the importance of literature in the construction of different kinds of femininity, and her own intertextual use of women's and men's European fiction forms part of such commentary. Like Mary Wollstonecraft, she recognized the dangers of romantic fiction for young girls—and it is significantly unstable or unreliable women characters who are shown as romance readers (Claire, in "At Chênière Caminada," taunting Tonie by giving him a silver chain she remembered a romantic character giving away; Liza in "The Going Away of Liza," who pursues fruitlessly the good life she has read about; and the alcoholic and aimless Fanny Hosmer in *At Fault*). European *realist* literature is always associated with sexual behavior and attitudes: in "A Shameful Affair" (1893) Mildred Orme is sexually aroused by her reading of Ibsen and Tolstoi; the flirtatious creole women in *The Awakening* read Daudet and the de Goncourts. And as for her fictional women, the realist Maupassant unpacked Chopin's repressed feelings and gave permission for her to explore female sexuality in fiction.

The two works of Maupassant that were appropriated by Chopin for her own countertext are the novel *Une Vie* and the short story "Réveil," both published in 1883.[65] Unlike the stories Chopin translated, they each have a female protagonist. In *Une Vie,* Jeanne is a romantic woman who marries and becomes sensually aroused by her husband; he then engages in many acts of adultery and is killed by a cuckolded husband. She then lives for her only son, who initially rejects her but finally sends his motherless daughter to be cared for by Jeanne, with the promise that he will return

65. Guy de Maupassant, *A Woman's Life,* trans. H. N. P. Sloman (Harmondsworth, 1965); Guy de Maupassant, "Réveil," *Contes et Nouvelles I* (Paris, 1974), 745–49.

home soon. "Réveil" is perhaps another version of the story, since its protagonist is also called Jeanne. A sickly wife, she leaves her unhealthy country home for a winter in Paris. After a wretched beginning, she soon enjoys a busy social life and the attentions of two men, with one of whom she falls in love. Resisting his advances (of which she dreams), she is seduced by the other man, then realizes with horror what she has done and rushes home to her husband.

In *Une Vie,* like his master Flaubert, Maupassant ridicules the girlhood reading and aspirations of his heroine. Just as Emma Bovary read Walter Scott and dreamed of châtelaines and princes, so Jeanne is the daughter of a mother who reads sentimental novels and examines her "relic-drawer" of old letters. In most respects, the novel follows the traditional narrative trajectory of sentimental *and* realist nineteenth-century fiction: a young girl's convent education is followed by a country house courtship, then marriage and sexual awakening, followed by male betrayal. The female protagonist Jeanne passively suffers humiliation from an unfaithful husband, but becomes a deeply satisfied mother, then grandmother—both of which roles replace her desire for sexual fulfillment and personal autonomy. The alternative model of womanhood, spinster aunt Lison, is pathetically envious of young lovers and women giving birth.

The Awakening follows a different trajectory that challenges and acts as a rebuttal of this biological determinist pessimism. In Chopin's novel, a woman's arousal/awakening of the senses and emotions is not merely associated with the illusions of adolescence or immaturity, nor is it easily satisfied by childbirth and forms of motherhood. Edna's awakening occurs in relative maturity, and with a clear understanding of what is entailed. Unlike Jeanne, she discovers the joys of swimming and sex *after* marriage and free from familial security and constraints. It is she, rather than her husband, who commits adultery and breaks kinship rules and safeguards; but it is her response to *another* woman's childbirth that makes her recognize the strong ties of women to reproduction and motherhood, leading to a sense of defeat and finally suicide. The heroine's growing sense of her own power and freedom is allowed to develop to its logical conclusion, and she breaks away from the conventional defeat and containment of Maupassant's Jeanne, who is offered a vicarious life as compensation for her ruined hopes and destroyed independence. Mademoiselle Reisz may be eccentric and ungainly throughout *The Awakening,* but she is never pathetic like Aunt Lison, nor does she offer a sad commentary on the lot of unloved, unmarried womanhood. She has powers and a beauty (pianoplaying) of her own, and her vicarious sexual experience—the go-between role she plays to Edna and Robert—acts to mock rather than support the bourgeois patriarchal family.

The Jeanne of "Réveil"—like Edna—finds her sexual arousal away from home and, though not in a resort like Grand Isle, in a socially relaxed and permissive place (Paris).[66] Like Edna, too, she is reluctantly and gradually aroused from torpor and sexual frigidity, but unlike Edna is horrified by the means of her sexual gratification. The tone of the story is somber and cynical; the wife is half-unaware of what is happening, "in a kind of hallucination" (288), imagining with her real lover that she is with the beloved other; she thus appears deluded and foolish. Edna Pontellier is absolutely clear about the nature of her adultery, only regretting that the full sexual arousal she experiences did not derive from the love she feels for Robert. Furthermore, Jeanne's flight back to her husband, with the lie that she could not live far from him, is a retreat from the fullness of experience to the safety of patriarchal marriage. When her husband notes how unhappy she seems, she responds, "Happiness exists only in our dreams in this world" (289). But through adultery and the sense of freedom it gives her, Edna refuses merely to dream and insists on awakening fully, even if this is not to "happiness" but to freedom from illusions. "Réveil" concludes with Jeanne's platonic lover mystified at the change in his erstwhile passionate mistress, saying that women are "really very strange, complicated, and inexplicable beings."[67]

These two works clearly suggested characters and situations to Kate Chopin; the adultery story concluding in suicide was a common European theme, and Maupassant proposed ways in which Chopin could adapt it for her own purposes. But as I suggested with the translations, Chopin could not adopt Maupassant's ironic view of women as mere victims or irresponsible creatures. There is a considerable difference between Edna and the two Jeannes, the latter out of control of and frightened by their husbands and their own sexuality, and reduced to accepting a destiny determined in one case by a husband, the other by a son. Edna gains in assurance and self-determination throughout the novel, and her death is ironically intended as a greater triumph than the uneasy compromises of her French predecessors. Furthermore, her awakening is not a furtive, guilty, uncontrollable process, nor is sexual expression to be feared and suppressed. And at least she is not spoken *for* at the conclusion. Whereas in the Maupassant works, other characters comment ironically and somewhat patronizingly on the protagonists, Chopin's heroine is given the last word. Of course, the conclusion of *The Awakening* is ambiguous, since the

66. In her story "A Point at Issue!" Chopin ironically acknowledges the wicked reputation of this city. Professor Faraday leaves his wife alone there, to everyone's horror: "And in Paris, of all places, to leave a young woman alone! Why not at once in Hades?" *CW*, 51.

67. "The Awakening," in Guy de Maupassant, *The Complete Short Stories* (London, 1970), 284–89.

female protagonist (like Cathy in *Wuthering Heights*) is acting defiantly only in order to commit suicide; but as with Cathy's death, its tone is exultant. Maupassant's work repeatedly demonstrates the ways in which society represses and contains the individual, but never in his fiction does he go beyond the sardonic timidity of the cynical bourgeois to suggest rebellion and a refusal of social recuperation. Chopin's *The Awakening* refuses Maupassant's irony and chooses tragedy, while much of her work revises and obliquely comments on his pessimism and stultifying nihilism.

Finally, of all the works to which *The Awakening* refers, there is one that has never been noted, but the details of which bear a striking resemblance to Chopin's novel. This is a story by Thomas Hardy, "An Imaginative Woman." Both works are set in summer resorts in warm, languid weather; Hardy's female protagonist is Ella, Chopin's Edna; both are married to an insensitive businessman husband and are somewhat casual mothers; both fall in love with a romantic young man called Robert. Ella has minor success as a poet, Edna as a painter; both women are drawn to unsuitable, unrequited love affairs because of the deeply unfulfilling state of their marriages. The significant difference lies in the fact that Hardy makes the beloved man, poet Robert Trewe, commit suicide for lack of a devoted, loving woman, with Ella dying inconsolable in childbirth; while Chopin's Robert Lebrun lives but flees from Edna, who witnesses her friend Adèle's painful childbirth then takes her own life.[68]

These strong parallels between the two suggest that Chopin knew the story and followed Hardy's plotting details, but as with Maupassant she emulated only to a point. While Hardy characteristically gives the story a bitterly ironic twist, making the widowed husband turn from his motherless son believing him to be Robert's child, Chopin concludes with her heroine's suicide and gives it no ironic distance or final narrative surprise. Her focus on the heroine's suicide is undeviating, free of the ironic fatalism of Hardy and his European realist counterparts—far closer to the writings of European *women*. In fact, Chopin criticism has tended to dwell excessively on the parallels that exist between her and male writers (European and American), with Ibsen, Flaubert, and Henry James recurring.[69] The far more direct, obvious borrowings from women writers have been discussed much less. Their critical neglect has tended to distort, isolate, and/or exaggerate the originality of Chopin's ideas.

68. Thomas Hardy, *Wessex Tales* (1888), in *Tales from Wessex* (London, 1973), 124–50. I am indebted to Elaine Showalter for pointing me to the connection.

69. See, for instance, Lewis Leary, "Introduction," in Kate Chopin, *The Awakening and Other Stories,* ed. Lewis Leary (New York, 1970), and Cyrille Arnavon, who calls *The Awakening* "this American *Madame Bovary," KCM,* 181.

As I discussed earlier, by the time she wrote *The Awakening* Chopin was very experienced with publishers and critics, and well aware of the way Genteel Tradition standards had operated on her contemporaries. Her second published novel is thus not only the most accomplished expression of her central themes; it is also the most allusive of all her works. The novel is often praised for its economy; I would argue that its economy derives from a deliberately restrained style that is nonetheless pregnant with meaning, and highly suggestive. The reader must tease out those meanings and resonances from Chopin's biography and earlier writings, from close reading of the novel itself, and from an examination of the specific social and historical conditions that are the work's contexts.

A frequent feature of Chopin's fiction is the escape from gender definition by a female protagonist. *The Awakening* is no exception. Edna tries to discover what kind of woman she might be through refusal of "feminine" behavior and style. It is not surprising that, as she begins to find her freedom, she has more in common than before with her father; she shares his enthusiasm for the races and, when she goes there, talks like him. She begins to earn money from gambling and selling her paintings; walks everywhere alone and stays out late; at Mademoiselle Reisz's drinks brandy from a glass like a man; and takes the initiative in lovemaking with Robert, who (she suggests) thinks her "unwomanly" (104). The novel can be read as an elaborate and subtle gloss on the notion of the "New Woman" of whom Chopin had heard and read much. As several critics have suggested, Chopin's impatience with organized women's clubs and the women's movement probably stemmed from her sense of the reductive nature of women's demands for freedom—seen in terms of suffrage, education, jobs, and so on—and *The Awakening* is an interesting contribution to the debate on the complexities of female growth and metamorphosis, especially in the South.

The night Edna has first admitted to loving Robert, she tells Arobin, "By all the codes which I am acquainted with, I am a devilishly wicked specimen of the sex" (82). Chopin's use of the word *codes* is surprising here, but with its legal implications entirely apt. Edna knows well enough the meaning of her departures from the "codes" of acceptable female behavior, but increasingly she takes upon herself the role of lawbreaker. So completely has she succeeded that Robert, who has dreamed and agonized over the possibility of her divorcing Pontellier and marrying him, is dumbfounded at her scorn for his notion that she is the property of her husband. He, of course, is no lawbreaker and runs away, unwilling to compromise them both in the eyes of society.

In creole eyes, women who flout the codes governing female behavior are dangerous or mad. Arobin reports that the spinster Mademoiselle Reisz is widely thought to be "partially demented" (while to Edna she is "wonderfully sane" [83]); Pontellier wonders if his wife's neglect of household management indicates she is "growing a little unbalanced mentally" (57). This compares significantly with Corinne's wry thought when reading Nelvil's uncomprehending letter about Italy: "Perhaps the best way for a woman of superior mind to regain her coolness and dignity is to withdraw into herself as into an asylum."[70] To everyone who sees her, Edna Pontellier is physically transformed and indeed a *new woman*: her husband sees her as " 'not herself' " (57); Victor Lebrun remarks that she looks " 'ravishing' " and " 'doesn't seem like the same woman' " (61); and Dr. Mandelet recognizes her erotic awakening when he compares her to " 'some beautiful, sleek animal waking up in the sun' " (70). The narrator, repudiating Pontellier's suspicion of madness, observes that Edna was simply "becoming herself and daily casting aside that *fictitious* self which we assume like a garment with which to appear before the world" (57, my emphasis). That fictitious self is socially defined and determined southern womanhood and ideal femininity, which Chopin knew had been reinforced and reified throughout nineteenth-century fiction.

Yet, new creature/woman as she undoubtedly becomes (and the animal imagery associated with her growth seems to suggest that monster which Ellen Moers, Adrienne Rich, Robin Morgan, and other women writers have associated with women's notion of change), Edna recognizes how solitary and potentially destructive this reborn figure is. Her exhilaration at the casting off of responsibilities, unwanted duties, and codes is finally defeated by her loyalty and sense of "right." Though she tells Robert at a moment of intense desire, " 'We shall be everything to each other. Nothing else in the world is of any consequence' " (107), in the next breath she tells him she must go to attend Adèle's childbirth. Later, she claims to Dr. Mandelet that " 'nobody has any right—except children, perhaps' " (109). The most oppressive demands of patriarchal society (embodied during her final swim in thoughts of her sons, father, and the spur-clanging cavalry officer, as well as the scorn of the true rebel Mademoiselle Reisz) must be evaded if they cannot be defied. If women like Edna must always "witness the scene [of] torture" with only "an *inward* agony," "*speechless* with emotion" (109, my emphases), there is no way in which a woman may speak herself in such a society—except negatively.

In some ways, following the European tradition of Flaubert and Maupassant, the novel is profoundly deterministic, demonstrating as it does the ways in which women—far more than men—are locked into

70. De Staël, *Corinne*, 97.

socially prescribed roles and definitions. Ellen Moers argues that Madame de Staël uses *Corinne* to show that

> regional or national or what we call cultural values determine female destiny even more rigidly, even more inescapably than male. For as women are the makers and transmitters of the minute local and domestic customs upon which rest all the great public affairs of civilization . . . so women suffer more, in their daily and developing lives, from the influences of nationality, geography, climate, language, political attitudes, and social forms.[71]

To a certain extent, *The Awakening* shows Edna at the mercy of a patriarchal husband, a hot climate, a creole lifestyle, and the circumscribed expectations of a particular class of Louisiana women.

In the first chapter of *The Awakening*, Mr. Pontellier is described much like a patriarchal planter of antebellum Grand Isle: as the novel begins, he is seated on the gallery of the main (*i.e.,* planter's) house overlooking the cottages (old slave quarters), and when he sits in his own cottage smoking a cigar the activities around him must have recalled to Chopin's readers the idyllic plantation settings of many southern novels—birds chattering, girls playing piano, a woman "giving orders in a high key" to yardboy and house servants, Pontellier's children playing under the supervision of a quadroon nurse. The habits of a slave culture are referred to in a later scene, when Madame Lebrun works a sewing machine while "a little black girl" pumps the treadle on the floor: "the creole woman does not take any chances which may be avoided of imperiling her health" (22). When his wife returns from swimming, Pontellier comments on Edna's burnt skin, "looking at his wife as one looks at a valuable piece of personal property which has suffered some damage" (4); without the need for words they both assume his ownership when Edna holds out her hand into which he drops the rings she had removed for bathing (one of which, her wedding ring, she will later remove and try to crush with her heel). Later in the novel, Chopin describes Pontellier walking round his house examining all his possessions, which "he greatly valued . . . chiefly because they were his" (50).

Again, after Edna asks Pontellier if he will return for dinner, he adopts the patriarch's privilege of declining to decide. Feeling the ten-dollar bill in his vest pocket, he knows he has the economic power to choose, and Edna—again without words spoken—knows it, too. This sense of his power extends to ostentatious generosity toward Edna's penniless young admirer Robert Lebrun: Pontellier has "presented him with" a cigar that the young man cannot afford to buy himself. In the second chapter, Edna

71. Moers, *Literary Women*, 207.

tells Lebrun about her father's Mississippi plantation, and in the third chapter, Pontellier returns very late from gambling, having forgotten the gift he promised his children, only to assert his lordly right to awaken his wife from sleep, resent her lack of interest in his doings, and claim unreasonably that one of his sons has fever and is being neglected by Edna. Pontellier's concern with his own money is emphasized heavily in the first three chapters both to demonstrate his economic power and muscle, and to underline Edna's dependence and vulnerability. The cash he fingers lovingly buys dinner at his club rather than at home; it enables him to accumulate more by gambling and then to heap it on his bureau "indiscriminately with keys, knife, handkerchief, and whatever else happened to be in his pockets" (7); it is used to humor his wife the next day when he returns to the city; and it pays for a food hamper that is regularly sent to Edna on Grand Isle, confirming the other wives' view that "Mr. Pontellier was the best husband in the world" (9).

In subsequent chapters, pessimistic determinism is refused. Edna Pontellier refuses to be named and delimited as a southern patriarch's wife within creole society. She is not one of the "mother-women" of plantation legend who "idolized their children, worshiped their husbands, and esteemed it a holy privilege to efface themselves as individuals and grow wings as ministering angels" (10). Adèle Ratignolle, the personification of this role, is seen in mythic terms: Chopin claims the only words fit to describe her are "the old ones that have served so often to picture the bygone heroine of romance and the fair lady of our dreams," and all her features are those of legendary heroines—"spun-gold hair," lips red as "cherries or some other delicious crimson fruit," a "sensuous Madonna" with the "lofty chastity" of all creole women (10, 13, 11). But Adèle is by no means idealized. In the very first description of this quintessential creole lady, Chopin shows her "engaged in sewing upon a diminutive pair of night-drawers" (10) for winter wear (something Edna finds rather odd in midsummer) and talking persistently of her "condition" (11), which Edna suspects she exploits to attract attention. Indeed, everything about Adèle indicates anachronism and frivolity—until her painful childbirth confirms Edna's pessimism about the possibilities available to all women. Not only is Adèle self-absorbed and engaged in unnecessary activity (reminiscent of *Middlemarch*'s Rosamond Vincy, she cannot abandon her needlework even for the duration of a short walk), but she also advises Robert to leave Edna alone because "the law and the gospel" of her community (21) dictate that married women and young gentlemen flirt with one another without seriousness.

Thus Adèle herself, apparently the paradigm of perfect southern womanhood, is a muddle of contradictions and absurdities. And it is perhaps precisely because Edna senses that the careful construction of femininity which Adèle represents cannot work without a great deal of self-deception and hard labor (in both senses of the word), that she warms to and identifies with her creole friend. It is always in the company and/or under the roof of women that Edna feels really free and joyful, never with men, who give her ecstasy but never peace—a parallel I have discussed in relation to Sand's Lélia and Pulchérie. Adèle's sensuality and gentleness lead Edna back to presexual girlhood reminiscence and romantic memory; make her feel "flushed" and "intoxicated" with such unusual intimacy; and "muddled her like wine, or like a first breath of freedom" (20). Edna relishes her own physical and emotional autonomy on the beach, before the arrival of the patriarchal band of "Robert, surrounded by a *troop* of children" (20, my emphasis); and later in Madame Antoine's simple cottage on Chênière Caminada, in Mademoiselle Reisz's garret, and in Catiche's garden in New Orleans.

The "pigeon-house" that she buys for herself is a woman's sphere where men may enter only by invitation. Edna explains to Mademoiselle Reisz her reason for moving: "that big house . . . never seemed like mine, anyway—like home. . . . The house, the money that provides for it, are not mine" (79). These words find an interesting echo in a contemporary New Orleans journalist, Dorothy Dix, who wrote on the *Picayune* woman's page, "no matter how much a woman loves her husband . . . to have to go to any man and ask him for money, and receive his 'What do you want with it?' is bitter shame, against which she revolts in her soul."[72] Alcée Arobin calls her final dinner at the old house a "*coup d'état*," especially when he learns that Edna has ordered the best of everything and plans to "let Léonce pay the bills" (85). Installed in her "pigeon-house," she feels that she has "descended in the social scale . . . [and] risen in the spiritual" (93).

Edna is seen throughout the novel breaking out of repressive structures of various kinds, and her rebellion is described in political as well as personal terms, always as something that increases her individual power: "Every step which she took toward relieving herself from obligations added to her strength and expansion as an individual" (93). Patriarchal houses—metaphoric as well as real—recur throughout the novel as embodiments of the constraints and taboos operating on Edna. And the novel's movement is a series of denials and ruptures of those structures by

72. Dorothy Dix, New Orleans *Picayune*, June 21, 1896, quoted in Margaret Culley, "Sob-Sisterhood: Dorothy Dix and the Feminist Origins of the Advice Column," *Southern Studies*, XVI (Summer, 1977), 206.

movements into the only free spaces available—notably, adultery and the source of legend and destruction itself, the waters of the Gulf. The oppressive resonances of the "house" of marriage have already been demonstrated; Edna's decision to marry Pontellier was an attempt to "take her place . . . in the world of reality, closing the *portals* forever behind her upon the realm of romance and dreams" (19, my emphasis). Edna breathes easily only outside her husband's house and area of influence.

The patriarchal house is nowhere more oppressively described than in chapter 23, when Edna sits at dinner with her husband (and, under the Napoleonic Code, owner of her home and children); her visiting father, a Confederate colonel who embodies male militaristic attitudes; and the old family doctor, Mandelet, who has been invited by Pontellier to drop a few words of advice into the wayward Edna's ear. In the previous chapter, Pontellier had visited Mandelet to consult him about the changes in his wife. Complaining about her neglect of housework, he also confides that " 'she's got some sort of notion in her head concerning the eternal rights of women; and—you understand—we meet in the morning at the breakfast table' " (65). To both men, Edna's refraining from the sexual duties of married life is an alarming signal, and the doctor wryly asks Pontellier if his wife has been associating lately " 'with a circle of pseudo-intellectual women—super-spiritual superior beings' " (66). These brief comments reflect the threat posed to harmonious patriarchal marriages by the burgeoning women's movement and especially by the women's clubs that (as I have discussed earlier) had spread from the North to southern cities like St. Louis and New Orleans. Even though Chopin resisted close identification with women's clubs and the women's movement, nevertheless references to them recur in her work. In *The Awakening,* the women's movement provides a context in which Edna, "solitary soul" as she is, may grow and resist female roles and definitions constructed and compounded by contemporary discourses of power.

Edna's new independence of spirit, as well as her uncharacteristic recklessness, are demonstrated by her narration to the assembled company at dinner of a story she pretends Madame Antoine told her, about a woman paddling away with her lover in a pirogue, never to return and lost forever amid the Baratarian Islands. This is significantly her erotic fictional response to the admonitory story told by Dr. Mandelet about "the waning of a woman's love, seeking strange, new channels, only to return to its legitimate source after days of fierce unrest" (70). Although Edna is still living with her husband and has not yet made love with Arobin, she indicates clearly here that she defies all these patriarchal figures who in their different ways are concerned about her new spirit of freedom and irresponsible pleasure. Dr. Mandelet leaves the dinner muttering " 'I hope to heaven it isn't Alcée Arobin,' " while the next day the colonel gives his son-in-law the advice of a military man: " 'You are too lenient, too lenient by far, Léonce. . . . Authority, coercion are what is needed. Put your foot down good and hard; the only way to manage a wife. Take my word for it' " (71). This is advice upon which Chopin casts doubt in the next sentence: "The Colonel was perhaps unaware that he had coerced his own wife into her grave." The link between society's authoritarian power structures and the marriage relationship provides a comment on the institutional contraints on all women, however successful their individual marriages may be—after all, Pontellier himself is relatively permissive.

In the previous chapter I discussed Charlotte Perkins Gilman's relationship with Dr. Weir Mitchell and late nineteenth-century definitions of femininity and woman's domestic role. Barbara Ehrenreich and Deirdre English have argued that Mitchell was characteristic of a newly ascendant medical profession which was taking the place of friends and female healers in women's lives, and which defined woman as "weak, dependent, and diseased," and her role as that of "a patient." But as Foucault has pointed out, in the nineteenth-century bourgeois and aristocratic family, the first figure to be "sexualized" was the " 'idle' " woman, that very " 'nervous' " creature whom the medical profession defined as "hysterical."[73] It is thus no coincidence that Léonce Pontellier refers his wife to the family doctor, who assures him that woman is " 'a very peculiar and delicate organism' " and that most are " 'moody and whimsical' " (66). And it is symbolically accurate that the doctor should be the last person to speak to Edna before she decides to take her life. When she rejects his counsel and diagnoses her own condition by telling him " 'I don't want anything but my own way' " (110), she is repudiating both his cloying paternalist concern and also his definition of her as "in trouble" and disturbed.

While Edna refuses to be simply her husband's property and the "mother-woman" of patriarchal and medical discourse, Pontellier circumvents her rebellion and prevents the scandal that would ensue were her independence fully understood, and that would undermine his business interests. He takes the doctor's advice to leave her alone until she gets over this strangeness, and when she moves out of his house he immediately instructs rebuilding work to begin to "explain" her abrupt departure. Furthermore, he—like other creole husbands—relies on the admonition and discipline of other women. Elaine Showalter argues of *Jane Eyre* that "the feminine heroine grows up in a world without female

73. Ehrenreich and English, *For Her Own Good*, 92; Foucault, *The History of Sexuality*, I, 121.

200 GENDER, RACE, AND REGION

solidarity, where women in fact police each other on behalf of patriarchal tyranny," and although there is considerable solidarity in Edna's world, the women perform a similar function for each other in this novel.[74] The creole women on Grand Isle maintain marital and thus social stability by refusing to treat flirtation and extramarital desire seriously, and indeed by rendering it invisible. In New Orleans, Edna's maid hastily sweeps up the pieces of the vase Edna has broken in frustration, and returns to her the wedding ring she tried to crush into the carpet. Adèle Ratignolle, especially, tries to prevent Robert from pursuing his relationship with Edna, who is apparently responding too strongly and visibly for comfort; she later calls on Edna at the "pigeon-house" to urge her to drop Arobin for her reputation's sake—being *seen* with a known roué will lead to social ostracism. Finally, Adèle tells Edna to think of the children— ironically, her only injunction to be taken to heart, as Edna recognizes the bitter wisdom of her words. The anarchic, socially disruptive implications of fulfilled desire are spoken from all sides, leaving Edna little alternative but the welcoming sensual release of death in the Gulf waters.

A problem that various critics have raised is Edna's apparently malevolent attitude toward her children just before she swims to her death. But it is no coincidence that Edna's children are *sons* (rather than daughters) who can be seen ominously to embody the patriarchal laws that their mother now refuses to acknowledge. She thinks of them as "antagonists who had overcome her; who had overpowered and sought to drag her into the soul's slavery for the rest of her days" (113). This analogy with slavery is carried through all male law-bearers and patriarchal figures, however young and "innocent"—from Pontellier through the Confederate colonel, to the conservative doctor and the shocked young lover who cannot face the consequences of the free love Edna offers him, and finally to the two boys who remind Edna of her "duties" and of the enslavement of the soul and denial of desire that they entail.

Earlier I quoted Anne Goodwyn Jones's statement that Chopin used blacks as an objective correlative for her feelings about oppression. Throughout this book I have demonstrated the frequency of this "conceit" and have argued that it derives from a class- and race-bound perspective on blacks (and especially slaves) that is both dishonest and politically outrageous. Self-conscious as Chopin was about her use of imagery in other ways, and subtle as some of the regional allusions are to Louisiana's slave past, her analogy between bourgeois white marriage and slavery reveals the limitations of contemporary southern women's racist feminism. In *The Awakening,* it comes close to allying Chopin with the distasteful

74. Showalter, *A Literature of Their Own,* 117.

excesses of journalist Dorothy Dix, whose articles on Louisiana women frequently made this comparison:

> There comes a time in the life of almost every woman when she has to choose between a species of slavery and freedom, and when . . . she must hoist the red flag of revolt and make a fight for her rights. It counts for nothing that the oppressor is generally of her own household. . . . [We give in to our oppressors till we are] nothing more than bond slaves to the tyrant on our hearth.
> Chief and foremost among these oppressors are children.[75]

The Awakening is the novel that best brings together those concerns, analogies, and contrasts that made up white middle-class women's preoccupations in the postbellum decades. Its focus on marriage, its use of the slavery correlative, and the suggestive use of topographical and historical materials, mediated through European intertextual readings, all combine to produce a feminist regionalist work that nonetheless lapses into unexamined racism. And I suspect that the shock with which it was read by contemporary critics, and the startled disappointment its conclusion gives to modern readers, derive from a similar source. The novel appropriates male romantic concerns for women, concerned as it is with the problem of achieving full subjectivity through that "unmediated and eroticised relation to art and life" that it was presumptuous for an 1890s southern woman to desire. In her attempt to become a full subject, Edna negotiates her way through various versions of femininity, rejecting each model as she goes and refusing all definitions of what she should be—including that of artist (which is the crucial point at which the author departs from her protagonist). Julia Kristeva offers a suggestive way of explaining our profound disturbance at the novel's closure. She argues that the role women have in challenging phallic dominance lies in "assuming a *negative* function: reject everything finite, definite, structured, loaded with meaning, in the existing state of society. [This] places women on the side of the explosion of social codes: with revolutionary moments." Of course, Kristeva's "negative function" dangerously allies women with a kind of death. But Edna's suicide does symbolically "explode" codes in a revolutionary moment, hence her exhilaration as she swims to her death and the romantic natural associations of the last line: "There was the hum of bees, and the musky odor of pinks filled the air" (114).[76]

But the novel is by no means unequivocally triumphant. Its closure,

75. Dorothy Dix, New Orleans *Picayune,* October 29, 1899, quoted in Chopin, *The Awakening,* ed. Margaret Culley, 131–32.
76. Kaplan, "Wild Nights," 27; Julia Kristeva, "Oscillation Between Power and Denial," in Elaine Marks and Isabelle De Courtivron (eds.), *New French Feminisms: An Anthology* (New York, 1981), 166.

which leaves so many readers uneasy, speaks the contradictory concerns and tensions of much of the late nineteenth-century regionalist fiction by Louisiana women. Better than any other text, perhaps, *The Awakening* brings together the romantic but deadly associations of the historic and mythic Gulf waters, the mingled voices of European and American naturalistic determinism and progressive or utopian feminism, and the hopelessness and joyous defiance of the "New Woman" who refuses political, social, and personal compromise.

Kate Chopin was disheartened at the critical reception of *The Awakening* and wrote little more before her death in 1904. As Thomas Hardy's disgust with the critical reception of *Jude the Obscure* silenced him as a novelist, so Chopin appears to have recognized the limited imaginative capacity and generosity of contemporary critics and to have capitulated to the critical double standard. She had not consciously sought notoriety, though her experiences with publishers must have prepared her for the storm over her second novel. But as a southern woman with little taste for self-revelation and a strong bent for irony, she must have found hard to swallow the implicitly adverse judgments on her as a *woman,* identified as she immediately was with Edna Pontellier.

The Awakening and "The Storm," written before the novel but pragmatically never offered to an editor, were the logical conclusion of all Chopin's writing about women. Both celebrate woman as an infinitely desiring and versatile subject, and both demonstrate the power of erotic bliss in the creation of a new kind of woman. Chopin's departure from orthodox American and southern themes is usually read as an interesting kind of aberration, inspired by the English romantic poets and by Walt Whitman, and accomplished by individual genius. But as I have tried to show, most of Chopin's work made relatively conventional use of Local Color themes and techniques, and was as deeply embedded in southern racist ideology as the writings of Grace King and Ruth McEnery Stuart—though her project was very different. Her originality as a woman writer, as I see it, derives from her complex and subtle intertextual reworkings of European fictional works to produce a critique of the social meanings of southern womanhood. *The Awakening,* which is thus the crucial text, is of considerable importance to this study since it embodies most of the regional and feminist concerns of southern women writers. Its unconsciously racist elements cannot be excused, but its feminist subtext manages to explore and explode the various meanings of femininity in the postbellum South.

IV

Afterword

In a radical reinterpretation of the American nineteenth-century sentimental novel, Jane P. Tompkins argues that in order to understand the significance of this very popular phenomenon, it must be seen "not as an artifice of eternity answerable to certain formal criteria and to certain psychological and philosophical concerns, but as a political enterprise, halfway between sermon and social theory, that both codifies and attempts to mold the values of its time."[1] Tompkins offers a useful way of thinking about popular literature, and especially genres and areas of women's writing that were successful and widely read in their own time but have since been critically dismissed and thus hidden from literary history. I would suggest that the southern Local Color movement, in which a number of prolific and critically acclaimed women writers were prominent, must also be seen as a political enterprise codifying and to some extent molding the values of its time, especially in relation to issues of gender, race, and region in the postbellum South.

For instance, it is important not simply to condemn the writers' unexamined or jingoistic racism, which clearly limited their literary experimentation and achievement. It is crucial to stress the connections between their capitulation to or defense of racism and the construction of a South that they all encouraged and in which they colluded. There were other versions of the South and the Civil War available to them—from male writers such as George W. Cable and the Mark Twain of *Huckleberry Finn* and *Pudd'nhead Wilson,* and women writers and activists like Harriet Beecher Stowe and the Grimké sisters. The literary success of the Loui-

---

1. Jane P. Tompkins, "Sentimental Power: *Uncle Tom's Cabin* and the Politics of Literary History," in Elaine Showalter (ed.), *The New Feminist Criticism: Essays on Women, Literature, and Theory* (London, 1986), 84–85.

siana writers and the careers they forged from regional materials depended on a politically acceptable and soft-edged interpretation of southern experience and social relations that ignored real conflicts and struggles. They all supplied the North with those ideal and romantic myths of the South that each knew distorted or evaded the truth; their particular relationships to southern history and culture, as well as personal ambition and desire to make a good living, finally obscured their pursuit of the sharpest historical and social accuracy and criticism.

It now seems clear that white women's writing about the Civil War and its aftermath follows a different trajectory from men's, in ways that are linked inextricably to women's specific experiences and relationships in the South, and to the ideological constructions of the defeated South and its white and black population around gender and race images and stereotypes. As a result, since most southern women's writing is what Anne Goodwyn Jones describes as "a pentimento sort of fiction that hid sometimes even from themselves as authors the more disturbing voices within the work," so its meanings must be located primarily in historical, social, and ideological terms.[2]

This raises a general problem in studying women's writing, namely the need to confront unwholesome and invidious political and social attitudes of writers whose feminist project and/or writing one admires and wishes to celebrate. But in order to understand the history of women's fiction and the kinds of pressure (positive and negative) that facilitated their literary production, it is vital not to excuse or explain away problematic or reactionary elements in the work. As with male writers, women must be understood as products of their age, however marginal or radical they may appear. Just as it is important for feminists not to see writers (male and female) as irrevocably locked into certain ideological positions, so we must also be wary of claiming as progressive or even revolutionary a work that breaks gender taboos while confirming reactionary positions on class or race. Such a judgment would apply to male as well as female writers, and should temper readings of D. H. Lawrence and William Faulkner as well as Virginia Woolf and Eudora Welty. I am not arguing for crude reflectionist readings which (like Kate Millett's powerful but reductive condemnation of male fiction) judge a work to be valuable as long as it betrays no overtly racist, sexist, ageist, etc., etc., views.[3] Rather, the best

2. Anne Goodwyn Jones, "Southern Literary Women as Chroniclers of Southern Life," in Hawks and Skemp (eds.), *Sex, Race, and the Role of Women in the South,* 92.

3. Kate Millett, *Sexual Politics* (London, 1971). For an excellent critique of Millett, see Cora Kaplan, "Radical Feminism and Literature: Rethinking Millett's *Sexual Politics,*" in Mary Evans (ed.), *The Woman Question* (London, 1982), 386–400.

kind of materialist criticism must locate a writer and text as accurately as possible in his/her place, time, and ideological context, and consider the ways in which those determinants are both accepted and acceded to, and countered and challenged within the framework of the text. In this way we may avoid attributing excessive originality to single writers and works, and we can begin systematically to map the field of the more obscure and neglected periods of literary history.

Bibliography

PRIMARY SOURCES

Grace King

"An Affair of the Heart." *Harper's,* LXXXVIII (April, 1894), 796–99.
"Annette: A Story of the Streets." *New Orleanian,* September 20, 1930, pp. 16–17, 36–37.
"At Chênière Caminada." *Harper's,* LXXXVIII (May, 1894), 871–74.
Balcony Stories. New York, 1893.
The Chevalier Alain de Triton. In *Chautauquan,* XIII (July, 1891), 409–64.
"The Clodhopper." *McClure's,* XXVIII (March, 1907), 487–91.
Creole Families of New Orleans. Baton Rouge, 1971.
La Dame de Sainte Hermine. New York, 1924.
"Destiny." *Harper's,* XCVI (March, 1898), 541–48.
"A Domestic Interior." *Harper's,* XC (February, 1895), 407–11.
Earthlings. In *Lippincott's Magazine* (November, 1888), 601–79.
"The Evening Party." *Harper's,* LXXXIX (July, 1894), 192–95.
"The Flitting of 'Sister.'" *Youth's Companion,* LXXVII (June 25, 1903), 305–306.
Grace King of New Orleans: A Selection of Her Writings. Edited by Robert Bush. Baton Rouge, 1973.
"Heroines of Novels." New Orleans *Times-Democrat,* May 31, 1885.
"An Interlude." *Harper's,* LXXXIX (November, 1894), 918–20.
"Making Progress." *Harper's,* CII (February, 1901), 423–30.
Memories of a Southern Woman of Letters. New York, 1932.
Monsieur Motte. New York, 1888.
New Orleans: The Place and the People. New York, 1895.
"One Woman's Story." *Harper's Bazaar,* XXIV (March 21, 1891), 218–19.

"On the Prairie." *Appleton's Booklover's Magazine,* VII (March, 1906), 324–26.

The Pleasant Ways of St. Médard. New York, 1916.

"A Quarrel with God." *Outlook,* LV (March 6, 1897), 687–94.

"The Self-Made Man: An Impression." *Harper's Bazaar,* XIV (April 5, 1890), 258–59.

A Splendid Offer: A Comedy for Women. In *The Drama,* XVI (March, 1926), 213–15, 235–37.

Stories from Louisiana History. New Orleans, 1905.

"Sympathy." *Harper's Weekly,* XXXII (May 12, 1888), 338.

Tales of a Time and Place. New York, 1892.

"A War-Time Santa Claus." *Collier's,* XLIV (December 11, 1909), 12.

Ruth McEnery Stuart

"American Backgrounds for Fiction, VI—Arkansas, Louisiana and the Gulf Country." *Bookman,* XXXIX (August, 1914), 620–30.

Aunt Amity's Silver Wedding, and Other Stories. New York, 1909.

Carlotta's Intended and Other Tales. New York, 1894.

The Cocoon: A Rest-Cure Comedy. New York, 1915.

Daddy Do-Funny's Wisdom Jingles. New York, 1913.

George Washington Jones: A Christmas Gift That Went A-Begging. Philadelphia, 1903.

Gobolinks, or Shadow-Pictures for Young and Old. With Albert B. Paine. New York, 1896.

A Golden Wedding and Other Tales. New York, 1893.

A Haunted Photograph and Other Stories. New York, 1911.

Holly and Pizen, and Other Stories. New York, 1899.

In Simpkinsville: Character Tales. New York, 1897.

Moriah's Mourning, and Other Half-Hour Sketches. New York, 1898.

Napoleon Jackson: The Gentleman of the Plush Rocker. New York, 1902.

Plantation Songs and Other Verse. New York, 1916.

The River's Children: An Idyl of the Mississippi. New York, 1904.

The Second Wooing of Salina Sue, and Other Stories. New York, 1905.

The Snow-Cap Sisters: A Farce. New York, 1897.

Solomon Crow's Christmas Pockets, and Other Tales. New York, 1896.

Sonny. New York, 1896.

Sonny's Father. New York, 1910.

The Story of Babette, a Little Creole Girl. New York, 1894.

Kate Chopin

At Fault. St. Louis, 1890.

The Awakening. New York, 1976.

Bayou Folk. Boston, 1894.

The Complete Works of Kate Chopin. Edited by Per Seyersted. Baton Rouge, 1969.

A Kate Chopin Miscellany. Edited by Per Seyersted. Natchitoches, La., 1979.

A Night in Acadie. Chicago. 1897.

Other Primary Sources

Bonner, Sherwood. *Like Unto Like*. New York, 1878.

———. "Two Storms." *Harper's,* LXII (April, 1881), 728–48.

Boucicault, Dion. *The Octoroon*. London, 1859.

Boyle, Virginia Frazer. "How Jerry Bought Malvinny." *Century,* XL (1880), 892.

Cable, George W. *Bonaventure: A Tale of Louisiana*. New York, 1888.

———. *The Grandissimes*. London, 1898.

———. *Old Creole Days*. New York, 1879.

Coltharp, Mrs. Jeanette. *Burrill Coleman, Colored: A Tale of the Cotton Fields*. Franklin, La., 1896.

Flaubert, Gustave. *Madame Bovary*. Harmondsworth, Engl., 1950.

Gilman, Charlotte Perkins. *The Yellow Wallpaper*. Old Westbury, Conn., 1973.

Hardy, Thomas. *Tales from Wessex*. London, 1973.

Harris, Joel Chandler. *Uncle Remus: His Songs and His Sayings*. Edited by Robert Hemenway. Harmondsworth, Engl., 1982.

Hearn, Lafcadio. *Chita: A Memory of Last Island*. New York, 1889.

Hildreth, Richard. *The Slave: or Memoirs of Archy Moore*. Upper Saddle River, N.J., 1968.

Howe, Maud. *Atalanta in the South: A Romance*. Boston, 1886.

Jewett, Sarah Orne. *The Country of the Pointed Firs*. London, 1927.

———. *Strangers and Wayfarers*. Boston, 1896.

Jones, Alice Ilgenfritz. *Beatrice of Bayou Têche*. Chicago, 1895.

Longfellow, Henry Wadsworth. *The Poetical Works of Henry Wadsworth Longfellow*. London, 1893.

Maupassant, Guy de. *Oeuvres Complètes de Guy de Maupassant*. Paris, 1926.

———. *A Woman's Life*. Harmondsworth, Engl., 1965.

Mitchell, Margaret. *Gone With the Wind*. New York, 1936.

Page, Thomas Nelson. *In Ole Virginia, or Marse Chan and Other Stories*. New York, 1887.

———. *Red Rock*. London, 1898.

Reid, Mayne. *The Quadroon*. New York, 1856.

Sand, George. *Lélia*. Translated by Maria Espinosa. Bloomington, Ind., 1978.

Staël, Madame de. *Corinne: or Italy*. London, 1911.

Stowe, Harriet Beecher. *Uncle Tom's Cabin*. Columbus, Ohio, 1969.

Styron, William. *The Confessions of Nat Turner*. New York, 1968.

Tourgée, Albion W. *Bricks Without Straw*. Baton Rouge, 1969.

Twain, Mark. *Adventures of Huckleberry Finn*. Boston, 1958.

————. *Pudd'nhead Wilson*. Harmondsworth, Engl., 1968.

Von Arnim, Elizabeth [Mary Russell]. *Elizabeth and Her German Garden*. New York, 1898.

Walworth, Mrs. J. H. *Without Blemish: Today's Problem*. New York, 1886.

Wetmore, Elizabeth Bisland [Louisiana]. *Blue and Gray, or, Two Oaths and Three Warnings*. New Orleans, 1885.

Wilkins, Mary E. *Pembroke: A Novel*. New York, 1894.

Wollstonecraft, Mary. *Mary and The Wrongs of Woman*. Oxford, 1980.

Woolson, Constance Fenimore. *Rodman the Keeper: Southern Sketches*. New York, 1880.

SECONDARY SOURCES

Aaron, Daniel. *The Unwritten War: American Writers and the Civil War*. London, 1973.

Abel, Elizabeth. *Writing and Sexual Difference*. Brighton, Engl., 1982.

Alderman, Edwin A., Joel C. Harris, and Charles W. Kent, eds. "Ruth McEnery Stuart." In *Library of Southern Literature*, XI (New Orleans, 1907), 5145–61.

Allen, J. S. *Reconstruction: The Battle for Democracy, 1865–1876*. New York, 1937.

Anderson, John Q., ed. *Brokenburn: The Journal of Kate Stone, 1861–1868*. Baton Rouge, 1955.

Andrews, Eliza Frances. *The War-Time Journal of a Georgia Girl, 1864–1865*. Edited by Spencer B. King. Macon, Ga., 1960.

Andrews, Kenneth R. *Nook Farm: Mark Twain's Hartford Circle*. Cambridge, Mass., 1950.

Andrews, Matthew Page, ed. *The Women of the South in War Times*. Baltimore, 1927.

Aptheker, Herbert. *Nat Turner's Slave Rebellion*. New York, 1966.

Armstrong, Judith. *The Novel of Adultery*. London, 1976.

Arner, Robert. "Special Kate Chopin Issue." *Louisiana Studies*, XIV (Spring, 1975), 1–139.

Auerbach, Nina. *Communities of Women: An Idea in Fiction*. Cambridge, Mass., 1980.

Avary, Myrta Lockett. *Dixie After the War: An Exposition of Social Conditions Existing in the South, During the Twelve Years Succeeding the Fall of Richmond*. New York, 1906.

Bain, Robert, Joseph M. Flora, and Louis D. Rubin, Jr., eds. *Southern Writers: A Biographical Dictionary*. Baton Rouge, 1979.

Baldwin, James. *Notes of a Native Son*. London, 1965.

Banks, Olive. *Faces of Feminism: A Study of Feminism as a Social Movement*. Oxford, 1981.

Barker, Francis, *et al.*, eds. *Literature, Society and the Sociology of Literature*. Colchester, Engl., 1977.

————, *et al.*, eds. *1848: The Sociology of Literature*. Colchester, Engl., 1978.

Barker-Benfield, G. J. *The Horrors of the Half-Known Life: Male Attitudes Toward Women and Sexuality in Nineteenth-Century America*. New York, 1976.

Barry, John D. "A Chat with Ruth McEnery Stuart." *Illustrated American*, June 6, 1896.

Barthes, Roland. *S/Z*. London, 1975.

Baym, Nina. *Woman's Fiction: A Guide to Novels By and About Women in America, 1820–1870*. Ithaca, N.Y., 1978.

Beer, W. "List of Writings About Grace King." *Louisiana Historical Quarterly*, VI (1923), 353–59.

Beers, Mrs. Fannie A. "Memories: A Record of Personal Experience and Adventure During Four Years of War." In Louisiana and Lower Mississippi Valley Collection, Hill Memorial Library, Louisiana State University, Baton Rouge.

Belsey, Catherine. *Critical Practice*. London, 1980.

Bentzon, T. "Les Romanciers du Sud en Amérique." *Revue des Deux Mondes*, CXVI (April, 1893), 652–83.

Berg Collection. New York Public Library, New York, N.Y.

Berzon, Judith R. *Neither White nor Black: The Mulatto Character in American Fiction*. New York, 1978.

Blassingame, John W. *Black New Orleans, 1860–1880*. Chicago, 1973.

Bone, Robert A. *The Negro Novel in America*. Rev. ed. New Haven, 1965.

Brown, Dorothy, and Elizabeth Sarkodie-Mensah, eds. *A Selected Bibliography of Louisiana Women Writers*. New Orleans, 1986.

Buck, Paul H. *The Road to Reunion, 1865–1900*. Boston, 1937.

Bush, Robert. "Charles Gayarré and Grace King." *Southern Literary Journal* (Fall, 1974), 100–31.

————. "Grace King." *American Literary Realism 1870–1910*, VIII (Winter, 1975), 42–51.

————. "Grace King and Mark Twain." *American Literature*, XLIV (March, 1972), 31–51.

————. *Grace King: A Southern Destiny*. Baton Rouge, 1983.

———. "Grace King: The Emergence of a Southern Intellectual Woman." *Southern Review,* XIII (April, 1977), 272–88.

———. Interview with author. New York, N.Y., November 1, 1980.

———. "Louisiana Prose Fiction, 1870–1900." Ph.D. dissertation, State University of Iowa, 1957.

Butcher, Philip. *George W. Cable.* New York, 1962.

Carleton, Mark T., Perry H. Howard, and Joseph B. Parker, eds. *Readings in Louisiana Politics.* Baton Rouge, 1975.

Cash, W. J. *The Mind of the South.* New York, 1941.

Century Collection. New York Public Library, New York, N.Y.

Christian, Barbara. *Black Women Novelists: The Development of a Tradition, 1892–1976.* Westport, Conn., 1980.

Coleman, Charles W., Jr. "The Recent Movement in Southern Literature." *Harper's,* LXXIV (May, 1887), 837–55.

Conrad, Susan Phinney. *Perish the Thought: Intellectual Women in Romantic America, 1830–1860.* Oxford, 1977.

Cott, Nancy F., ed. *Root of Bitterness: Documents of the Social History of American Women.* New York, 1972.

Cott, Nancy F., and Elizabeth H. Pleck, eds. *A Heritage of Her Own: Toward a New Social History of American Woman.* New York, 1979.

Coxe, John M. Private Collection. New Orleans, La.

———. Interview with author. New Orleans, Louisiana, April 10, 1980.

Culler, Jonathan. *The Pursuit of Signs.* London, 1981.

Culley, Margaret, ed. *The Awakening,* by Kate Chopin. New York, 1976.

———. "Sob-Sisterhood: Dorothy Dix and the Feminist Origins of the Advice Column." *Southern Studies,* XVI (Summer, 1977), 201–10.

Cunningham, Gail. *The New Woman and the Victorian Novel.* London, 1978.

Davis, Angela. *Women, Race and Class.* London, 1982.

Davis, David Brion. *The Problem of Slavery in Western Culture.* Ithaca, N.Y., 1966.

Dawson, Sarah. *A Confederate Girl's Diary.* Edited by James I. Robertson, Jr. Bloomington, Ind., 1960.

Dimitry, Adelaide Stuart. "The Battle of the Handkerchiefs." *Confederate Veteran,* XXXI (May, 1923), 182–83.

Douglas, Ann. *The Feminization of American Culture.* New York, 1977.

Douglass, Frederick. *Narrative of the Life of Frederick Douglass, An American Slave.* New York, 1968.

Du Bois, Ellen Carol. *Feminism and Suffrage: The Emergence of an Independent Women's Movement in America, 1848–1869.* Ithaca, N.Y., 1978.

DuBois, W. E. B. *Black Reconstruction in America, 1860–1880.* New York, 1935.

Dunbar-Nelson, Alice. "People of Color in Louisiana, Parts I and 2." *Journal of Negro History,* I (October, 1916), 361–76; II (January, 1917), 51–78.

Ehrenreich, Barbara, and Deirdre English. *For Her Own Good: 150 Years of the Experts' Advice to Women.* London, 1979.

Ewell, Barbara C. *Kate Chopin.* New York, 1986.

Fiedler, Leslie. *Love and Death in the American Novel.* Rev. ed. New York, 1966.

Fitzhugh, George. "Women of the South." *DeBow's Review,* XXXI (August, 1861), 147–54.

Fletcher, Marie. "Grace Elizabeth King: Her Delineation of the Southern Heroine." *Louisiana Studies,* V (Spring, 1966), 50–60.

————. "The Southern Heroine in the Fiction of Representative Southern Women Writers, 1850–1960." Ph.D. dissertation, Louisiana State University, 1963.

Fletcher, Mary Frances. "A Biographical and Critical Study of Ruth McEnery Stuart." M.A. thesis, University of Virginia, n.d.

Flexner, Eleanor. *Century of Struggle: The Women's Rights Movement in the U.S.* New York, 1973.

Foucault, Michel. *The History of Sexuality: Volume I, An Introduction.* Harmondsworth, Engl., 1981.

Franklin, John Hope. *From Slavery to Freedom.* New York, 1969.

————. "Mirror for Americans: A Century of Reconstruction History." *American Historical Review,* LXXXV (February, 1980), 1–14.

————. *Reconstruction After the Civil War.* Chicago, 1961.

Fryer, Judith. *The Faces of Eve: Women in the Nineteenth-Century American Novel.* New York, 1976.

Gaines, Francis Pendleton. *The Southern Plantation: A Study in the Development and the Accuracy of a Tradition.* New York, 1924.

Gaudé, Pamela. "Kate Chopin's 'The Storm': A Study of Maupassant's Influence." *Kate Chopin Newsletter,* I (1975), 1–6.

Genovese, Eugene D. *Roll, Jordan, Roll: The World the Slaves Made.* New York, 1976.

————. *The World the Slaveholders Made.* New York, 1971.

Gilbert, Sandra M. " 'Soldier's Heart': Literary Men and Literary Women, and the Great War." Paper presented at the annual meeting of the Modern Languages Association, December 28, 1980.

Gilbert, Sandra M., and Susan Gubar. *The Madwoman in the Attic: The Woman Writer and the Nineteenth-Century Literary Imagination.* New Haven, 1979.

Gilman, Charlotte Perkins. *The Home: Its Work and Influence.* Urbana, Ill., 1972.

Grace King Papers. Louisiana and Lower Mississippi Valley Collection, Hill Memorial Library, Louisiana State University.

"Grace King Tributes." *Louisiana Historical Quarterly*, VI (July, 1923), 344–79.

Grimké, A. E. *Appeal to the Christian Women of the South*. New York, 1836.

———. *An Appeal to the Women of the Nominally Free States*. Boston, 1838.

Grimké, Sarah. *Letters on the Equality of the Sexes and the Condition of Women*. Boston, 1838.

Gutman, Herbert G. *The Black Family in Slavery and Freedom*. New York, 1976.

———. "Persistent Myths About the Afro-American Family." *Journal of Interdisciplinary History*, VI (Autumn, 1975), 181–210.

Hair, William Ivy. *Bourbonism and Agrarian Protest: Louisiana Politics, 1877–1900*. Baton Rouge, 1969.

Hall, Mrs. Frances. *Major Hall's Wife: A Thrilling Story of the Life of a Southern Wife and Mother, While a Refugee in the Confederacy, During the Late Struggle*. Syracuse, N.Y., 1884.

Hartman, Mary S., and Lois Banner, eds. *Clio's Consciousness Raised: New Perspectives on the History of Women*. New York, 1974.

Hawks, Joanne V., and Sheila L. Skemp, eds. *Sex, Race, and the Role of Women in the South*. Jackson, Miss., 1983.

Hayden, Dolores. *The Grand Domestic Revolution: A History of Feminist Designs for American Homes, Neighborhoods, and Cities*. Cambridge, Mass., 1981.

Hensen, Mrs. Nell W. "Women's Clubs of New Orleans." *New Orleans Life*, II (February 17, 1927).

Hofstadter, Richard, and Michael Wallace, eds. *American Violence: A Documentary History*. New York, 1971.

Hooks, Bell. *Ain't I a Woman: Black Women and Feminism*. London, 1982.

Hubbell, Jay B. *The South in American Literature: 1607–1900*. Durham, N.C., 1954.

James, Henry. *The American Scene*. Bloomington, Ind., 1968.

Jones, Anne Goodwyn. *Tomorrow Is Another Day: The Woman Writer in the South, 1859–1936*. Baton Rouge, 1981.

Jones, K. M. *Heroines of Dixie: Confederate Women Tell Their Story of the War*. Indianapolis, Ind., 1955.

Kane, Harnett. *The Bayous of Louisiana*. New York, 1963.

Kaplan, Cora. Introduction to *Aurora Leigh*, by Elizabeth Barrett Browning. London, 1978.

———. "Radical Feminism and Literature: Rethinking Millett's *Sexual Politics*." In *The Woman Question*, edited by Mary Evans. London, 1982.

————. "Wild Nights: Pleasure/Sexuality/Feminism." In *Formations of Pleasure,* edited by Formations Editorial Collective. London, 1983.

Kaplan, Sidney. "*The Octoroon*: Early History of the Drama of Miscegenation." *Journal of Negro Education* (Fall, 1951), 547–57.

Kendall, John S. "A New Orleans Lady of Letters." *Louisiana Historical Quarterly,* XIX (April, 1936), 28.

————. "Who Killa de Chief?" *Louisiana Historical Quarterly,* XXII (1939), 498–512.

King, Edward. *The Great South.* Edited by W. Magruder Drake and Robert R. Jones. Baton Rouge, 1972.

King, Frederic Delaybache, III, and R. Richardson King. Interview with author. New Orleans, Louisiana, March 13, 1981.

Kirby, David K. *Grace King.* Boston, 1980.

Kirkham, Margaret. *Jane Austen, Feminism and Fiction.* Brighton, Engl., 1983.

Kraditor, Aileen S. *Up from the Pedestal: Selected Writings in the History of American Feminism.* Chicago, 1968.

Kristeva, Julia. *Desire in Language: A Semiotic Approach to Literature and Art.* Oxford, 1980.

Leary, Lewis, ed. *The Awakening and Other Stories,* by Kate Chopin. New York, 1970.

LeGrand, Julia. *The Journal of Julia LeGrand: New Orleans, 1862–1863.* Edited by Kate Mason Rowland and Mrs. Morris L. Croxall. Richmond, Va., 1911.

Lerner, Gerda, ed. *Black Women in White America: A Documentary History.* New York, 1972.

Lestage, H. Oscar, Jr. "The White League in Louisiana and Its Participation in Reconstruction Riots." *Louisiana Historical Quarterly,* XVIII (July, 1935).

Loewenberg, Bert James, and Ruth Bogin. *Black Women in Nineteenth-Century American Life: Their Words, Their Thoughts, Their Feelings.* University Park, Penn., 1976.

Lunt, D. S. *A Woman's Wartime Journal.* Macon, 1927.

Macherey, Pierre. *A Theory of Literary Production.* London, 1978.

Mainiero, Lina, ed. *American Women Writers, from Colonial Times to the Present.* New York, 1979.

Marks, Elaine, and Isabelle De Courtivron, eds. *New French Feminisms: An Anthology.* New York, 1981.

Marxist-Feminist Literature Collective. "Women's Writing: *Jane Eyre, Shirley, Villette, Aurora Leigh.*" In *Ideology and Consciousness,* III (Spring, 1978), 27–48.

Maurois, André. *Lélia: The Life of George Sand.* London, 1952.

M'Caleb, Thomas, ed. *The Louisiana Book: Selections from the Literature of the State.* New Orleans, 1894.

McAlexander, Hubert Horton. *The Prodigal Daughter: A Biography of Sherwood Bonner.* Baton Rouge, 1981.

McClave, Heather, ed. *Women Writers of the Short Story.* Englewood Cliffs, N.J., 1980.

McCoy, Mrs. Mildred. Interviews with author. New Orleans, Louisiana, September 9, 1976, and April 2, 1980.

McHatton-Ripley, Eliza. *From Flag to Flag: A Woman's Adventures and Experiences in the South During the War, in Mexico, and in Cuba.* New York, 1896.

McVoy, Lizzie Carter. *Louisiana in the Short Story.* Baton Rouge, 1940.

McVoy, Lizzie Carter, and Ruth Bates Campbell. *A Bibliography of Fiction by Louisianians and on Louisiana Subjects.* Baton Rouge, 1935.

Merrick, Caroline E. *Old Times in Dixie Land: A Southern Matron's Memories.* New York, 1901.

Millett, Kate. *Sexual Politics.* London, 1971.

Mills, Elizabeth Shown. "Colorful Characters from Kate's Past." *Kate Chopin Newsletter,* II (1976–77), 7–12.

Mills, Gary B. *The Forgotten People: Cane River's Creoles of Color.* Baton Rouge, 1977.

Moers, Ellen. *Literary Women.* London, 1978.

Moore, T. O. "Governor Moore's Proclamation, Concerning General Butler's Infamous Order, Dated Opelousas, La. May 24, 1862." *Southern Historical Society Papers,* VI (November, 1878), 228–29.

Muhlenfeld, Elizabeth S. "Grace King." *American Literary Realism,* VIII (Autumn, 1975), 295–96.

Musselwhite, David. "*Wuthering Heights*: The Unacceptable Text." In Francis Barker *et al.,* eds. *Literature, Society and the Sociology of Literature.* Colchester, Engl., 1977.

Northup, Solomon. *Twelve Years a Slave.* Edited by Sue Eakin and Joseph Logsdon. Baton Rouge, 1968.

O'Brien, Sharon. "The Limits of Passion: Willa Cather's Review of *The Awakening.*" *Women and Literature,* III (1975), 11, 13–14.

———. "Sentiment, Local Color and the New Woman Writer: Kate Chopin and Willa Cather." *Kate Chopin Newsletter,* II (1976–77), 16–24.

O'Connor, Flannery. "The Regional Writer." In *Mystery and Manners: Occasional Prose.* Edited by Sally Fitzgerald and Robert Fitzgerald. London, 1972.

Olsen, Tillie. *Silences.* New York, 1978.

Page, Thomas Nelson. "Literature in the South Since the War." *Lippincott's Monthly,* XLVIII (December, 1891), 740–56.

―――. *The Old South: Essays Social and Political.* New York, 1892.

Papashvily, Helen Waite. *All the Happy Endings: A Study of the Domestic Novel in America, The Women Who Wrote It, The Women Who Read It, in the Nineteenth Century.* Port Washington, N.Y., 1956.

Parish, Peter J. *Slavery: The Many Faces of a Southern Institition.* Durham, Engl., 1979.

Parker, Gail, ed. *The Oven Birds: American Women on Womanhood, 1820– 1920.* New York, 1972.

Parrington, Vernon Louis. *The Beginnings of Critical Realism in America, 1860–1920.* New York, 1930. Vol. 3 of *Main Currents in American Thought.* 3 vols. New York, 1927–30.

Pattee, Fred Lewis. *The Development of the American Short Story: An Historical Survey.* New York, 1923.

―――. *A History of American Literature Since 1870.* New York, 1915.

Patty, James S. "A Woman Journalist in Reconstruction Louisiana: Mrs. Mary E. Bryan." *Louisiana Studies,* II (Spring, 1964), 77–104.

Prichard, Walter, ed. "The Origin and Activities of the 'White League' in New Orleans (Reminiscences of a Participant in the Movement)." *Louisiana Historical Quarterly,* XXIII (April, 1940).

Rankin, Daniel S. *Kate Chopin and Her Creole Stories.* Philadelphia, 1932.

Raymond, Ida, ed. *Southland Writers: Biographical and Critical Sketches of the Living Female Writers of the South.* Philadelphia, 1870.

Reid, Ian. *The Short Story.* London, 1977.

Reinders, Robert C. *End of an Era: New Orleans, 1850–1860.* New Orleans, 1964.

Roller, David C., and Robert W. Twyman, eds. *The Encyclopedia of Southern History.* Baton Rouge, 1979.

Roosevelt, Theodore. "What Americanism Means." *Forum,* XVII (April, 1894).

Rose, Willie Lee. "American Women in Their Place." *New York Review of Books,* July 14, 1977, pp. 3–4.

―――. "The Emergence of American Women." *New York Review of Books,* September 15, 1977, pp. 19–22, 24–26, 31–32.

―――. *Race and Region in American Historical Fiction.* Oxford, 1979.

Rossi, Alice S. *The Feminist Papers: From Adams to de Beauvoir.* New York, 1973.

Rothblatt, Sheldon. "George Eliot and the New Intellectuals." Paper read at the George Eliot Centennial Conference, Rutgers University, November 21–23, 1980.

Rozwenc, Edwin C. *Reconstruction in the South*. 2nd ed. Lexington, Mass., 1972.

Rubin, Louis D., Jr., ed. *A Bibliographical Guide to the Study of Southern Literature*. Baton Rouge, 1969.

———. *George W. Cable: The Life and Times of a Southern Heretic*. New York, 1969.

———. *William Elliott Shoots a Bear: Essays on the Southern Literary Imagination*. Baton Rouge, 1975.

———. *The Writer in the South: Studies in a Literary Community*. Athens, Ga., 1972.

Rubin, Louis D., Jr., and C. Hugh Holman. *Southern Literary Study: Problems and Possibilities*. Chapel Hill, N.C., 1975.

Rubin, Louis D., Jr., and Robert D. Jacobs. *Southern Renascence: The Literature of the Modern South*. Baltimore, 1953.

Ruth McEnery Stuart Clan: A Brief History on the Occasion of Its Sixtieth Anniversary. New Orleans, 1975.

Ruth McEnery Stuart Collection. Special Collections Division, Tulane University Library, New Orleans, Louisiana.

Ryan, Mary P. *Womanhood in America from Colonial Times to the Present*. New York, 1975.

Schuler, Kathryn Reinhart. "Women in Public Affairs in Louisiana During Reconstruction." *Louisiana Historical Quarterly,* XIX (July, 1936).

Scott, Anne Firor. *The Southern Lady: From Pedestal to Politics, 1830–1930*. Chicago, 1970.

Seidel, Kathryn Lee. *The Southern Belle in the American Novel*. Tampa, Fla., 1985.

Sellers, C. G., Jr., ed. *The Southerner as American*. Chapel Hill, N.C., 1960.

Seyersted, Per. *Kate Chopin: A Critical Biography*. Baton Rouge, 1969.

Showalter, Elaine. *A Literature of Their Own: British Women Novelists from Brontë to Lessing*. London, 1978.

Simpson, Lewis P. *The Brazen Face of History: Studies in the Literary Consciousness in America*. Baton Rouge, 1980.

———. *The Dispossessed Garden: Pastoral and History in Southern Literature*. Athens, Ga., 1975.

———. *The Man of Letters in New England and the South: Essays on the History of the Literary Vocation in America*. Baton Rouge, 1973.

Sinfield, Alan. "Four Ways with a Reactionary Text." *LTP: Journal of Literature Teaching Politics,* II (1983), 81–95.

Smith-Rosenberg, Carroll. "The Female World of Love and Ritual: Relations Between Women in Nineteenth-Century America." *SIGNS,* I (Autumn, 1975), 1–29.

Spiers, Patricia Loraine. "The Woman Suffrage Movement in New Orleans." M.A. thesis, Southeastern Louisiana College, 1965.

Springer, Marlene, ed. *What Manner of Woman: Essays on English and American Life and Literature.* New York, 1977.

Spruill, Julia Cherry. *Women's Life and Work in the Southern Colonies.* Chapel Hill, N.C., 1938.

Sampp, Kenneth M. *The Era of Reconstruction, 1865–1877.* New York, 1965.

Stanton, Elizabeth Cady, Susan B. Anthony, and Matilda Joslyn Gage, eds. *History of Woman Suffrage.* 6 vols. Rochester, N.Y., 1881–1922.

Stark, Myra. "No Transformation, No Ecstasy: Short Stories by Women." *Regionalism and the Female Imagination,* IV (Fall, 1978), 4–7.

Stielow, Frederick. "Grand Isle, Louisiana, and the 'New' Leisure, 1866–1893." *Louisiana History,* XXIII (1982), 239–57.

Stubbs, Patricia. *Women and Fiction: Feminism and the Novel, 1880–1920.* Brighton, Engl., 1979.

Swanson, Betsy. *Historic Jefferson Parish from Shore to Shore.* Gretna, La., 1975.

Taylor, Helen. "The Case of Grace King." *Southern Review,* XVIII (October, 1982), 685–702.

————. Introduction to *Portraits,* by Kate Chopin. London, 1979.

Taylor, Joe Gray. *Louisiana: A Bicentennial History.* New York, 1976.

————. *Louisiana Reconstructed, 1863–1877.* Baton Rouge, 1974.

Taylor, William R. *Cavalier and Yankee: The Old South and American National Character.* New York, 1961.

Thomson, Patricia. *George Sand and the Victorians: Her Influence and Reputation in Nineteenth-Century England.* London, 1977.

Thornton, Lawrence. "*The Awakening:* A Political Romance." *American Literature,* LII (1980), 52–53.

Tillett, Wilbur Fisk. "Southern Womanhood as Affected by the Civil War." *Century Magazine,* XLIII (November, 1891), 9–16.

Tinker, Edward Larocque. *Lafcadio Hearn's American Days.* New York, 1924.

Tompkins, Jane P. "Sentimental Power: *Uncle Tom's Cabin* and the Politics of Literary History." In *The New Feminist Criticism: Essays on Women, Literature, and Theory,* edited by Elaine Showalter. London, 1986.

Toth, Emily. "Bibliography of Kate Chopin's Writings." In *A Kate Chopin Miscellany,* edited by Per Seyersted. Natchitoches, La., 1979.

———. "The Independent Woman and 'Free' Love." *Massachusetts Review,* XVI (Autumn, 1975), 647–64.

Tourgée, Albion. "The South as a Field for Fiction." *Forum,* VI (December, 1888), 404–13.

Turner, Arlin. *George W. Cable: A Biography.* Durham, N.C., 1956.

Tutwiler, Julia R. "Ruth McEnery Stuart: The Southern Woman in New York." *Bookman,* XVIII (February, 1904), 633.

Twelve Southerners. *I'll Take My Stand: The South and the Agrarian Tradition.* Baton Rouge, 1980.

Vaughan, Bess. "A Bio-Bibliography of Grace Elizabeth King." *Louisiana Historical Quarterly,* XVII (October, 1934), 752–70.

Veblen, Thorstein. *The Theory of the Leisure Class: An Economic Study in the Evolution of Institutions.* New York, 1899.

Vicinus, Martha, ed. *Suffer and Be Still: Women in the Victorian Age.* Bloomington, Ind., 1972.

———. *A Widening Sphere: Changing Roles of Victorian Women.* London, 1980.

Wall, Bennett H., ed. *Louisiana: A History.* Arlington Heights, Ill., 1984.

Weaver, Richard Mervin. *The Southern Tradition at Bay: A History of Postbellum Thought.* New Rochelle, N.Y., 1968.

Welter, Barbara. "The Cult of True Womanhood: 1820–1860." *American Quarterly,* XVIII (Summer, 1966), 151–74.

———. *Dimity Convictions: The American Woman in the Nineteenth Century.* Athens, Ga., 1976.

Wilds, John. *Afternoon Story: A Century of the New Orleans 'States-Item.'* Baton Rouge, 1976.

Williams, Raymond. *The Country and the City.* London, 1973.

———. "Region and Class in the Novel." In *The Uses of Fiction: Essays on the Modern Novel in Honor of Arnold Kettle,* edited by Douglas Jefferson and Graham Martin. Philadelphia, 1982. Pp. 57–68.

Williams, Susan Millar. "Love and Rebellion: Louisiana Women Novelists, 1865–1919." Ph.D. dissertation, Louisiana State University, 1984.

Wilson, Edmund. *Patriotic Gore: Studies in the Literature of the American Civil War.* New York, 1962.

Wilson, Mary Helen. "Kate Chopin's Family: Fallacies and Facts." *Kate Chopin Newsletter,* II (1976–77), 25–29.

Winters, John D. *The Civil War in Louisiana.* Baton Rouge, 1963.

Wolff, Cynthia Griffin, ed. *Classic American Women Writers.* New York, 1980.

Wood, Ann Douglas. "The Literature of Impoverishment: The Women

Local Colorists in America, 1865–1914." *Women's Studies,* I (1972), 3–45.

Woodward, C. Vann. *The Burden of Southern History.* Rev. ed. Baton Rouge, 1968.

————, ed. *Mary Chesnut's Civil War.* New Haven, 1981.

————. *Origins of the New South, 1877–1913.* Baton Rouge, 1951.

————. *The Strange Career of Jim Crow.* 3rd ed. New York, 1974.

Yellin, Jean Fagan. *The Intricate Knot: Black Figures in American Literature, 1776–1863.* New York, 1972.

Young, Thomas D., *et al.,* eds. *The Literature of the South.* Glenview, Ill., 1968.

Zanger, Jules. "The 'Tragic Octoroon' in Pre-Civil War Fiction." *American Quarterly,* XVIII (Spring, 1966), 63–70.

Ziff, Larzer. *The American 1890s: Life and Times of a Lost Generation.* New York, 1967.

Index

Cooper, Fenimore, 87
Cotton Centennial Exposition. *See* New Orleans Cotton Centennial Exposition
Crane, Stephen, 159

Darwin, Charles, 147
Daudet, Alphonse, 158
Davis, Angela, 9, 14
Davis, Mollie Moore, 20, 40
Dawson, Sarah Morgan, 12–13, 72
DeMenil, Alexander, 146, 158
De Staël, Madame, 41, 153, 154, 162, 183, 184, 185, 186, 195
Dewey, John, 146
Dialect: authors' use of black dialect, 20, 98–99; Stuart's use of black dialect, 84, 86–87, 88, 97–99, 109–10, 114–15, 121–22, 156, 157; definition of, 87; European authors' use of, 87–88; as feature of Local Color movement, 87; significance of, 87–88; Stuart's use of Italian dialect, 87, 88; Chopin's use of, 156–57, 164, 166, 169
Dickens, Charles, 162
Dix, Dorothy, 197, 201
Dixon, Thomas, 42n
Douglas, Judith Hyams, 96
DuBois, Ellen, 10
Dunbar, Paul, 105
Dunbar-Nelson, Alice, 7, 23–24, 80n
Durham, Robert Lee, 42n

Eggleston, Edward, 87
Ehrenreich, Barbara, 199
Eliot, Charlotte, 146–47
Eliot, George, 36, 40, 41, 105, 158, 186, 196
Eliot, Henry Ware, 146
Eliot, T. S., 146
Elliott, Sarah Barnwell, 85
English, Deirdre, 199
Esposito, Giuseppe, 107
Evans, Augusta, 16

Faulkner, William, 42n, 204
Fields, Annie, 35, 40
Flaubert, Gustave, 17, 157, 158, 190, 192, 194
Fletcher, Mary, 90, 92, 105

Foucault, Michel, 199
Franklin, John Hope, 1n-2n, 3
Freeman, Mary Wilkins. *See* Wilkins Freeman, Mary E.
Friedman, Jean E., xi, 6
Fuller, Margaret, x, 185, 186

Garesché, Kitty, 142, 153, 162
Garland, Hamlin, 95, 136, 149, 159, 164–65
Garnett, Edward, 71
Gautier, Théophile, 17
Gayarré, Charles, 30, 32, 32n, 33, 34
Genovese, Eugene, 49, 49n
Gibson, William Hamilton, 63
Gilbert, Sandra, 13
Gilder, Richard Watson, 19, 33, 34–35, 35n, 46, 50, 66, 86, 149
Gilman, Charlotte Perkins, 103, 126, 131–32, 134, 188–89, 199
Glasgow, Ellen, 15n, 17, 30, 81–82, 85, 100, 130
Grand Isle, 173, 174, 175, 177
Grenier, Edouard, 31
Grimké sisters, 14, 26, 203
Grimm brothers, 162
Gulf of Mexico, 172–78

H.D., 13
Hardy, Thomas, 87, 105, 150, 192, 202
Harper, Frances, 9
Harper's, 35, 36, 86, 92
Harper's Bazaar, 93
Harper's Monthly Magazine, 19
Harper's New Monthly Magazine, 35
Harris, Joel Chandler, 18, 19, 85, 87, 91, 97, 98–100, 105, 107, 156
Harte, Bret, 17
Hawthorne, Nathaniel, 150
Hearn, Lafcadio, 30, 173–74, 177
Hemenway, Robert, 99
Hennessey, David, 108, 136
Higginson, Thomas Wentworth, 20
Hildreth, Richard, 42
Hooker, Isabella Beecher, 39, 40
Houssaye, Sidonie de la, 173
Howe, Julia Ward, 7, 10, 33, 38, 103, 146, 186
Howe, Maud, 19n, 25, 38, 146, 186